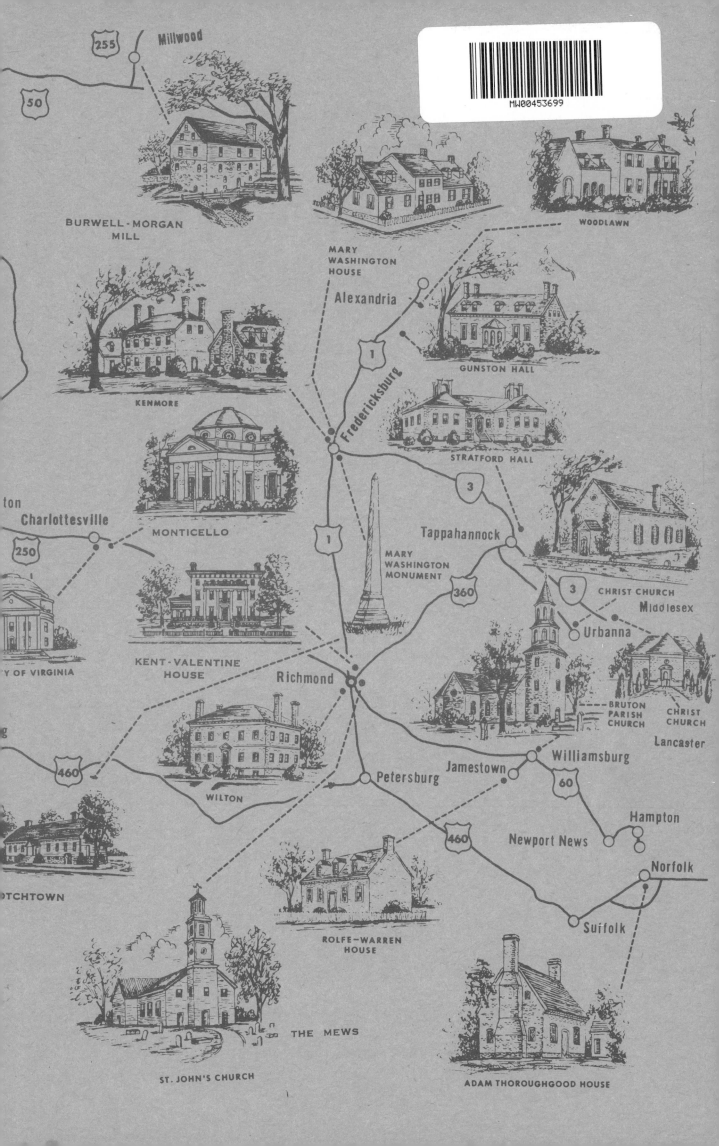

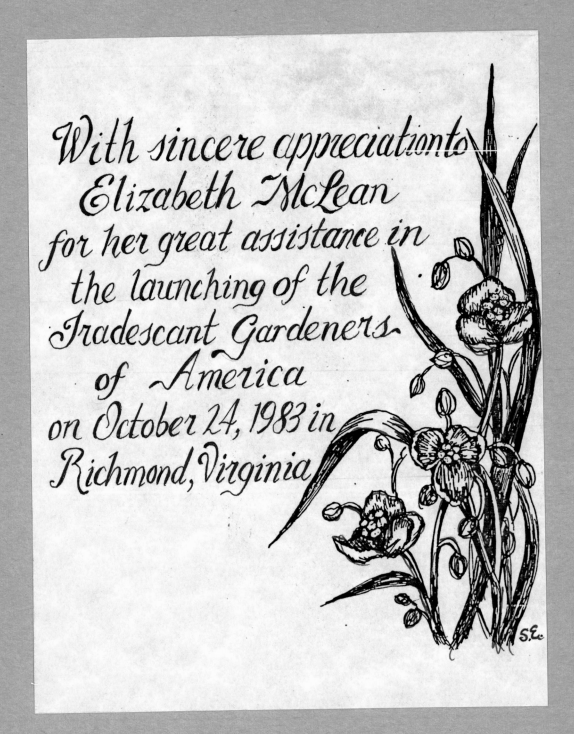

With sincere appreciation to
Elizabeth McLean
for her great assistance in
the launching of the
Iradescant Gardeners
of America
on October 24, 1983 in
Richmond, Virginia

S.E.

Historic Virginia Gardens

Preservations by

The Garden Club of Virginia

Historic Virginia Gardens

Preservations by The Garden Club of Virginia

Dorothy Hunt Williams

Published for The Garden Club of Virginia

by the University Press of Virginia, Charlottesville

THE UNIVERSITY PRESS OF VIRGINIA
Copyright © 1975 by The Garden Club of Virginia

First published 1975

Library of Congress Cataloging in Publication Data

Williams, Dorothy Hunt.
  Historic Virginia gardens.

  Bibliography: p.
    1. Gardens—Virginia. 2. Gardens—Conservation and
restoration. 3. Garden Club of Virginia. 4. Virginia
—Historic houses, etc.—Conservation and restoration.
I. Garden Club of Virginia. II. Title.
SB466.U65V88 635.9′09755 74-19422 ISBN 0-8139-0604-0

Printed in the United States of America

This Book
is dedicated to all
who have opened their houses
and gardens for
Historic Garden Week

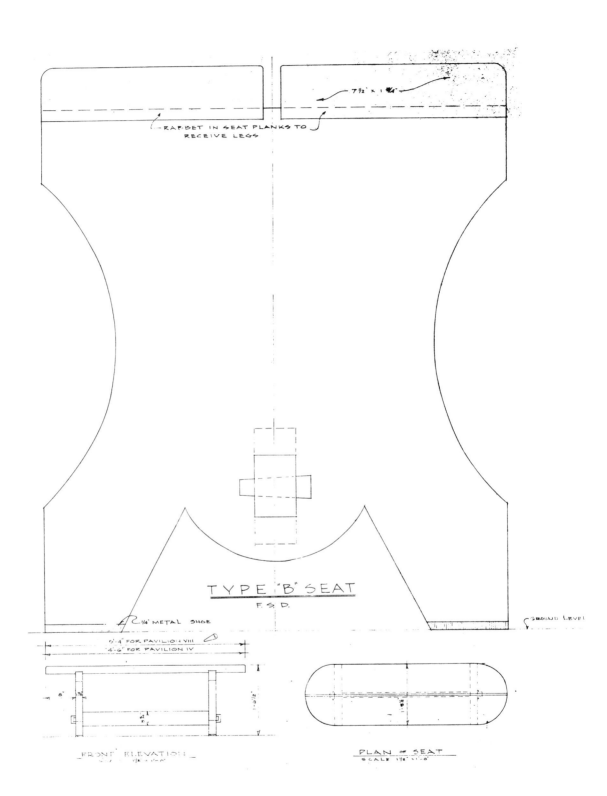

7½" × 1¾"

RABBET IN SEAT PLANKS TO
RECEIVE LEGS

TYPE "B" SEAT
F. S. D.

¼" METAL SHOE

GROUND LEVEL

5'-4" FOR PAVILION VIII
4'-6" FOR PAVILION IV

8"

FRONT ELEVATION

PLAN OF SEAT
SCALE 1½" = 1'-0"

Foreword

FINE GARDENING came naturally to Virginians. Coming originally from England, they brought with them an inherent love of the land and things that grow. They lived on their land, creating great plantations with noble houses and handsome gardens. They found Virginia soils, climates, and plant life congenial to gardening. Magnificent waterfronts—ocean, bays, rivers, and mountain streams with a challenging diversity of topography—and temperate climate from Tidewater flatlands to Blue Ridge mountains offered an infinite variety of flora and fauna.

Pioneer English naturalists—John Banister, Sr., John Clayton, and Mark Catesby—were enticed to this botanical and biological wonderland and identified many plants destined to ornament American gardens. Among the patrons of these scholarly naturalists were distinguished plantation owners and statesmen—William Byrd II, George Washington, Thomas Jefferson, and George Mason. Their own writings, gardens, and libraries helped establish the traditional love of gardening in Virginia. To this day Jefferson's Garden Book is the most comprehensive record of early American horticulture and gardening. That he knew the difference between utilitarian and ornamental gardening at this early date (1805) is apparent in a letter he wrote to his granddaughter explaining the status of gardening as a fine art. "Not horticulture, but the art of embellishing grounds by fancy" was his succinct way of expressing the art that was perfected by Virginia aristocrats. By preserving their historic gardens and the grounds of their churches and universities, the entire state has become an outdoor museum of an art that has, since the beginning, challenged man's ingenuity. Visitors may now see irrefutable evidence that the founders of this nation thought not alone of their plantation crops but were equally concerned with the beauty of their natural landscape and its embellishment "by fancy."

Without organized protection of this irreplaceable inheritance, The Garden Club of Virginia foresaw its inevitable destruction. They made it their most important work to preserve Virginia's historic gardens. An adequate source of funds had to be found. The usual flower shows would not suffice. Furthermore, for such an enterprise there was as yet no precedent. They had to be pioneers. This book is a history of that pioneer effort. It is, therefore, the record of a unique American conception for preservation of historic American gardens.

The idea of charging admission to see the gardens they were trying to preserve was a stroke of genius that has made the scheme self-perpetuating. More admission fees produce more money to invest in more garden restorations which, in turn, mean more admission fees. This self-reliant method seems especially admirable at a time when such enterprises are preceded by seeking government subsidy, high-pressure fund raising, or huge foundation grants. With the proceeds of their own resourcefulness, The Garden Club of Virginia forged ahead in typical early American grass-roots style.

For any kind of garden preservation the greatest obstacle to be avoided is sentimentalism. So many poetic descriptions have created romantic illusions about the realities of gardening that it is sometimes difficult to keep them out of authentic restorations. This danger has been successfully overcome by the Restoration Committees with whom I have worked. Previously, they had worked with Morely Williams, Charles Gillette, Arthur Shurcliff, and Alden Hopkins, all conscientious, capable garden historians and landscape architects. The interpretation of sketches for the East Lawn Gardens of the University of Virginia was entrusted to Donald Parker, landscape architect, with myself as consultant. There has always been an abhorrence of an amateur attitude toward gardening by the members of the Restoration Committees and their professional advisers. They have made every effort to discover historical evidence by documentary research, archaeological excavation, and study of contemporary precedent.

This preservation of historic gardens and grounds has accomplished more than was originally intended. It has not only preserved these historic places but has also memorialized the garden interest of their distinguished owners: can anyone think of the complete Jefferson without having seen his garden at Monticello? Moreover, there has developed, since The Garden Club's first restoration in 1929 at Kenmore, an entire new attitude toward authentic historic restoration. What once passed for archaeological research on the history and restoration of gardens and grounds would be unacceptable under present-day standards. Progress in the accuracy of historic preservation has advanced concurrently with The Garden Club of Virginia's accomplishments. In this record of twenty-three projects undertaken in about a half century is found the full range of American garden design before the advent of the industrial age. Although the methods of preservation have changed considerably, the motives have remained the same: to preserve the past for the enlightenment of the future.

From the early English-born Tidewater dynasties of the Byrds and Carters to the late American-born Piedmont statesmen—Jefferson, Madison, and Monroe—the full diversity of garden character is represented. Visitors may now see the traditional geometric parterres compared to the naturalistic English gardens of famous Americans preserved in their original environment. No monetary appraisal can be adequately made of the enjoyment and cultural stimulation created by these gardens. They are an ever-changing exhibit of living natural beauty.

Unlike the other arts—architecture, painting, sculpture—that are judged by their immediate effect, gardening, like fine wine, requires years for perfection. Nature's fourth dimension—growth—cannot be achieved except on her own schedule, which is beyond man's control. Those who scorn age as the greatest embellisher of gardens can have no appreciation of what maintenance means to the preservation of historic gardens. Even a year of neglect can obliterate a lifetime of a gardener's skill. Realizing that restoration without intelligent maintenance was as foolish as expecting plants not to grow, The Garden Club wisely required owners to guarantee perpetual maintenance and provided for periodic inspection to ensure the fulfillment of that guarantee. Without this firm provision there might not have been any restorations to illustrate this bicentennial report. No artist possesses the magic to reproduce the beauty that nature bestows on a fine old garden. But for those masterpieces that have escaped total obliteration, The Garden Club of Virginia has been able to serve as protector, restorer, reconstructor, and preserver, letting nature pursue her unmolested course.

As the creation and maintenance of any pleasure garden becomes ever more difficult, traditional gardening is threatened with extinction. It is consoling to know that some of our finest historic gardens are being conscientiously preserved.

RALPH E. GRISWOLD

*Fellow of the American
Society of Landscape
Architects and Fellow of the
American Academy in Rome*

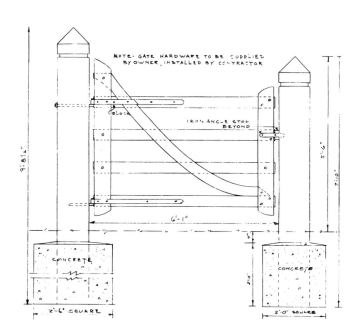

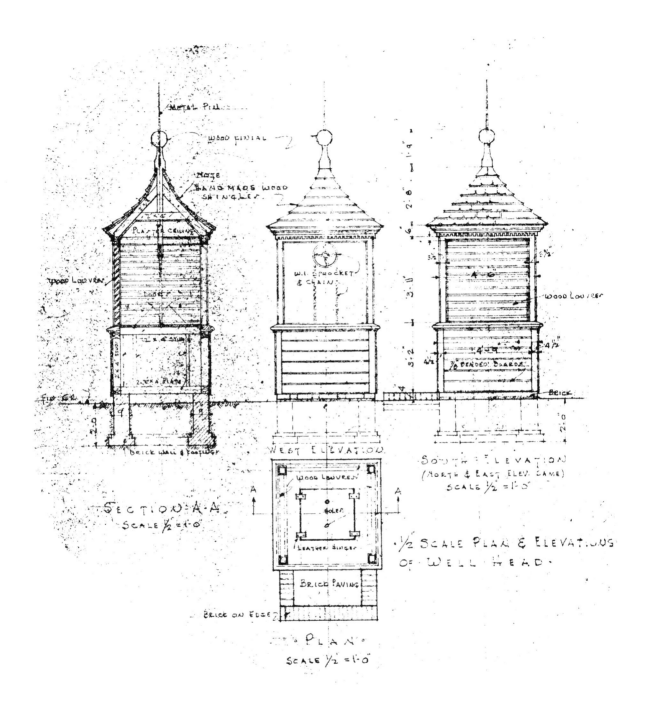

METAL PINN.

WOOD FINIAL

NOTE
HANDMADE WOOD
SHINGLES.

PLASTER CEILING

2"x 4"

WOOD LOUVER

HOOD

2"x 4" STUD

2"x 4" PLATE

FIN. GR.

BRICK WALL & FOOTING

SECTION·A·A·
SCALE ½"=1'-0"

W.I. SPROCKET
& CHAIN

WEST ELEVATION

A

WOOD LOUVER

HOLE

A

LEATHER HINGE

BRICK PAVING

BRICK ON EDGE

PLAN
SCALE ½"=1'-0"

A-A

WOOD LOUVER

⅞ BEADED BOARDS

BRICK

SOUTH ELEVATION
(NORTH & EAST ELEV. SAME)
SCALE ½"=1'-0"

½ SCALE PLAN & ELEVATIONS
OF WELL HEAD.

Preface

THE PRIVATE FILES of The Garden Club of Virginia contain documents, plans, and illustrations that record a comprehensive story of restoration. The purpose of this book is to share this information. Though this story is one that records the history of garden restoration within the Commonwealth of Virginia, its relevance is national, for these gardens are of significance to all Americans. It is appropriate that this history should be presented as a gift to the nation on the occasion of the bicentennial year of our country.

To understand this gift it is necessary to know something of The Garden Club of Virginia. In the years between 1911 and 1919, eight garden clubs were formed in Virginia. They all came into being in the same way—a small group of friends deciding that horticulture and companionship made a happy combination. Most of these clubs were the result of casual conversation among friends. One even evolved from a bridge club. It was not until 1920 that these individual clubs banded together as a statewide organization. Their number has increased from the original eight clubs to the present forty-four, but the essential character of the organization has never changed. It was, and still is, a small group of friends sharing an interest in gardening and expressing this interest by creative endeavor. The empathy of this group, together with its appreciation of the past, present, and future hopes of this state, is responsible for the unique character of The Garden Club of Virginia.

The observance of the national bicentennial year reminds us that we are, indeed, a young nation. Because of our national youth it is understandable that historic restoration in the United States is also in its infancy. National interest in restoration and the active expression of this interest by The Garden Club of Virginia are concurrent developments. In the very early years of The Garden Club two projects of preservation were sponsored. The first was assistance to the College of William and Mary in saving a beautiful grove of trees on the edge of the campus. The second was financing tree surgery at Monticello. But the decision in 1928 to restore the grounds at Kenmore was the step that led this organization into a continuing interest in restoration. From that time until the present, restoration has been its dominant interest.

The Kenmore restoration posed many problems, not the least of which was its financing. As no funds were available, some means had to be found to finance the project. After much discussion, it was decided to sponsor a statewide tour of homes and gardens. These private properties would be opened to the public for a week at the height of the spring blooming season. The proceeds from admissions would be used to finance the restoration. As an adjunct to this first Garden Week, a guide book was prepared. It was such a success that it ran through four editions and seven printings and was used as a guide for the twelve Garden Week tours before World War II. Income from this book was used to restore the churchyard of Old Saint John's in Richmond. This book was republished in 1950 and again in 1962; in these editions it was revised as a reference book.

These were the beginnings—Kenmore, the first in a long line of restorations; its supporting garden tour the initiation of Historic Garden Week in Virginia; its directory the forerunner of all subsequent guide books. Thus was established a pattern to be repeated annually.

The beneficiaries of this endeavor are selected through long and thoughtful study. Application must be made to the Restoration Committee of The Garden Club of Virginia. A file of all applications is kept and from year to year reviewed and reconsidered before a choice is made. An application contains the historical significance of the site, the financial ability of the foundation to support the garden once it has been created, and the stated promise that the garden will be kept open to the public. To insure that the restoration is maintained according to plans agreed upon between the owner and The Garden Club of Virginia, the Restoration Committee and its landscape architect make an annual inspection. When a garden is selected as worthy of restoration, the committee presents it to the membership. Final approval is made by representatives of the entire organization in annual meeting.

The extreme care with which a garden is studied before being selected for restoration avoids superficiality. Each garden restored is of unquestionable historic significance, thus insuring a project of national interest. For the serious student of restoration, these gardens offer valuable information historically, horticulturally, and aesthetically.

Historically, a visit to any of these restorations is a rewarding experience. Here is encounter with the major personalities who formed our nation. For a garden is a revealing reflection of its owner and his era. In conveying a sense of antecedents and the continuity of generations, these gardens restate enduring, basic values upon which this country was founded.

Horticulturally, plants that embellish the individual gardens provide an instant index of plant material indigenous to, or popular in, the period in which the garden was originally created. In this book a list of plant material used within the garden follows all but one of the monographs. These lists were compiled before each restoration was executed. Only plant material used in the particular period and in the specific location of the original garden is used in restoration. For those who are interested in determining plants of a certain period, these lists provide ready reference. In the plant lists authority for both scientific and common names of plants is Liberty Hyde and Ethel Zoe Bailey's authoritative dictionary *Hortus* and his *Standard Cyclopedia of Horticulture;* in text, *Webster's New Collegiate Dictionary.*

It must be understood that certain deviations have had to be made from the original plans. Some flowers included in the original plans no longer flourish, having fallen victim to pollution. These varieties must be judiciously replaced by plants that can survive. The Japanese beetle has wreaked havoc with the old roses in such gardens as Woodlawn and the Woodrow Wilson Birthplace. The difficulty of obtaining, and the expense of keeping, gardeners has forced simplification in many instances. Plantings within parterres increasingly are restricted to ground covers interplanted with bulbs.

The original variety of blooming plants must often give way to a mass of a single variety. These are practical solutions to the very real problems of maintaining properties constantly exposed to public scrutiny. Rather than being a discouraging bow to necessity, these deletions have revealed the strength of the original, basic plan and demonstrate the importance of superior design.

Aesthetically, much is to be learned from the diversity of these gardens. Many years intervene between the periods of the Adam Thoroughgood or the Rolfe-Warren gardens and those of Woodrow Wilson or Kent-Valentine. These gardens and the others that lie between provide a review of the entire history of the American landscape tradition. A few examples will illustrate this point.

Before and after the Revolutionary War, English influence was the dominating factor in American landscape design. Because England was so far away, garden fashions in America followed, rather than paralleled, those of England. Our forebears were steeped in the English idea that a garden was an integral part of the domestic building scheme. The ready availability of many illustrated English garden books provided patterns for the gardens of the New World. The formality of these early gardens of traditional form is exemplified in the Adam Thoroughgood garden and in the garden of Gunston Hall.

After American independence was established, a radical change appeared in landscape design, as dramatically illustrated by the plan drawn by Jefferson for his garden at Monticello. His design was based upon curving lines embellished with native plant material. This naturalistic trend reflected the new English style of landscape gardening. It is interesting to note that the gardens of the more liberal politicians of the period seem to express a freedom of design in keeping with their political views.

Not all the restorations reviewed in this book are of the seventeenth and eighteenth centuries. Gardens at the Woodrow Wilson Birthplace and the Kent-Valentine House are examples of the landscape styles of the late nineteenth and early twentieth centuries. This was an era of changing approach as demands for city gardens increased. The restrictions and requirements of urban life strongly influenced landscape design of this period.

It should be noted that some of these projects are preservations, some restorations, and some interpretations of varying life-styles. Established policy of The Garden Club of Virginia dictates that if a true restoration is possible, it is carried out. If preservation is the need, that is undertaken; if no valid basis for design can be found in existing conditions, an interpretation based upon historical research is executed. But whether it be restoration, preservation, or interpretation, each garden illustrates a chapter of American history and landscape development.

Monographs preceding the plans and illustrations are summaries of the correspondence and reports of the people immediately responsible for the execution of each restoration. These letters and papers constitute the essential bibliography for this presentation. A brief perusal of this bibliographic material makes it clear that the successful, sustained salvation of any historic landmark must depend upon the cooperative effort of several organizations. The demands upon resources of time and money are so great that few organizations could bear the responsibility alone. Usually one organization purchases the property, another furnishes the interior of the house, and yet another provides the landscaping. It requires the greatest restraint on the part of all involved to restore and maintain a shrine. In this book every effort has been made to avoid infringement on the accomplishments of the organizations with which The Garden Club of Virginia has been associated. No plans are shown that were not specifically executed under the jurisdiction of The Garden Club of Virginia. A case in point is the additional plans for Stratford. These are not shown here because their execution was the accomplishment of another organization. Another case is the omission of the Hopkins plan for the front lawn of Kenmore. This plan was superimposed upon the original Gillette design, which is included.

As with the plans, so with the illustrations. The views here shown are of vistas of landscapes created or embellished at the direction of The Garden Club of Virginia. The exception to this policy is the inclusion of views of central structures. Building and landscape are one, the landscape providing a setting for the structure. The character of the landscape sets the mood for appreciation and understanding of the structure.

For the celebration of this nation's bicentennial year, The Garden Club of Virginia presents this book illustrating the development of our nation through the evolution of the art of landscape design. These gardens belong to all Americans to visit and to enjoy. Their beauty, created by past generations, speaks to us today through restoration. These gardens transmit an awareness of history, tradition, and antecedents: they are the nation's own, its past and its recreated present. Come, America, and enjoy them.

This book is a composite of the thoughtful consideration of many people. Grateful acknowledgment is here tendered the various organizations and individuals who have given hearty and helpful support to this study. Thanks in particular are due Christine Hale Martin and her committee, who made the collection of the plans possible. Frank Davis's photographs illustrate the majority of the monographs. Additional photographs were secured by Mary Wise Boxley Parrott, Decca Gilmer Frackelton, Mary Stuart McGuire Gilliam, Marion Lee Cobb Stuart, Lee Stuart Cochran, and Rosalie Nelson Bell. Each monograph has been scrutinized by a member of The Garden Club of Virginia knowledgeable in that particular restoration and by a representative of the shrine itself. The guidance of these reviewers was an essential aid in my effort to distinguish between fact and legend; to them I am humbly grateful.

Richard Stinely rendered invaluable service in ordering the contents of the book. The publication of this book was financially underwritten by the Restoration Committee of The Garden Club of Virginia. Action initiating publication was taken through the leadership of Lee Stuart Cochran, president of The Garden Club of Virginia. Dorothy Douglas Kellam, chairman of the Restoration Committee, has been responsible for many decisions of publication. Katherine Peatross and Jenny Gray Hill have patiently and efficiently typed and retyped manuscript. Kathleen Westlake Young has assisted in verifying and arranging plant lists. Charlotte Taylor Massie has rendered incalculable assistance in evaluating material for inclusion in the monographs. She and Francis Berkley have read text ad infinitum. To all these individuals I express profound gratitude. Binding these gifts together has been Ralph Esty Griswold, consultant for this work. His background of historical, literary, and architectural study has enabled him to give essential advice in the writing and compilation of this book. He has long insisted such a book be published, and his aid has brought it to fruition.

DOROTHY HUNT WILLIAMS

Little Yatton
March 1975

Contents

Foreword by Ralph E. Griswold	vii
Preface	xi
Kenmore	3
Stratford	15
Woodrow Wilson Birthplace: The Manse	29
Lee Memorial Chapel	39
Rolfe-Warren House: Smith's Fort Plantation	43
Wilton	53
Bruton Parish Church	61
Mary Washington Monument	69
Monticello	75
Christ Church: Middlesex	87
Christ Church: Fincastle	91
Barter Theatre: Abingdon	95
Gunston Hall	99
The University of Virginia	115
West Lawn	
Pavilion I	125
Pavilion III	131
Pavilion V	135
Pavilion VII	139
Pavilion IX	142
East Lawn	
Pavilion II	151
Pavilion IV	157
Pavilion VI	161
Pavilion VIII	167
Pavilion X	173
Woodlawn	189
Adam Thoroughgood House	205
The Mews: Richmond	217
Christ Church: Lancaster	229
Mary Washington House	235

Scotchtown   249
Burwell-Morgan Mill   261
Kent-Valentine House   269
Historic Virginia Gardens in Color   277
Bibliography   337
Index   343

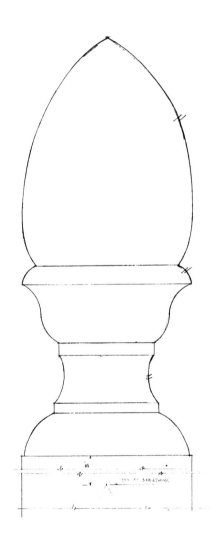

Historic Virginia Gardens
Preservations by
The Garden Club of Virginia

A Note Regarding
the Validity of the Plant Lists

The plant lists accompanying the subjects are the ones used by the Restoration Committees and landscape architects for the original projects. For reasons stated in the Preface there have been subsequent changes, all of which have been approved by the Committee. No attempt has been made to keep these original lists up to date because the problem arises immediately—what date? Every gardener realizes that a plant list that is valid today may, by nature's caprices, be obsolete tomorrow. Nevertheless, the visitor will find the essential plant character of these gardens unchanged since they were planted according to these lists.

Kenmore

IN 1752 George Washington surveyed a tract of 863 acres along the upper Rappahannock for Fielding Lewis, son of the Honorable John Lewis III of Warner Hall, Gloucester County. After the survey the land was purchased by Lewis, and upon it he built a house as a wedding gift to his sixteen-year-old bride, Betty Washington, only sister of George Washington. The original holding of 863 acres was, in time, increased to 1,100 acres. Lewis was a man of prominence who engaged actively in business and civic affairs. He and his young wife were also deeply interested in the church and contributed liberally to the community. It is upon the Lewis lands that much of the city of Fredericksburg developed.

For almost thirty years Betty and Fielding Lewis occupied their home, which we now know as Kenmore, and raised their children there. George Washington was a frequent visitor. The Lewis home made a convenient place to spend the night when traveling north or south between Mount Vernon and Williamsburg. Washington often sought the intimate companionship of his sister's household during the harrowing days of the Revolution. In later years there was the added attraction of a visit with his mother, whom he had established in a cottage bordering the Lewis property.

In the early years of the Revolution, Washington's troops were armed and fed principally by Virginians. The gun factory in Fredericksburg was under the joint supervision of Lewis and Charles Dick. In financing the gunnery, Lewis sacrificed his private fortune. As a last resort, he raised further funds by mortgaging house and lands to pay for the arms used by Washington's troops at Yorktown. Lewis died in comparative poverty shortly before this victory. In appreciation of this sacrifice, Washington provided financial assistance to his sister that enabled her to stay on in her home until the children were grown. Eventually she moved to Culpeper County to live with her daughter.

Following her death in 1797 the estate was sold. From the date of this sale until 1922, ownership of Kenmore changed many times. One owner was Samuel Gordon of Falmouth, who purchased the estate in 1819 and occupied it until 1859. It was during the ownership by the Gordon family that the name Kenmore was given. The years between 1850 and 1881 were years of constant change for the estate. Lots were sold off; during the cannonading of the Civil War battle of Fredericksburg, the ornamental

Entrance walk

Entrance lawn

plaster ceilings of the house were heavily damaged; and use of the mansion as a hospital and subsequently as a boys' academy caused further damage.

In 1881 the property was purchased by William Key Howard of Baltimore, who literally saved the house and grounds and whose son repaired the plaster ceilings. Upon his death his son inherited the estate and preserved it intact until 1914. After Howard's ownership the property continually decreased in size until, in 1921, the total land comprised only a single city block. Several houses had been built on the east side of the block, and the owner planned to subdivide further.

Alarmed by impending destruction of this significant landmark, private citizens banded together to form the Kenmore Association. Their aim was the purchase of Kenmore and its restoration. The Washington-Lewis Chapter of the Daughters of the American Revolution (DAR) in Fredericksburg was the outgrowth of this effort. With only fourteen members this chapter effected the organization of the Kenmore Association. Though this undertaking was encouraged by both the national and state DAR, it was the determination of the small local group that wrought the miracle. So successful was this organization that the house and grounds were purchased; the last payment was made in 1925.

In 1924 the president of The Garden Club of Virginia personally became interested in improving the grounds of Kenmore. To this end she wrote James Greenleaf, presi-

The enclosing garden wall (photo by Frackleton)

Garden pavilion (Copied from Federal Hill, Fredericksburg)

dent of the Landscape Architects of America, and asked him to meet with her and with Charles Gillette, landscape architect of Richmond, to help formulate plans for the grounds. This meeting produced the nucleus of a plan, and it was agreed that Greenleaf would serve as consultant with Gillette as architect. The initial idea was for The Garden Club of Virginia to present a plan for landscaping that would be carried out by the Kenmore Association as money became available. Gillette made a survey and executed a plan at the expense of The Garden Club of Virginia. This plan was approved and accepted by the Kenmore Association. The original watercolor sketch was to be framed and hung in the mansion as a guide for future development.

In the meantime the Kenmore Association had generated national enthusiasm by appointing a regent in each state. From many quarters much interest was expressed in restoration of the outlying buildings on the Kenmore property. This diverted money from landscaping. Consequently, an appeal was made to The Garden Club of Virginia to carry out the Gillette-Greenleaf plan. The affirmative vote by The Garden Club on this suggestion was contingent upon finding some means of financing the project without taxing the individual member clubs of The Garden Club of Virginia. The answer to

Garden walk

this problem was the idea of opening many historic gardens simultaneously throughout the state for an admission fee. The plan was a remarkable success.

From this visitation money was now available for landscaping. A meeting was held at Kenmore to discuss the possibility of carrying out a true restoration of the grounds as they existed in Col. Fielding Lewis's time. To this end the Kenmore Association had made every effort to obtain data on the original design of the grounds either in letters or records, but to no avail. After thorough study it was determined that the original estate of Colonel Lewis had been so encroached upon and the boundaries so restricted that a restoration with any degree of fidelity was impossible.

It was resolved that the Kenmore Association would undertake to buy the residences adjoining the Kenmore grounds so that the plan presented by The Garden Club of Virginia might include this addition to the property. The Garden Club agreed to build the enclosing wall and, following completion of the kitchen and other outbuildings, to plant the grounds according to the Gillette plan. After a study of many walls in various sections of the Commonwealth, the wall surrounding Ware Churchyard in Gloucester County was selected as a model, and plans were drawn to adapt the design to the Kenmore property.

As soon as the Kenmore Association completed rebuilding the old kitchen, the grounds were turned over to The Garden Club of Virginia for landscaping. The wall was built, and during late summer and autumn of 1931 grading and planting carried out the Gillette plan. On February 22, 1932, the completed garden was turned over to the president of the Kenmore Association by The Garden Club of Virginia. A bronze tablet on the wall establishes the beginning of this project as February 1924 and its completion as February 22, 1932. This was the first major historic garden restoration by The Garden Club of Virginia.

Initially it had been hoped that the Kenmore Association might acquire the land between Kenmore and Mary Washington's cottage, but investigation proved this unreasonable because of expense and the difficulty of obtaining property titles. This impracticality having been determined, the Association turned its attention to acquiring the six houses on the east side of the Kenmore block. The intrusion of these houses made it impossible to carry out the complete Gillette plan in 1924–32. However, by February 22, 1932, when the wall and front grounds were presented, two of the houses had been purchased by the Association. Following this, other houses were purchased in 1934, 1936, and 1940. With acquisition of these properties, it was possible for The Garden Club, in 1940–41, to complete the wall and to carry out the deferred portion of the Gillette plan for the eastern grounds of the mansion. The garden is a series of terraces descending toward the east. Each terrace is bordered by dwarf boxwood hedges. At the time he designed this garden, Gillette had in his possession a letter which indicated that the original garden at Kenmore contained two bowers. Exactly what these bowers were was not clear; so he copied the very beautiful garden pavilion at nearby Federal Hill.

Today Kenmore is a memorial to both the Lewis and Washington families and is an outstanding example of a typical fine house of the mid eighteenth century. The fortuitous relation of dwelling and grounds recalls a way of life as lived by a patriot whose influence was instrumental in determining the future of our country.

TREES

Aesculus hippocastanum, Horse-Chestnut
Albizzia Julibrissin, Mimosa, Silk-Tree
Celtis occidentalis, Hackberry
Liquidambar styraciflua, Sweet Gum

Liriodendron Tulipifera, Tulip-Tree
Magnolia grandiflora, Southern Magnolia
Morus alba, Mulberry
Prunus angustifolia, Plum

SHRUBS

Buxus sempervirens, Common Boxwood
   (true tree)

Buxus sempervirens suffruticosa, Dwarf
   Boxwood (true dwarf)

VINES

Hedera helix, English Ivy

HERBACEOUS PLANTS—ANNUALS AND PERENNIALS

Althea rosea, Hollyhock
Iris var., Iris

Narcissus var., Daffodil
Yucca filamentosa, Adams-Needle

Vinca minor, Periwinkle

A proposed arrangement of the Kenmore grounds, Charles F. Gillette, landscape architect

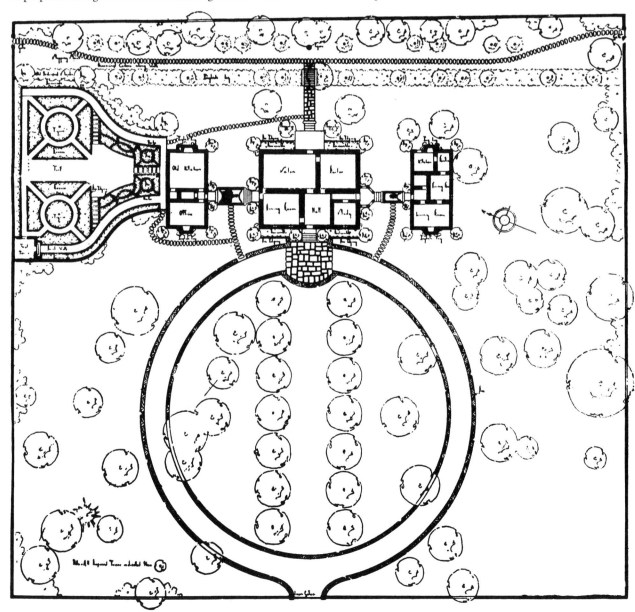

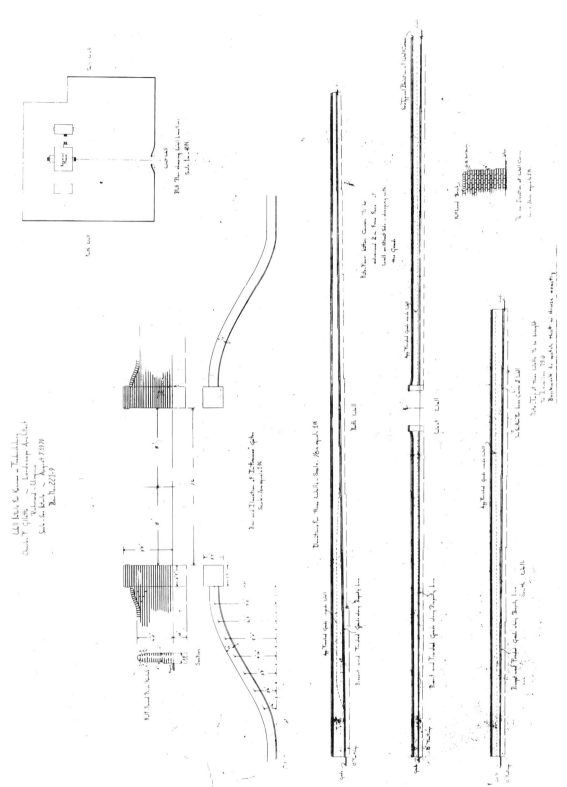

Garden wall details at Kenmore by Charles F. Gillette, landscape architect, 1930

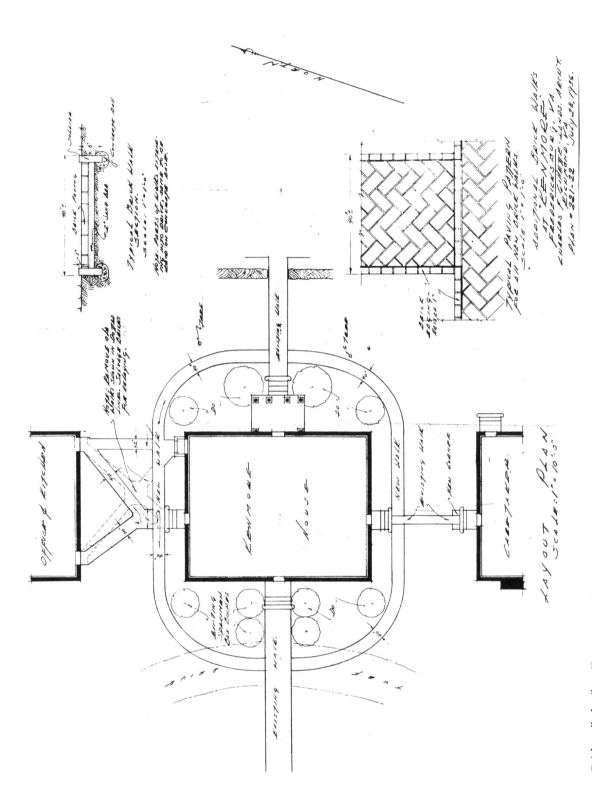

Brick walk details at Kenmore, 1936

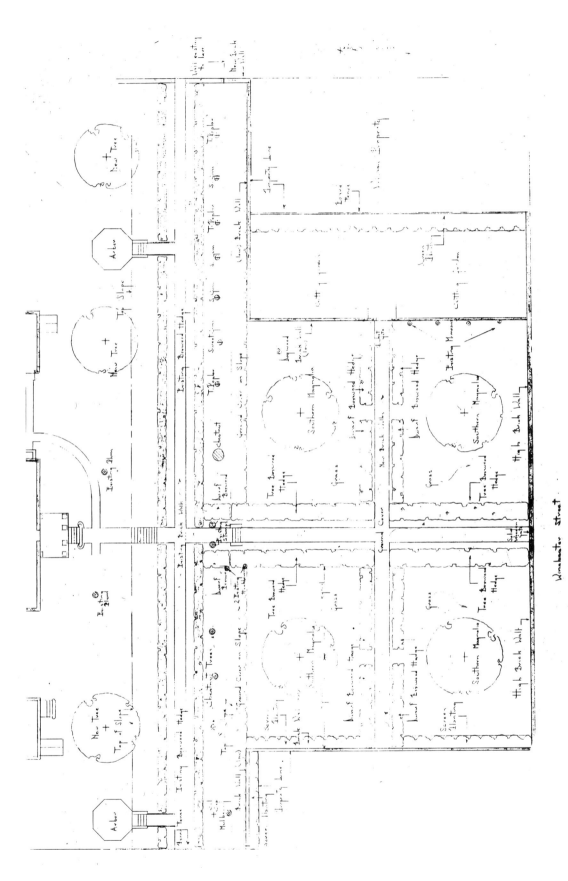

New Kenmore garden plan, Charles F. Gillette, landscape architect, 1940

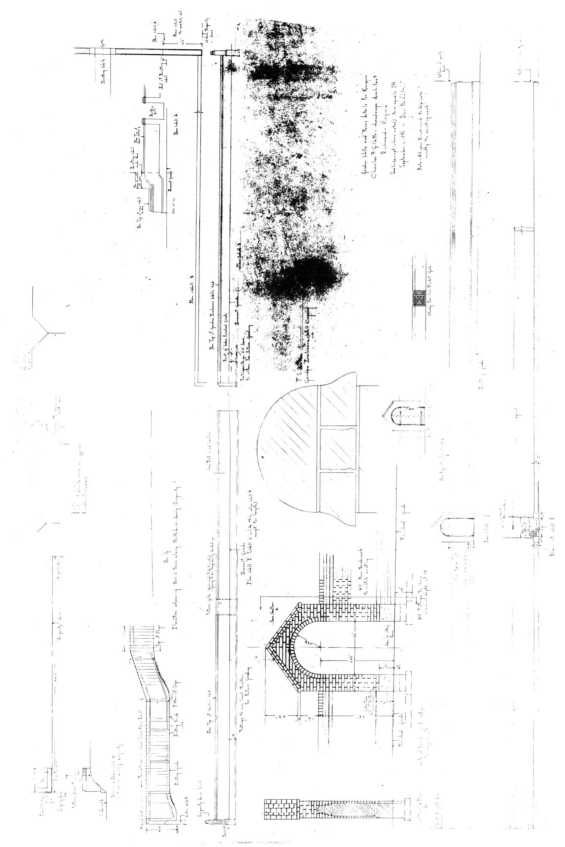

Details of the enclosure wall and gate at Kenmore, Charles F. Gillette, landscape architect, 1940

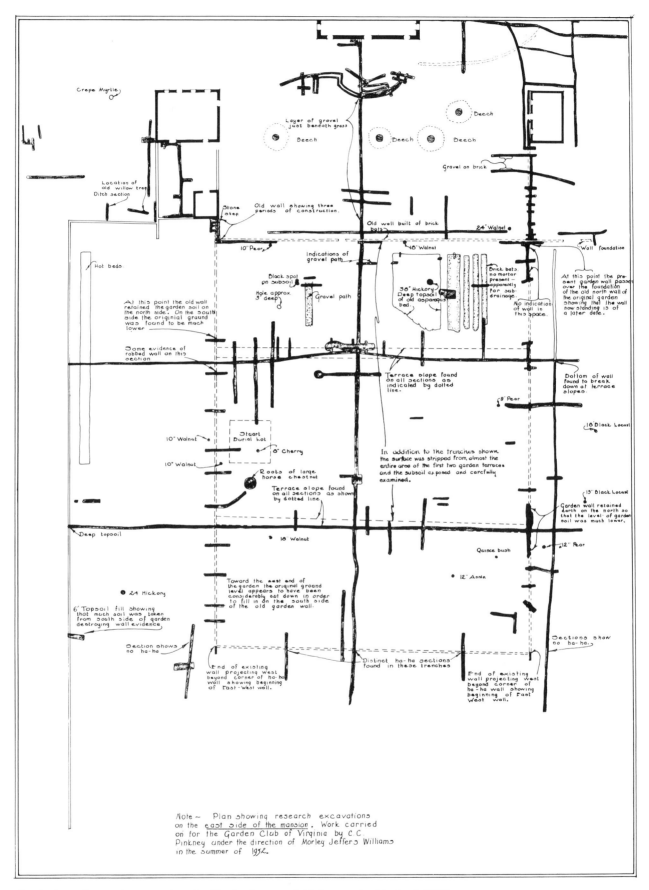

Sketch plans of excavations carved out by Charles Coatsworth Pinkney under Morley J. Williams, 1932

Stratford

STRATFORD IS LOCATED upon commanding ground on the south bank of the Potomac River, southeast of Fredericksburg and about fifty miles below Washington. As nearly as can be determined, the building of Stratford was begun about 1729 by Thomas Lee to replace his older house, Mount Pleasant, which had burned earlier that year. To help defray the costs of construction, friends sent funds from England. Queen Caroline, wife of George II, also sent a gift of money in appreciation for Lee's outstanding services to the Crown.

This house that Thomas Lee and his wife built reflected the new style and proportion for domestic design that was inaugurated by the Governor's Palace in Williamsburg. During the seventeenth century the important brick dwellings of Virginia had been rather small and had shown distinct Jacobean characteristics. But with the building of the new mansion for the governor, the influence of Wren brought changes in design and an increase in size for the great houses, such as Stratford and Rosewell.

The H-plan of Stratford has many counterparts in the period around 1700, both in England and in the colonies. Many illustrations of this basic plan were shown in Stephen Primatt's *The City and Country Builder*, published in 1667. But there are certain distinctive features that make Stratford unique. Placing the main floor above a high basement was unusual in the colonies at this period. The great flight of steps that leads to this floor and the two chimney groupings with connecting arches are also features seldom seen in early houses along the Potomac.

A survey of private documents of the Lee family was made by Fiske Kimball, architect and adviser to the Stratford Foundation, in 1931, but nothing was found to date the order of development of the various components of the total Stratford establishment. Chronology was determined primarily from surviving evidence in the buildings themselves, such as materials, designs of roofs, and window arches.

These studies produced evidence that the brick walls of the mansion were bonded continuously, indicating that the house was built as a whole. This was in contrast to the building of many large houses, where a wing was first constructed, followed later by the building of the main portion of the house. To build such a large house in its entirety must have taken a period of years. Kimball surmised from the style of the Corinthian

Central garden walk with crape myrtles

capitals in the great hall that it was completed by 1740. Work continued on the supporting buildings of the estate until Thomas Lee died in 1750.

Little building seems to have been done by Thomas Lee's oldest son, Philip Ludwell Lee, who inherited the estate. But he may have developed the garden, for there is a note in the estate accounts for "bricklaying at the M.H., Garden Walls and house in 1776, 77, 78."

In 1793 Henry Lee (the third of that name) married, as his second wife, Anne Hill Carter of Corotoman and Shirley. Of their six children, four were born at Stratford. The youngest of these was Robert Edward Lee.

Many changes were made in both the interior and exterior of the mansion during the years of ownership by Anne and Henry Lee. Most notable was the addition of a north portico and the removal of the impressive front staircase of Portland stone and its replacement by a narrower stairway of Rappahannock stone. None of the work during this period was comparable either in design or workmanship with that of the original construction. This decline in craftsmanship undoubtedly reflected the decline in prosperity of Tidewater Virginia. No longer was this section of preeminent influence in the developing nation. The tide of settlement had moved inland. Grave financial problems beset the family, and in 1810 Henry Lee moved to Alexandria. Stratford then became the home of Major Henry Lee, his son by an earlier marriage.

Young Henry Lee held Stratford for twelve years. In 1817 he married Anne McCarty, and together they made many changes outside the house. Short on funds but long on labor, they pulled down two of the original brick buildings and used the brick to build the great walls that surround the mansion area on the south and east.

Through mismanagement the estate became financially insolvent. In 1822 it was deeded to William C. Somerville, thus ending tenure of the Lee family. Four generations of the family had contributed to the building of Stratford as we know it today. There followed a century of varied ownerships in which Stratford gradually sank into disrepair. Certain additions, such as the portico of Henry Lee, collapsed, but the original fabric of the house, the dependencies and the yard, as built by Thomas Lee, remained essentially intact.

The well-preserved brick dwelling remained. Its brick outbuildings, in fair condition, flanked the four corners of the dwelling and their connecting brick walls remained. East of the house a ruined wall of brick and stone surrounded a large vegetable and fruit garden. To the south there were vestiges of a garden plot and lawn, and to the west indications of an orchard. To the north lay the remains of an old driveway leading over rough terrain to the old river landing. The area around the mansion was level and shaded by very old, remarkably well-preserved trees.

The preliminary steps for preserving and restoring Stratford were taken by a small group of southern women, residents in New England, all members of the William Alexander, Jr., Chapter, United Daughters of the Confederacy of Connecticut. It was this preservation-minded group who raised the money for the initial payment and signed the contract of purchase on January 19, 1929, the 122d anniversary of the birth

Side gate to garden

Boxwood parterre

of General Lee. Having received temporary title, they then formed the Robert E. Lee Memorial Foundation to complete the payments, take permanent title, and reestablish Stratford as an operating plantation.

On June 12, 1929, shortly after this final transaction, the Foundation sent a telegram to The Garden Club of Virginia, at its annual meeting in Winchester, asking that it restore the gardens at Stratford. This request was granted. Funds to carry out this initial restoration were raised by individual gifts and by proceeds from Historic Garden Week tours of 1930, 1931, and 1932.

Arthur Shurtleff (spelling later changed to Shurcliff) of Boston, landscape architect for Colonial Williamsburg, was retained to conduct archaeological investigations for the restoration. Active work was started July 28, 1930, and was continued until September 29, 1930.

Excavations began along a line of wire fences south of the mansion and soon uncovered the foundations of a ha-ha wall and a brick pavement to the south of it. The lines of the ancient road coming from the south and southwest that had been all but obliterated by ploughing of the fields were established and marked for future consideration. The list of discoveries grew rapidly.

Concurrent with the work of excavation, a thorough study was made of the inventories of Thomas Lee and Philip Ludwell Lee. Further research was made in the Library

Espaliered pears

of Congress, the Boston Athenaeum, and in other public and private libraries. Advertisements were published in Virginia newspapers for old pictures, letters, and personal recollections of Stratford. A permanent record was made through photography and measurements of brickwork, both above and below ground in walls, pavements, and structures. A field study was made of the similarities and differences between the bricks, mortar, and types of bonding in various walls and pavements in the hope of finding evidence of their age in relation to garden walls. The studies made of the mansion and associated buildings cast light on the grounds, just as the excavations and studies of the grounds cast light on the mansion.

By October 1930 this extensive archaeological and documentary study temporarily exhausted the funds available for preliminary investigation. It was agreed by Shurcliff and the Restoration Committee that it would be well to conclude this first phase and take time to assess the information gathered. There was assurance that, bit by bit, evidence was being assembled to provide proof of location of the garden.

By 1931 it was evident that the Stratford gardens were laid out with careful attention to levels and grading. This question of levels prompted the committee to engage Herbert Claiborne of Richmond to execute a topographic survey of the garden area. Claiborne's engineering experience and knowledge of Virginia colonial history, habits, and customs enabled him to give a new interpretation to some of the problems posed.

During the period of initial documentary research conducted by Shurcliff, correspondence had been exchanged between the Restoration Committee and the Harvard School of Landscape Architecture. This led to an arrangement with Harvard University whereby under a grant from the Clark Fund for Research in Landscape Design, Harvard would lend its associate, Morley Williams, to complete research at Stratford. Upon completion of his research in the spring of 1932, Williams was engaged to draw plans for restoration of the garden.

Coupled with the previous Shurcliff records, this latest research showed proof of the old layout of the gardens, the walls, and terrain, as well as verifying the original approach to the mansion and the vista from mansion to river. By October the plans were drawn by Williams and approved for execution by The Garden Club of Virginia with full sanction of the Robert E. Lee Memorial Foundation. The only deletions from the plans were the garden houses at the termination of the wall. These were disapproved, being considered by Kimball as unauthentic.

The period selected for the restoration was that of 1700–1812 as suggested by a letter written by Thomas Lee Shippen, a grandson of Thomas Lee, in which he described the Stratford gardens in 1790.

For construction of the walls, bricks similar to those used in the period of 1775 were selected. The north and south garden walls, the east ha-ha wall, separating the garden proper from the grove, or area leading to the tomb, and the long wall leading to the octagon foundation were reconstructed or repaired. The new brickwork matched the existing brickwork admirably. The coping chosen for these walls is an early pattern, examples of which can be seen at Mount Vernon.

Outside the garden walls extensive work was done. The octagon house was constructed, as were garden gates. A toolhouse was erected according to the Williams plan. The south ha-ha wall was reconstructed and the approach road built. To the north the vista was reestablished. At Stratford, on May 9, 1936, the Foundation held a meeting in honor of The Garden Club of Virginia, in recognition of the contribution made in restoring the gardens.

To alleviate the expense of maintenance of the gardens in their early stages, The Garden Club of Virginia agreed to establish a temporary trust, the interest from which would be used to help defray expenses of garden maintenance. By 1941 the financial affairs of the Foundation were in order and the principal of this trust was used for further restoration of the gardens.

Plans for this additional work were drawn by the landscape architect Umberto Innocenti, who had been engaged by the Foundation. The work was paid for by Garden Club funds formerly held in trust. Among the refinements of this phase were an improvement and enlargement of the vista to the river, the construction of brick walks, and a brick wall on the northern end of the west area of the yard. These walls were constructed as designed by Kimball but with openings introduced by Innocenti.

In 1955 The Garden Club of Virginia undertook further work at Stratford. This time it was under the guidance of Alden Hopkins, who succeeded Shurcliff as landscape architect for Colonial Williamsburg. The most urgent need of the garden was for shade. Other needs were for color and the creation of something to give a third dimension to the flat parterres. Fourteen yellow locusts were planted along the main axis, and the locust grove to the north of the garden was also replanted with yellow locust to replace the honey locust, which had not flourished. Flowering shrubs were added to the parterres to enhance, rather than conflict with, the pattern. Overgrown boxwood was removed from the Lee coat of arms parterre, and the parterre design was simplified where it could be accomplished without harm to the pattern. Side walks leading out of the center oval were closed. The long center walk, which had become badly twisted and curved because of necessary removal of large bordering boxwood, was realigned. To add color, a few thousand tulips and squills were planted. Along the walls iris, peonies, asters, and day lilies were also planted. Introduction of European cranberry bushes on the upper terrace and on the lower parterre were in recognition of General Lee's preference for this shrub.

The creation of a shady, restful, colorful garden with a mature appearance was the aim of this revival. The added trees and shrubs did not interrupt the views over and into the garden but rather created interesting vistas. The garden as viewed from the mansion retained its importance.

The major difficulty encountered in recreating the Stratford garden was its large area of plantation dimensions. The landscape depended upon the location and shape of the mansion and yard, which in turn depended upon the vistas and the complicated demands of plantation life. This was not a single house and garden. It was a highly organized way of life to be recreated.

The old spreading hickory tree

TREES

Carya pecan, Pecan
Celtis occidentalis, Hackberry
Cornus florida, Flowering Dogwood
Cornus florida rubra, Pink Flowering
  Dogwood
Crataegus phaenopyrum, Washington Thorn
Fagus americana, American Beech
Ilex opaca, American Holly

Koelreuteria paniculata, Goldenrain-Tree
Lagerstroemia indica, Crape-Myrtle
Prunus sp., Damson
Prunus cerasus var., Cherry
Prunus persica, Peach
Pyrus var., Pear
Robinia pseudoacacia, Black Acacia, Yellow
  Locust

SHRUBS

Buxus sempervirens, Common Boxwood (true tree)
Buxus sempervirens suffruticosa, Dwarf Boxwood (true dwarf)
Chionanthus virginicus, Fringe-Tree
Cotinus coggygria, Smoke-Bush
Gelsemium caroliniana, Carolina Yellow Jessamine
Hibiscus syriacus, Rose-of-Sharon, Shrubby Althea

Lonicera fragrantissima, Bush Honeysuckle
Pyracantha coccinea, Firethorn
Syringa vulgaris, Common Lilac
Viburnum Lentago, Nanny-Berry
Viburnum Opulus, European Cranberry-Bush
Viburnum Tinus, Evergreen Viburnum
Vitex Agnus-castus, Chaste-Tree or Hemp-Tree or Monks Pepper-Tree
Wisteria sinensis, Chinese Wisteria

VINES

Hedera helix, English Ivy

HERBACEOUS PLANTS—ANNUALS AND PERENNIALS

Anemone sp., Anemone
Crocus var., Crocus
Fritillaria meleagris, Checkered-Lilly
Hemerocallis var., Day-Lilly
Hyacinthus var., Hyacinth
Lavandula spica, Lavender
Muscari botryoides, Grape-Hyacinth
Narcissus Jonquilla, Jonquil

Paeonia var., Peony
Primula veris, Cowslip
Rosmarinus officinalis, Rosemary
Salvia officinalis, Sage
Santolina chamaecyparissus, Santolina
Scilla sibirica, Siberian Squill
Teucrium chamaedrys, Germander
Tulipa var., Tulip

Vinca minor, Periwinkle

ROSES

Rosa centifolia, Rose of Provence, Cabbage Rose, described by Theophrastus before 300 B.C.

Rosa laevigata, Cherokee Rose, introduced into America before 1759.

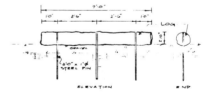

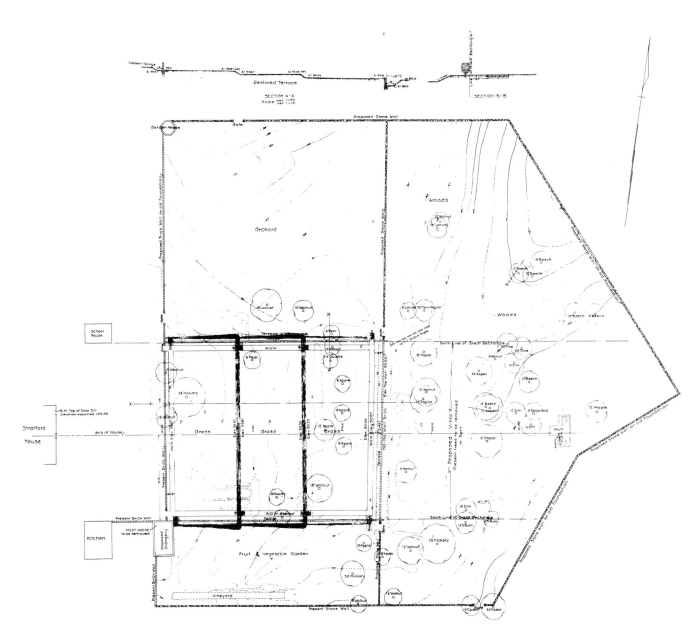

Tentative plan of the garden development at Stratford Hall, compiled by W. W. LaPrade and Bros., 1931

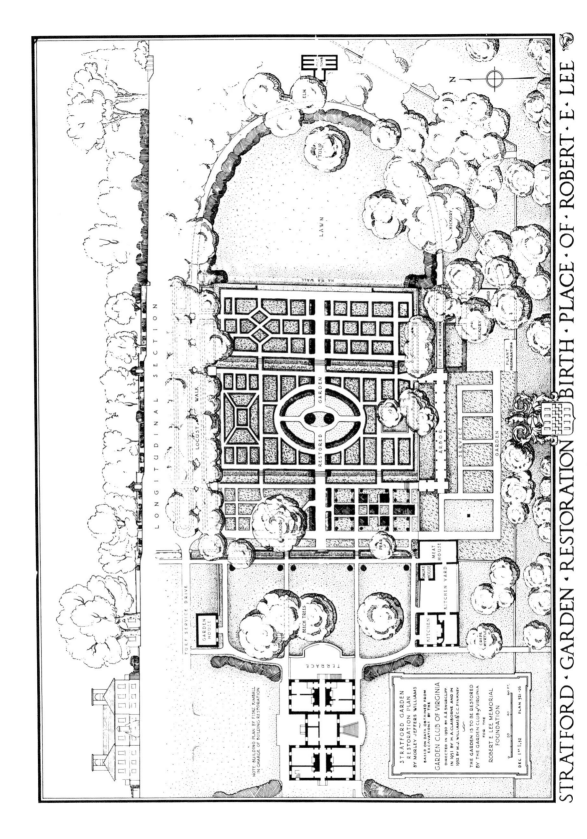

STRATFORD · GARDEN · RESTORATION BIRTH PLACE · OF · ROBERT · E · LEE

Garden presentation plan of Stratford Hall by Morley J. Williams, landscape architect, 1932

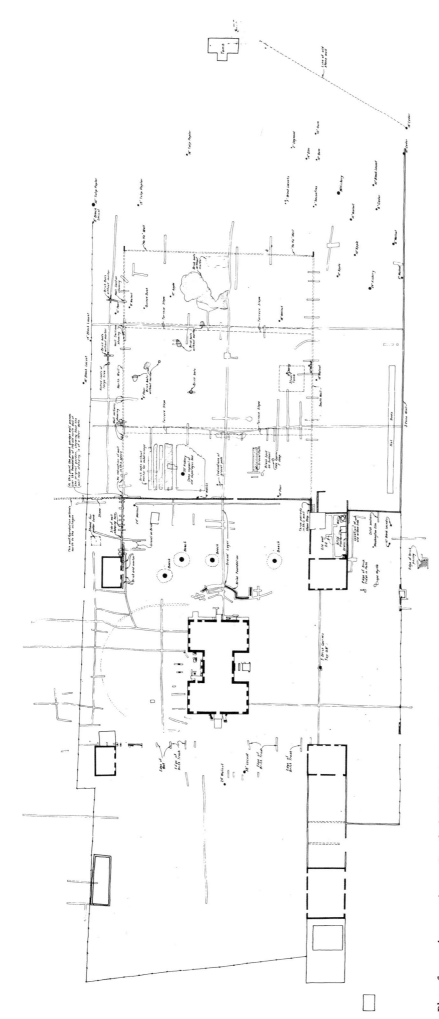

Plan of research excavations at Stratford Hall, Morley J. Williams, landscape architect, 1933

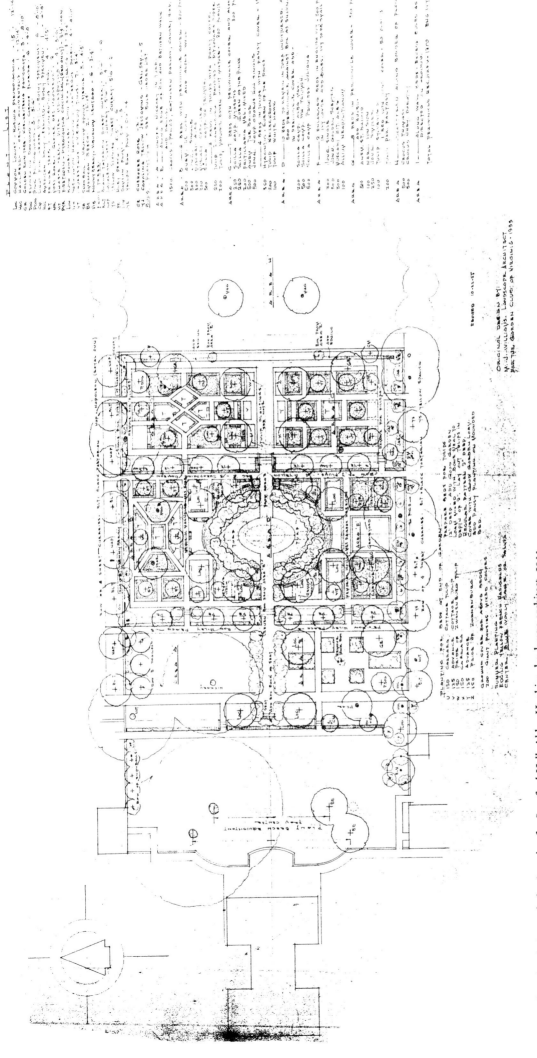

Revised garden design and planting plan for Stratford Hall, Alden Hopkins, landscape architect, 1955

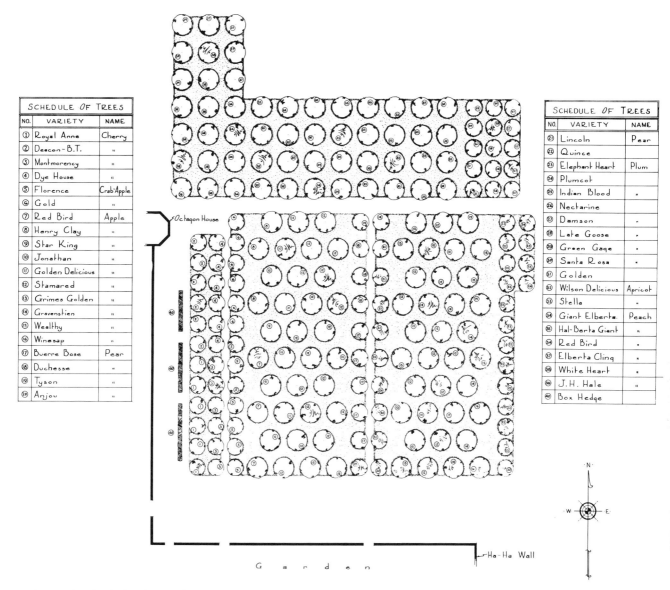

SCHEDULE OF TREES		
NO.	VARIETY	NAME
①	Royal Anne	Cherry
②	Deacon-B.T.	"
③	Montmorency	"
④	Dye House	"
⑤	Florence	Crab-Apple
⑥	Gold	"
⑦	Red Bird	Apple
⑧	Henry Clay	"
⑨	Star King	"
⑩	Jonathan	"
⑪	Golden Delicious	"
⑫	Stamared	"
⑬	Grimes Golden	"
⑭	Gravenstien	"
⑮	Wealthy	"
⑯	Winesap	"
⑰	Buerre Bose	Pear
⑱	Duchesse	"
⑲	Tyson	"
⑳	Anjou	"

SCHEDULE OF TREES		
NO.	VARIETY	NAME
㉑	Lincoln	Pear
㉒	Quince	
㉓	Elephant Heart	Plum
㉔	Plumcot	
㉕	Indian Blood	"
㉖	Nectarine	
㉗	Damson	"
㉘	Late Goose	"
㉙	Green Gage	"
㉚	Santa Rosa	"
㉛	Golden	
㉜	Wilson Delicious	Apricot
㉝	Stella	
㉞	Giant Elberta	Peach
㉟	Hal-Berta Giant	"
㊱	Red Bird	"
㊲	Elberta Cling	"
㊳	White Heart	"
㊴	J.H. Hale	"
㊵	Box Hedge	

Octagon House

Garden

Ha-Ha Wall

Proposed orchard plan for Stratford Hall (not planted), B. F. Cheatham III, 1933

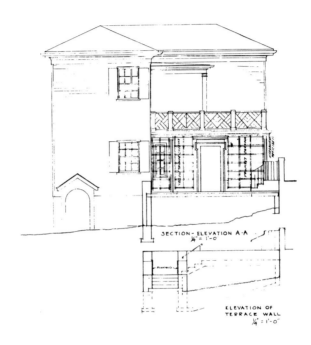

SECTION - ELEVATION A·A
¼" = 1'-0"

ELEVATION OF
TERRACE WALL
¼" = 1'-0"

Woodrow Wilson Birthplace: The Manse

ON THE CORNER of Frederick and Coalter streets, in the city of Staunton, stands the birthplace of the twenty-eighth president of the United States, Thomas Woodrow Wilson. The congregation of the First Presbyterian Church of Staunton built this manse in 1845 on top of the hill that rose above their church. The contractor and builder of the Manse was John Fifer, who not only helped lay the bricks in the house but also made the bricks in his yard on the turnpike just a mile from Staunton. The house is rectangular and of Greek Revival architecture. It has two stories on the east front facing Coalter Street, but on the opposite side the land falls away steeply, exposing a full lower story. This lower story opens directly onto a garden. At the rear of the house round pillars on pedestals extend the full height of the house, supporting porches for the two upper stories.

Thomas Woodrow Wilson was born in the Manse, December 28, 1856, but his first association with the house was brief, as his father resigned the Staunton pastorate to accept a church in Augusta, Georgia, when young Woodrow was scarcely a year old. Mrs. Wilson, however, had made many friends in Staunton and returned to visit often. One of her particular friends was Mary Julia Baldwin, headmistress of the Augusta Female Seminary (later Mary Baldwin College). The two Wilson girls attended this school for the 1866–67 session, and for this period Mrs. Wilson and her son were guests in the Manse. Later, while a student at the University of Virginia, Wilson was a frequent visitor at Staunton and to the Manse.

In 1911 as a candidate for the presidency of the United States, Wilson made a great effort to emphasize his Staunton birth. This did much to counter the South's objection to his having been governor of New Jersey. By special invitation of the people of Staunton, Wilson and his wife returned there on his birthday in 1912 during the brief time between his election as president and his assumption of that office. They stayed at the Manse as guests of the minister and his wife.

In the years following World War I there began to develop a strong movement to preserve and maintain Wilson's birthplace as a historical site. After prolonged negotiations the church sold the Manse in 1929 to Mary Baldwin College with the understanding that it could be conveyed later to "a society for the perpetuation of the name and

The Manse and central garden steps

fame of Woodrow Wilson." By this time part of the original garden of the Manse had
been sold and many structural changes had been made in the house.

Mary Baldwin College held title to the Manse until October 29, 1938. During these
nine years volunteer personnel kept the house open for a growing number of visitors.
In the meantime a foundation to purchase the birthplace was organized. Wilson's
widow, Edith Bolling Wilson, aided the movement financially, along with the General
Assembly of Virginia, the Woodrow Wilson Foundation of New York, and other
private donors.

In 1932, when The Garden Club of Virginia, responding to repeated requests,
agreed to undertake the rehabilitation of this garden, a fortuitous thing happened.
Charles Gillette, landscape architect of Richmond, who had been retained as architect
for the project, found in his files a letter containing a plan for this garden. The plan had
been drawn by a former resident of the Manse, some sixty years before. As far as possible,
suggestions in this letter as to plant material were incorporated in the Gillette plan. The
steep terrain necessitated terracing the original garden. On the lowest of these terraces
the Gillette plan suggested Victorian bowknot flower beds, outlined by low clipped
boxwood. On the terraces above, his plan included a Victorian summerhouse, well
house, and grape arbor, each of these brick floored. The existing cement sidewalks near
the house were replaced with brick for aesthetic reasons and because cement would not
have been used in the original garden. After much debate a brick wall was designed and
built on the Frederick Street boundary. Although the previous fence had been boards,

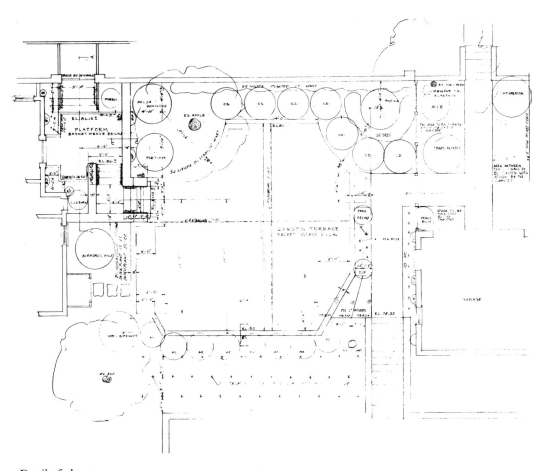

Detail of plan 13

The reception terrace

The garden pavilion

a wooden fence meant upkeep. The rake of the brick wall, as finally constructed, simply followed the ground and was topped with a molded brick coping. Appropriate furniture was placed to make the garden comfortably inviting.

The gift of the 1933 garden restoration inspired other gifts greatly needed for renovating and furnishing the house itself. In 1940 a front porch, which had been added in recent years, was removed and replaced by one of appropriate design. With its completion The Garden Club of Virginia made a further donation to help defray the cost of rebuilding the front wall on both sides of the new porch. This project was under the direction of Mrs. Woodrow Wilson. At the same time Garden Club funds were used to refine the planting of the Gillette plan of 1933.

With the constant increase of visitors to this memorial, it became difficult to maintain the grass paths in the garden. In the spring of 1960 The Garden Club replaced the worn grass of the lower garden paths with brick. Old bricks were used, laid in sand, following the pattern originally suggested by Gillette almost thirty years before. During this same period a small plot of ground adjacent to the Manse property and originally a part of the 1846 holding was acquired by the Woodrow Wilson Foundation. Under Gillette's supervision this made an integrated part of the garden plan.

Again in 1967–68 The Garden Club returned to the Manse. This time a lower terrace connecting the garden with a newly constructed parking lot immediately below the Woodrow Wilson property was added. For this additional terrace The Garden Club engaged Ralph E. Griswold as landscape architect. By preserving the Gillette garden and meeting the demands for parking access, the transitional terrace filled a practical necessity in an attractive way.

The hills of Staunton give it a unique beauty but also present very real problems in landscaping. Steep terrain demanded walls and steps that might have been ugly but were actually made beautiful features of the garden. Potential hazards were made assets. For forty years this garden has developed upon a sound initial plan, guided by care and expert advice to its present state of congeniality with the land upon which it is built.

The bowknot parterre

TREES

Cornus florida, Flowering Dogwood
Fagus americana, American Beech

Prunus glandulosa, Flowering Almond
Prunus serrulata, Flowering Cherry

SHRUBS

Buxus sempervirens, Common Boxwood
(true tree)
Buxus sempervirens suffruticosa, Dwarf
Boxwood (true dwarf)
Calycanthus floridus, Carolina Allspice
Chaenomeles lagenaria, Japanese Flowering
Quince

Kerria japonica, Kerria
Philadelphus coronarius, European Mock-
Orange
Spiraea prunifolia, Bridal Wreath
Syringa vulgaris, Common Lilac
Viburnum Opulus, European Cranberry-
Bush

VINES

Akebia quinata, Five-leaf Akebia

HERBACEOUS PLANTS—ANNUALS AND PERENNIALS

Althea rosea, Hollyhock
Anchusa capensis, Summer Forget-Me-Not
Chrysanthemum coccineum, Pyrethrum
Chrysanthemum coronarium, Crown Daisy
Delphinium cheilanthum, Garland Larkspur
Dicentra spectabilis, Bleeding-Heart
Digitalis purpurea, Foxglove
Hemerocallis flava, Lemon Day-Lily

Hosta subcordata, Plantain Lily
Lavandula spica, Lavender
Lilium candidum, Madonna Lily
Mertensia virginica, Virginia Bluebell
Paeonia albiflora, White Peony
Paeonia Moutan banksii, Tree Peony, first
grown in England (Kew Gardens) in
1789

Phlox paniculata, Summer Perennial Phlox

ROSES

Rosa centifolia, Rose of Provence, Cabbage
Rose, described by Theophrastus before
300 B.C.
Rosa centifolia muscosa 'Duchesse de Ver-
neuil' 1856, a moss rose
Rosa centifolia muscosa 'Gloire des Mous-
seux' 1852, a moss rose
Rosa chinensis bourboniana 'Général
Jacqueminot' 1852, an early hybrid
perpetual
Rosa chinensis bourboniana 'Hermosa' 1840,
a Bourbon rose
Rosa chinensis bourboniana 'Souvenir de la
Malmaison' 1843, a Bourbon rose
Rosa chinensis semperflorus 'Old Blush,'
known in England before 1759
Rosa damascena versicolor, the rose of York

and Lancaster; contrary to tradition this
was not known before the beginning of
the seventeenth century.
Rosa gallica 'Cramoisi des Alpes' 1838, a
French rose
Rosa gigantea 'Gloire de Dijon' 1853, a
climbing tea rose
Rosa 'Camille de Rohan' 1861, a hybrid
perpetual
Rosa 'Horace Vernet' 1866, a hybrid from
Général Jacqueminot
Rosa 'Paul Neyron' 1869, a hybrid
perpetual
Rosa odorata 'Duchesse de Brabant' 1857,
a tea rose
Rosa sempervirens 'Felicite et Perpetue'
1827, a sport from the species

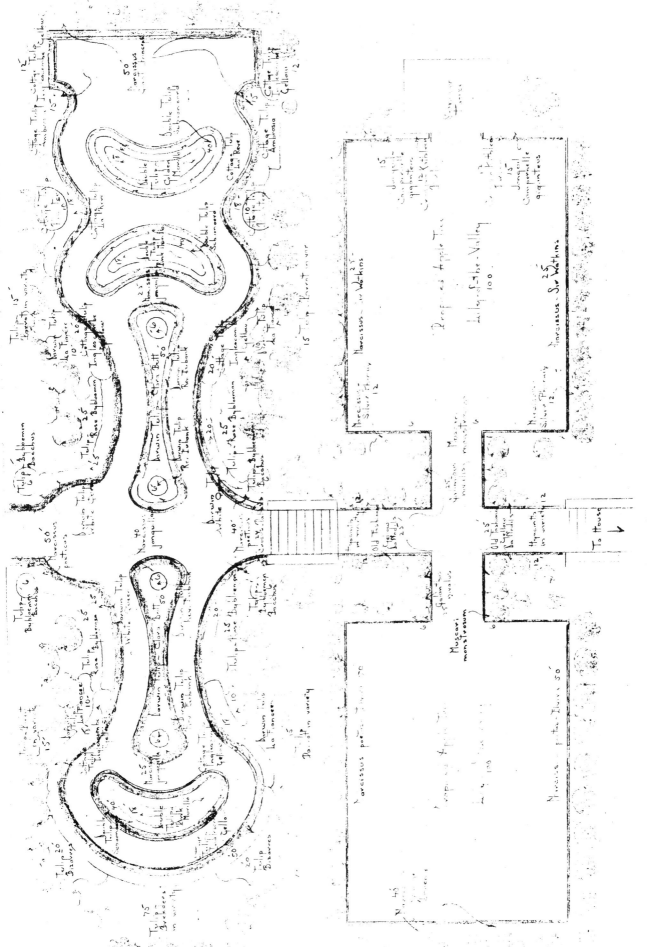

Bulb planting plan at the Woodrow Wilson Birthplace, Charles F. Gillette, landscape architect, 1933

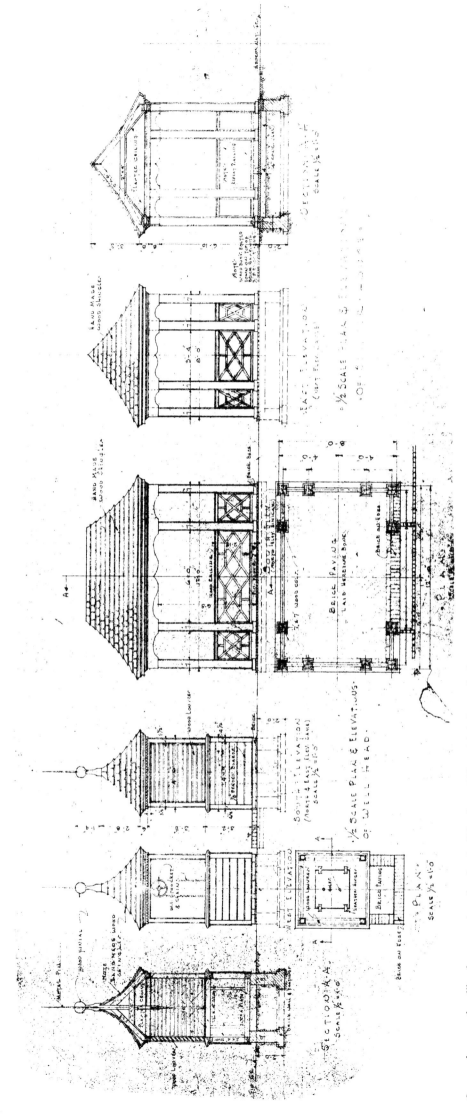

Summerhouse and wellhead construction plan for the Woodrow Wilson Birthplace, Charles F. Gillette, landscape architect, 1933

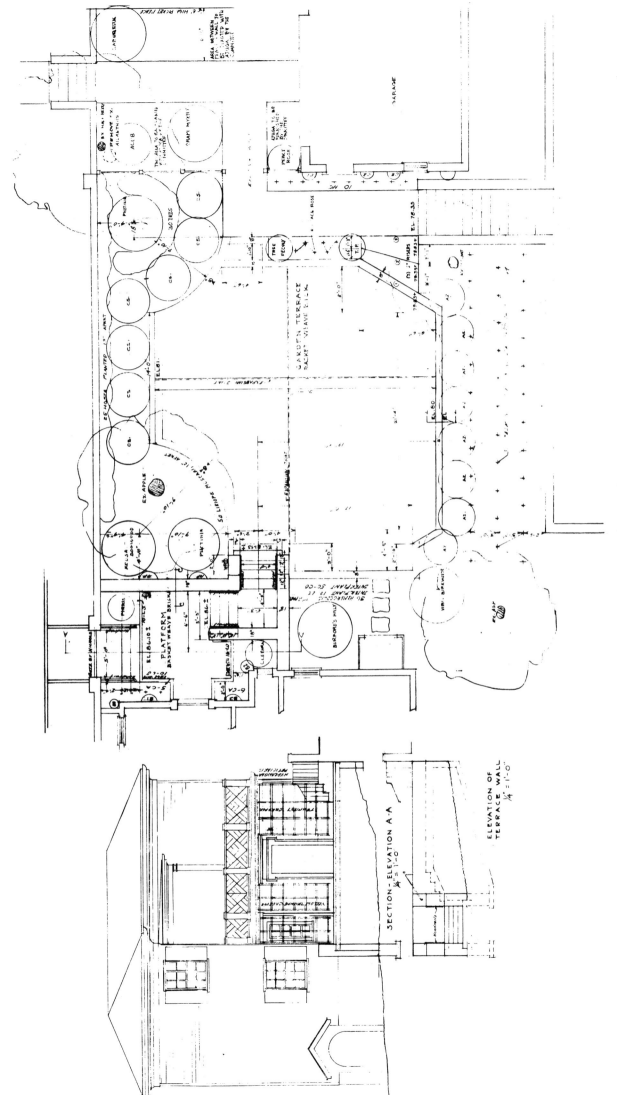

Plan for an additional terrace garden entrance at the Woodrow Wilson Birthplace, Griswold, Winters, and Swain, landscape architects, 1967

The Lee Chapel

Lee Memorial Chapel

FOUNDED IN 1749, Washington and Lee University is the sixth oldest institution of higher learning in America. Its front campus is of outstanding dignity and beauty. Washington Hall, which is the center of the columned buildings on the hill, and the Lee Chapel opposite are both National Historic Landmarks. These buildings are memorials to the men for whom the university is named.

The history of Washington and Lee reaches back to the middle of the eighteenth century and the establishment, a few miles north of Lexington, of a small classical school called Augusta Academy. In 1776 the school was patriotically renamed Liberty Hall, and at the end of the war was moved to a hill just west of the town of Lexington. Struggling to survive, the school received essential support in 1796 when George Washington endowed the institute with a gift of stock. A few years later the name was changed to Washington College. Following a disastrous fire the academy was moved in 1803 to its present location in Lexington.

During the 1820s the college undertook the construction of the columned and pilastered buildings that are the heart of the university today. Samuel Darst and John Jordan, Lexington builders and architects, were probably the designers of Washington Hall, the original building. Jordan, who had previously had experience in working with the building of the University of Virginia and Monticello, was influenced by the Classic Revival style of Jefferson.

Following the tragic years of the Civil War, a new era began for the college as Gen. Robert E. Lee became president. Under his inspiring leadership the small local college was transformed to a university of national stature. In 1867 the chapel of simple Victorian design was built under Lee's direction. It was the scene of his funeral in October 1870; his body is buried in the chapel crypt. In the statue chamber is the impressive marble recumbent figure by Edward Valentine representing Lee sleeping.

In the summer of 1933 the Blue Ridge Garden Club of Lexington petitioned The Garden Club of Virginia to "consider the building of a Boxwood Memorial Garden to Robert E. Lee at his tomb on the grounds of Washington and Lee University." The thought of a memorial planting appealed to The Garden Club, and Charles Gillette of Richmond was engaged to work out a plan. After study of the terrain it was realized that a boxwood walk or maze was not the solution, and a plan using other plant material was drawn for the chapel area.

The plan which Gillette submitted and which was carried out at the direction of The Garden Club was, appropriately, very simple. The front walk and entrance to the chapel were paved with brick laid over existing concrete. A brick coping was built around the grass plots before the entrance, and a new brick walk was laid leading from the side entrance to the main walk. Handsome yews, thickly underplanted with periwinkle, were placed at the entrance and behind the building. Yew hedges were planted along the old brick walks on either side of the chapel. A major expense of the project was for surgery on old trees in the area of the campus immediately around the chapel.

When this phase of the project was completed, attention was given to the entrance gates and to the parking space below the chapel. Gillette considered this a necessary part of the overall plan. The problem presented by this area is stated in a letter written January 11, 1935, from Gillette to a representative of the university:

Here, we have very large entrance gates that lead to nothing but a parking space . . . and I don't see any chance of ever carrying a roadway through these gates to the campus. The thought has finally come to me to make this parking space a memorial court. If it is enclosed with a planting of tree box and the paving is properly done. . . . it will look like a cool, green court. To make a final terminus to this court opposite the main gates, I am suggesting that a statue of either Washington or Lee be placed within a brick enclosure that will fit into the hillside. This paving I am suggesting to be of brick and old cobblestones, the brick to be a panel through the center that would be uninterrupted by automobiles, and the cobblestones would pave the two sides that would be the parking area, as indicated, for cars. The elm trees would be retained, and protected by a coping of cobblestones, and a planting of periwinkle around their base. The whole thing would be enclosed as indicated, with tree box.

As neither the university nor The Garden Club of Virginia had the money to execute this entire plan, a modification was carried out by The Garden Club.

In the simplified plan the parking court was encircled with a hedge of tree boxwood and the three existing elm trees were pruned and left to provide shade within the court. Since funds were not available to place a statue of Washington or Lee in the enclosure opposite the gates, a flag is flown there. On the hillside between the parking court and the chapel a few trees, including American holly, magnolia, beech, and maple were planted. By the fall of 1935 the planting was completed and turned over to the University.

This gift of The Garden Club of Virginia added beauty and dignity to the grounds around the Lee Chapel. It is a fitting memorial to the hero who made a new start here, leading his country through education to new achievement, unity, and greatness.

TREES

Fagus grandifolia, American Beech	*Magnolia grandiflora*, Southern Magnolia
Ilex opaca, American Holly	*Picea abies*, Norway Spruce

SHRUBS

Buxus sempervirens, Common Boxwood (true tree)	*Taxus baccata*, English Yew
	Taxus cuspidata, Japanese Yew
Taxus media Hicksii, Hicks Yew	

VINES

Hedera helix, English Ivy

HERBACEOUS PLANTS—ANNUALS AND PERENNIALS

Vinca minor, Periwinkle

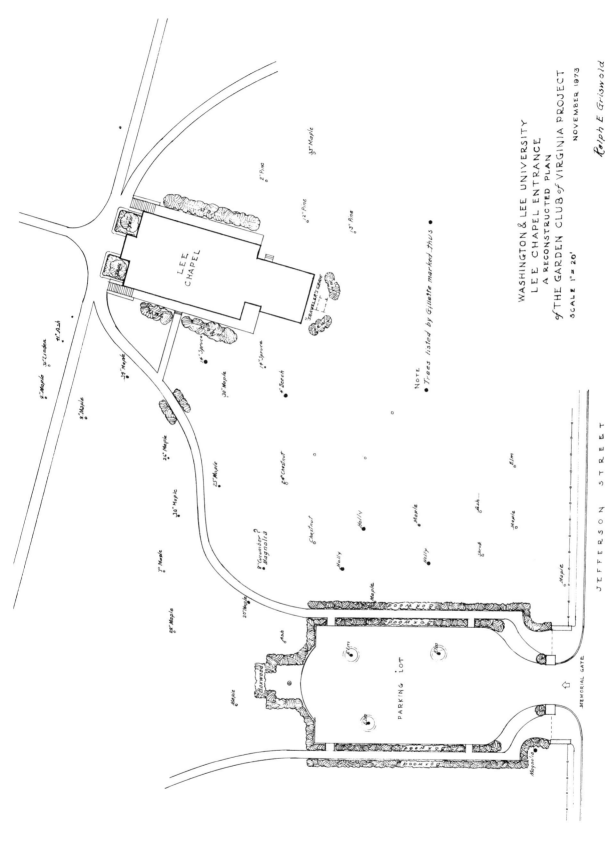

A reconstructed plan of the Lee Memorial Chapel entrance, Ralph E. Griswold, 1973; based on Charles Gillette plan of 1934

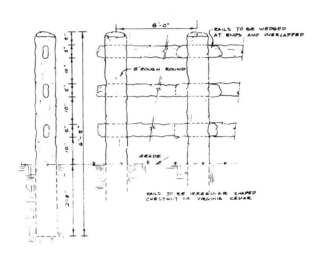

Rolfe-Warren House: Smith's Fort Plantation

OF ALL COLONIAL HISTORY stories perhaps the romance of John Rolfe and the Indian princess Pocahontas is the most appealing. Though Rolfe is chiefly remembered in this context, it is of much more importance to the Commonwealth of Virginia that he introduced to this colony the systematic cultivation of tobacco. Realizing that the strong coarse leaf of native Virginia tobacco could never be popular for export to England, he imported plants of two types of mild tobacco from the southern Spanish settlements. By this farsighted act he established the basis for the future economic prosperity of the colony and, ultimately, the Commonwealth.

It is a well-known story that Pocahontas, John Rolfe, and their baby son paid a visit to England in 1616 and were received cordially at Court. Unfortunately, after plans had been made for their return to the colony, Pocahontas died before the voyage was begun. The baby son, Thomas, was left in custody of his uncle, Henry Rolfe of London.

In 1640 Thomas came to America, where he had inherited a property called Smith's Fort Plantation. This is the same property upon which, in 1609, Captain John Smith built a fort for the protection of the beleaguered colonists. The land was a gift from Chief Powhatan to his daughter, Pocahontas, and John Rolfe upon their marriage in 1614.

A deposition of March 5, 1677, states that a house was built by Thomas Warren in 1652 at Smith's Fort Plantation. The house is described as being of brick and fifty feet in length. The land upon which the house was built had been purchased by Warren, who lived here until his death in 1669. The construction date of the present house is a subject of continuing debate. The large regular window openings and the subtle execution of the woodwork would indicate the house to be of early eighteenth-century construction. It seems unlikely, however, that a house of eighteenth-century date would fit exactly the recorded dimensions given in describing the 1652 structure. The uncertainty is increased by archaeological findings that revealed the presence of other early structures nearby. Whatever the date may be, the architectural merits of the house, coupled with the significance of Rolfe's ownership of this plantation, make this a property of importance.

The house is located in Surry County, situated about a half-mile from a promontory overlooking Gray's Creek. For many years the dwelling stood neglected. Located

Garden entrance

two miles from any maintained road and occupied by a succession of impoverished families who sold bricks from it, it is a wonder that anything survived. It was saved from complete destruction by John D. Rockefeller, Jr., who bought the ruin and gave it to the Association for the Preservation of Virginia Antiquities (APVA) in 1928. For the next six years the APVA gradually restored the house while the State Highway Department constructed a public road that gave vehicular access to what previously could only be reached on foot across fields.

In the spring of 1934 the APVA asked The Garden Club of Virginia to provide a seventeenth-century landscape setting for the house. The project was accepted in May 1934, and Arthur Shurcliff of Colonial Williamsburg was appointed landscape architect. Before any restoration plans were drawn, archaeological excavations were made that revealed previously existing buildings and walks. On these Shurcliff based his plan.

That any restoration could have been undertaken at this time of financial depression seems remarkable, and both the plans and their execution reflect the financial distress. Shurcliff's plan showed only the basic elements required for the appropriate setting of the house.

There was no money to construct the well and smokehouse that had been revealed by the excavations, and they were omitted. The two privies, however, were built because they formed an integral part of the design. Rail fences were built around the property to define its extent. As there was no money to buy shrubs to plant against this fence, it was embellished with vines—honeysuckle, clematis, and wisteria. Immediately around the house, as was the custom in those days, a picket fence was erected. The area between the outer and inner fences was plowed, harrowed, and leveled. Dogwood, redbud, sorrel trees, and other small native trees were encouraged to grow naturally.

In the choice of plant material strict adherence to plants supposed to have been used in the early part of the seventeenth century would have imposed an unrealistic limitation. It was decided, therefore, to include plants that were known from earliest days in Virginia to the time of the American Revolution. Native arborvitae was used as an evergreen screen for the newly constructed garden houses. Crape-myrtles, because of their long-enduring brilliant color and hardiness, were planted as accents. Boxwood and a persimmon tree were used in front of the house, holly trees at the back marked

Straight rows of tulip trees parallel the entrance road.

Garden area

the corners where the paths intersect. Fig trees indicated where the kitchen garden and orchard had been. Although these were practical plantings, they also maintained the sense of beauty that prevailed in pioneer gardens. Old-fashioned roses, such as the delicious scented Provence, were used.

By 1956 the financial outlook for all the shrines had changed, and The Garden Club of Virginia took another look at this particular project. It engaged Shurcliff's successor, Alden Hopkins, to make a restudy to attract more people to this shrine. It was concluded that something should be done to make a more inviting entrance. The existing pine trees at the entrance were thinned and cut to give the passing motorist a better view of the house. But a more emphatic attraction was created by planting a double row of tulip trees, sixty feet apart, from the entrance pine grove to the fence enclosure of the house. A new tulip tree was planted on the east side to balance the persimmon on the west. A few red cedars were scattered along the east-west fence, and another cedar was added to the south to emphasize the corner. The boxwood was reset, four at each corner of the house and three on each side of the steps. The study that brought about these suggestions was financed by The Garden Club of Virginia, but the revisions were carried out by the Association for the Preservation of Virginia Antiquities.

TREES

Cercis canadensis, Eastern Redbud
Cornus florida, Flowering Dogwood
Diospyros virginiana, Persimmon
Ficus carica, Fig

Juniperus virginiana, Eastern red cedar
Liriodendron Tulipifera, Tulip-Tree
Malus var., Apples
Oxydendrum arboreum, Sorrel-Tree

Pyrus communis var., Pears

SHRUBS

Buxus sempervirens, Common Boxwood
(true tree)
Buxus sempervirens suffruticosa, Dwarf
Boxwood (true dwarf)

Lagerstroemia indica, Crape-Myrtle
Myrica caroliniensis, Bayberry
Syringa vulgaris, Common Lilac

VINES

Campsis radicans, Trumpet-Vine

Lonicera japonica, Climbing Honeysuckle

Wisteria sinensis, Chinese Wisteria

ROSES

Rosa alba, Rose of York
Rosa centifolia, Rose of Provence, Cabbage
Rose, described by Theophrastus before
300 B.C.

Rosa centifolia muscosa 'Duchesse de Ver-
neuil' 1856, a moss rose
Rosa gallica officinalis, Rose of Lancaster
Rosa spinosissima, Scotch Hedge Rose

The plantation yard is enclosed with a picket fence.

The well outside the garden area

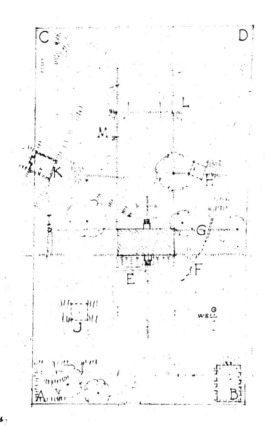

A· NO FOUNDATION FOUND BY A.A.S.
B· FOUNDATION WITH SMALL CHIMNEY,
  DISCONTINUOUS 14" SHALLOW BRICKWALL
  UNEARTHED BY A.A.S. NOV.14.1934·
C· DIGGING BY A.A.S. NOV.14.1934 REVEALED NO
  TRACES OF FOUNDATIONS IN REGIONS DUG.
D· MODERN FOUNDATIONS IN PLAIN
  SIGHT MOSTLY NORTH OF THIS CORNER.
E· STAIN REVEALED BY SHAVING THE
  GROUND WHICH INDICATED OLD
  GRAVEL PATH· A.A·S JULY.26.1934·
F· STAIN REVEALED BY SHAVING THE
  GROUND WHICH INDICATED OLD
  GRAVEL PATH. A.A.S. JULY 26.1934·
G· BRICK BAT PATH 12" TO 18" WIDE
  EXCAVATED TO FULL LENGTH SHOWN.
  DIGGING BY A.A.S. NOV.14.1934.
H· REMAINS OF SQUARE BRICK WALL 8" TO 12"
  WIDE IN FAIR CONDITION- A.A.S. JULY.26.1934.
I· BRICK AT 56'AND 59' DISTANT FROM BUILDING
  DIGGING BY A.A.S JULY.26.1934
J· REMAINS OF FOUR PIERS AND SOME
  SCATTERED BRICKWORK .A.A.S. JULY.26.1934
K· FINE FOUNDATION OF OLD BRICK VERY
  CAREFULLY LAID WALLS A DEEP
  ON INSIDE· A.A.S. NOV.14.19
  SEE DETAIL DRAWING LOWER CORNER
  OF THIS SHEET
L· SMEAR OF OLD BRICK. A.A.S. JULY.26.1934.
M· SMEAR OF OLD BRICK. A.A.S. JULY.26.1934

NOTE. LINES INDICATED THUS━━━ SHOW THE
POSITION OF TRENCHES OR AREAS
WHICH WERE THOROUGHLY EXAMINED
BY DIGGING ON JULY.26, AND NOV.14,1934
AREAS "H"·"J"AND "K" ARE NOT INDICATED IN
THIS MANNER AS THE HATCHED LINES WOULD
OBLITERATE THE DRAWING OF THE
FINDINGS AS SHOWN.

DETAIL OF FOUNDATION AT "K"
SCALE 10'=1"

Excavation plan of the Rolfe-Warren House, Arthur A. Shurcliff, landscape architect, 1934

Record of excavations of the Rolfe-Warren House, Arthur A. Shurcliff, landscape architect, 1934

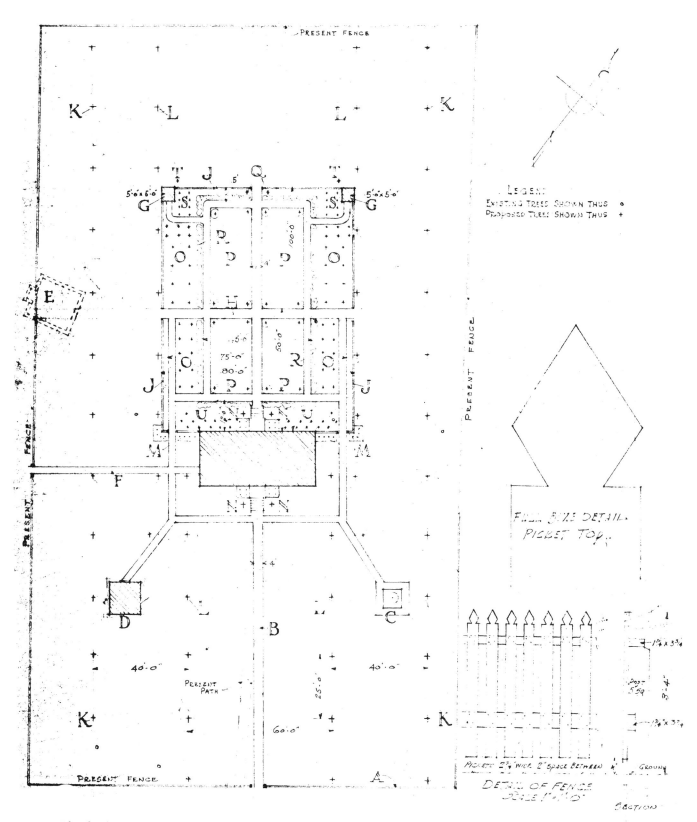

Plan for the arrangement of the grounds at the Rolfe-Warren House,
Arthur A. Shurcliff, landscape architect, 1935

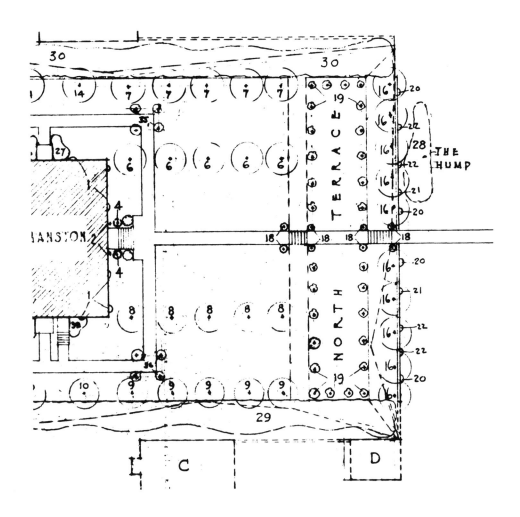

Wilton

WILTON IS a transplanted house surrounded by a recreated garden—a masterpiece of conservation and restoration. In 1933 the National Society of the Colonial Dames of America in the Commonwealth of Virginia dismantled and moved the house from its original site at World's End, six miles below Richmond on the James River, in order to save it from destruction by the industrial expansion of the city of Richmond. Its new site was farther west on a bluff above the Kanawha Canal and James River. Here in a residential section it was meticulously rebuilt and now serves as the Society's headquarters and as a public museum.

In the early days of the colony, the Randolph family built several homes along the James. One of the finest of these was Wilton. It was built by William Randolph III and his wife, Ann Carter Harrison of Berkeley. Though completed in 1753, the dwelling is known to have existed in part since 1751, when it was shown on the Fry-Jefferson map that was based on a survey made that year. The 2,000-acre tract upon which Wilton was located was purchased by William Randolph III in 1747. Possession of the estate remained in the Randolph family until 1859, when it was sold to Col. William C. Knight. Through six successive ownerships the house remained essentially intact, a remarkable record, since at one time it was used for the storage of grain.

Wilton is an example of exceptionally pure Georgian design. Built during the closing years of Virginia's Queen Anne architectural period, its perfect proportions and exquisite detail make it a distinguished domestic architectural monument. The exterior is enhanced by rubbed brick trim around the windows, doors, belt course, and corners. The interior is decorated in the original colors and is completely paneled, including halls and closets. The perfect harmony of interior and exterior architectural detail gives this mansion a special feeling of complete repose.

At the request of the Colonial Dames, The Garden Club of Virginia created an appropriate landscape setting for relocated Wilton. For this undertaking Arthur Shurcliff, landscape architect for Colonial Williamsburg, was engaged to draw plans and carry out the work, which was completed in 1936. The task of grading and planting the surrounding lawn was a monumental undertaking as the new site was exceedingly rocky and steep and quite barren of proper soil for planting. However, every effort was used to establish the former sense of surrounding spaciousness lost in the move from the original 2,000-acre site.

The firm of Claiborne and Taylor, which had moved the mansion, was employed to execute Shurcliff's plans. This was a fortunate choice as Herbert Claiborne was an experienced restorer under whose supervision archaeological excavations of the original site were made. This research delineated the form and dimensions of the immediate area around the house. Terraces descending from the mansion created an expansive vista. The high commanding view of canal and river compensated for the diminished acreage of the new location.

Wilton owes much of its charm to this ingeniously chosen location. Its broad terrace is halfway down the natural slope, with further terraces, walls, and slopes both above and below the mansion. Paralleling the long dimensions of the north and south facades, the horizontal lines of the terraces anchor the house and gardens comfortably on the slope. Necessity enforced a unique design.

In order to separate the house from the close proximity of the public street, a high brick wall that helps retain the steep slope was built. The top of this wall descends in a graceful profile from the main visitor entrance gate to the service gate below. The wrought-iron visitor gate is supported by brick piers topped with original handsome stone caps retrieved from the old plantation. The ironwork is genuine Swedish wrought iron skillfully finished with fine craftsmanship.

On this new site there were many trees that had to be cleared to a width of seventy-five feet across the property to open up a full view of the mansion. In the center of this open space a five-foot brick walk with the necessary steps between levels connects the

Recreated entrance gate

Vista from the house toward the James River

River view terraces

Recreated river terraces and memorial bench

entrance gate with the front door. This same axis carried through the house and down the steps on the lower terrace.

A circumferential walk that, as a square, surrounds the house is a feature made possible in reconstruction. It could not have been included had this been a restoration. Shurcliff introduced this surrounding walk to insure a view of the superb brickwork of the mansion from every angle. It also allows a visitor primarily interested in gardens to enjoy the grounds without entering the house.

After the terraces had been subgraded, topsoil had to be hauled in before any planting could be done. Large tree boxwood was planted, symmetrically framing both north and south entrance steps. Smaller dwarf boxwood outlined the south terrace. American holly was massed in hedges along the side boundaries. On the north wall vines—wisteria, cross vine, and honeysuckle—were planted. At either end of the house a few deciduous shrubs were used—virburnum, Carolina allspice, privet, and lilac. Care was taken not to overplant as it was important to preserve a feeling of spaciousness in proportion to the dignity of the mansion.

Located well away from the house are some aristocratic trees, such as beech, willow oak, and tulip. Beyond the artificially graded lawn the remaining property acquired by the Colonial Dames was kept in its native forest growth to provide a screen from the surrounding residential area.

As the grounds at Wilton matured, The Garden Club contributed necessary renovations to the landscape. In 1959 additional planting was made under the direction of Alden Hopkins. Trees and shrubs that had grown out of proportion to their intended purpose had to be pruned and some removed to reestablish the vistas as intended. Other maintenance items were necessary to rejuvenate the terrace banks. As the years passed operation of the mansion necessitated installation of sophisticated equipment that required outside receptacles. Twenty large boxwood were planted at the four corners of the house to hide the mechanics. At this same time an ivy edging was planted along the front walk and a specimen dogwood was planted to the left of the entrance.

In 1961 The Garden Club completed a small section of the front wall when a new

Entrance terrace

access road and parking area were built outside the north gate. This wall was a part of the original plan but could not be completed until the grading for the new driveway was finished.

If a visitor were not told that Wilton was a relocated house, it would be impossible for him to realize that it had not always rested upon its present site. The amazing sense of privacy and isolation that pervades the spot seems to indicate long years of congeniality with the landscape. The site provides a view of Williams Island in the center of the river. The city owns this island, which has remained a wilderness because of frequent flooding. Wilton stands today in privacy and beauty, protected by its wall and descending terraces from intrusions of the street and isolated from visual distractions on its river side by the wilderness of Williams Island.

TREES

Fagus americana, American Beech
Celtis occidentalis, Hackberry
Ilex opaca, American Holly
Lagerstroemia indica, Crape-Myrtle

Liriodendron Tulipifera, Tulip-Tree
Morus Broussonetia, Paper Mulberry
Quercus Phellos, Willow Oak
Thuja occidentalis, Arborvitae

SHRUBS

Buxus sempervirens, Common Boxwood
    (true tree)
Buxus sempervirens suffruticosa, Dwarf
    Boxwood (true dwarf)
Calycanthus floridus, Carolina Allspice

Ligusturm vulgare, Common Privet
Syringa vulgare, Common Lilac
Viburnum Opulus, European Cranberry-
    Bush

VINES

Bignonia capreolata, Cross-Vine
Hedera helix, English Ivy

Lonicera sempervirens, Trumpet Honey-
    suckle

Wisteria sinensis, Chinese Wisteria

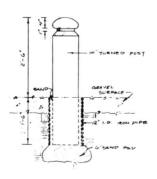

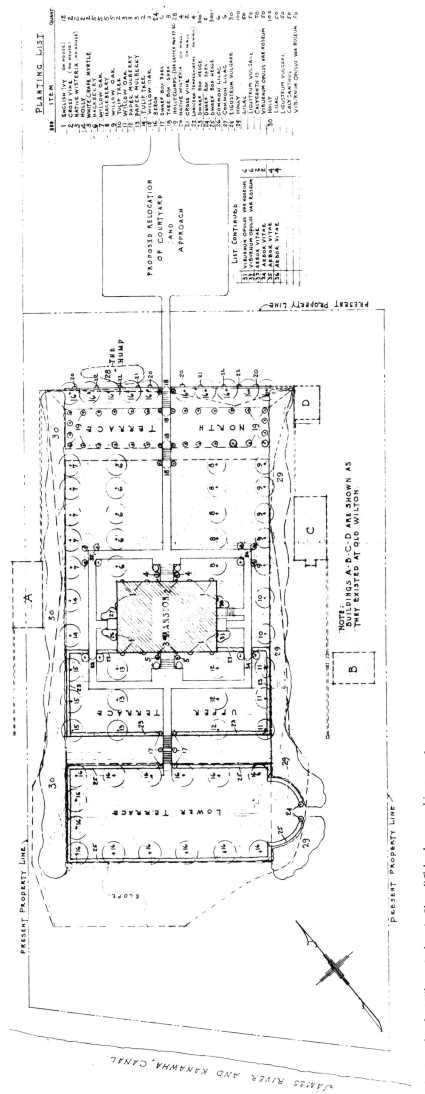

Planting plan for Wilton, Arthur A. Shurcliff, landscape architect, 1936

Bruton Parish Churchyard

Bruton Parish Church

BRUTON PARISH CHURCH is the oldest Episcopal church in the country in continuous use for worship. It is located on the northwestern corner of Duke of Gloucester Street and the Palace Green in Williamsburg. The original portion of the present structure was completed in 1715 and is the third Bruton Parish Church. The first church was built about 1660, probably of wood and possibly on the site of the present church. The second church was a Gothic brick structure built in 1683. The foundations of this second church were revealed by excavation in 1939. They are northwest of the existing building in the center of the churchyard.

The design of the present church was made by Lieutenant Governor Alexander Spotswood. Its construction was paid for principally by the General Assembly as this had become the Court church in 1699, when the colonial seat of government moved from Jamestown to Williamsburg. In this capacity it accommodated the governor, the council of state, the House of Burgesses, the faculty and students of the College of William and Mary as well as its own parishioners.

Following the Revolution, Bruton Parish Church continued in Anglican service. Both before and after the war there seems to have been a constant series of additions and repairs to the structure of the church. During the Civil War the church served as a hospital. Though no great damage resulted, further repairs were effected following the conflict.

It was the rector of Bruton Parish, William Archer Rutherfoord Goodwin, who conceived the idea of restoring Colonial Williamsburg and induced John D. Rockefeller, Jr., to undertake this project.

In 1936 The Garden Club of Virginia was approached by the Williamsburg Garden Club to help in restoring Bruton Parish Churchyard. Goodwin had already begun work on the ancient churchyard walls and the tombstones. The handsome brick wall, erected around the churchyard in 1745 by Samuel Spurr, has a coping of half-round brick set on sloping bricks on end. The foundations of this wall were in need of repair and this was done at the expense of the church.

Age and severe storms had played havoc with many of the old trees and shrubs within the enclosure. To counter this damage, The Garden Club replaced ten trees and planted a few shrubs to bring back the charm of the old churchyard. Damaged trees were removed and the deadwood taken from the remaining trees. This work was financed and supervised by The Garden Club of Virginia, which made payment directly to Bruton Parish Church to cover the cost. This is of interest because the next phase of this project involved the influence and cooperation of Colonial Williamsburg, separating this project into two eras.

In a letter of July 6, 1939, Vernon M. Geddy of Colonial Williamsburg wrote to the representative of The Garden Club of Virginia: "This is to confirm our telephone conversation of a few days ago in reference to the suggested landscaping of Bruton Churchyard. . . . I discussed this matter with Mr. Chorley and found that the Restoration had made no plans nor commitment in reference to doing landscaping work in the churchyard. Mr. Chorley, however, has authorized me to say that in order to cooperate with The Garden Club of Virginia, the Restoration would be glad to have Mr. Shurcliff make a landscape plan for the churchyard at the expense of the Restoration. If this plan is then approved by The Garden Club and the Vestry of Bruton Parish Church, the Restoration would then be very glad to execute the work proposed at the cost of The Garden Club."

By March of 1940 Shurcliff's plans had been approved by The Garden Club of Virginia and by the Vestry Committee of Bruton Parish Church. Work was begun immediately. An opening in the west churchyard wall was closed and a walk extending west from the church to the wall was taken up. A new pattern was established for walks within the churchyard. The new walks were laid in a rectangular herringbone pattern with borders of brick on edge. Around the sundial a flagstone paving was replaced by one of brick. A few additional trees and shrubs were added to the previous planting, the grass was reseeded, and a ground cover of periwinkle planted.

Because this project had extended over several years, the plan had been revised from time to time. In order to have a record of the final planting as completed, Shurcliff, in collaboration with The Garden Club, made a record plan dated March 21, 1942, in which he incorporated directions for future maintenance of the planting that became the obligation of the church.

Despite its wealth of historic interest, Bruton Parish Church conveys no air of a museum. In the architectural beauty of its structure and its surrounding yard it is as central to the life of Williamsburg today as it was two hundred and fifty years ago.

Entrance paving

Initial Planting

TREES

Cedrus libani, Cedar-of-Lebanon
Crataegus crus-galli, Cockspur Thorn

Quercus virginiana, Live Oak
Taxus baccata, English Yew

SHRUBS

Hibiscus syriacus, Rose-of-Sharon, Shrubby
  Althea

Ilex vomitoria, Yaupon

VINES

Hedera helix, English Ivy

HERBACEOUS PLANTS—ANNUALS AND PERENNIALS

Vinca minor, Periwinkle

Later Planting

TREES

Acer rubrum, Red Maple
Albizzia Julibrissin, Mimosa, Silk-Tree
Catalpa speciosa, Catalpa
Cedrus libani, Cedar-of-Lebanon
Crataegus spathulata, Hawthorn
Ilex opaca, American Holly
Juniperus virginiana, Virginia Red Cedar
Lagerstroemia indica, Crape-Myrtle

Magnolia virginiana, Swamp Bay, Sweet
  Bay Magnolia
Melia Azedarach, Pride-of-India-Tree
Quercus virginiana, Live Oak
Salix babylonica, Weeping Willow
Taxus baccata, English Yew
Ulmus americana, American Elm

SHRUBS

Hibiscus syriacus, Rose-of-Sharon, Shrubby
  Althea

Ilex vomitoria, Yaupon

VINES

Bignonia capreolata, Cross-Vine
Gelsemium sempervirens, Carolina Yellow
  Jessamine
Hedera helix, English Ivy

Lonicera sempervirens, Trumpet Honeysuckle
Wisteria macrostachys, American Wisteria

HERBACEOUS PLANTS—ANNUALS AND PERENNIALS

Vinca minor, Periwinkle

Bruton Parish Churchyard
Plan for Perpetual Maintenance
of Eighteenth Century
Trees, Roses, Vines, and Minor Structures
March 21, 1942

West Wall of Churchyard

This is a 35′ continuous border 160 feet long and is to contain the following as plotted on this plan:

2 Althea	1 Crepemyrtle	1 Live Oak
4 American Elm	1 English Yew	1 Magnolia
1 Cedar of Lebanon	1 Holly	1 Rose
		1 Hawthorn

Vines on wall must not cover more than 10% of the wall surface.
8 English Ivy

North Wall of Churchyard

This is a 25′ border in two parts, one of 205 lineal feet, the other 45 feet in length. The interspace of 90 feet is to be kept open for views to and from the Wythe House. This border is to contain the following as plotted on this plan:

1 English Yew	3 Maple
9 Hawthorn	1 Yaupon

Vines on wall must not cover more than 10% of the wall surface:
4 Carolina Yellow Jasmine
4 Native Honeysuckle
4 Native Wistaria

East Wall of Churchyard

This is a 35′ border of 160 feet long with an opening 30 feet wide to give uninterrupted views of the Churchyard from the Palace Green and on the center line of the site of the ancient Bruton edifice. This border is to contain the following as plotted on this plan. Street trees included in this border are not listed and are not in the custody of the Church.

4 Althea	1 Crepemyrtle	2 Rose
1 Cedar of Lebanon	1 Hawthorn	

Vines on wall must not cover more than 10% of the wall surface:
2 Crossvine
2 English Ivy
2 Native Wistaria

South Wall of the Churchyard

This continuous 26′ border of 342 feet is sparsely planted to allow ample views of the Church from the Duke of Glouchester Street and at the same time to give shade to the south windows by trees on the Duke of Glouchester Street, which trees are not listed and are not in the custody of the Church. This border within the Churchyard is to contain the following as plotted on this plan:

1 Live Oak	1 Rose	1 Weeping Willow
1 Mimosa	1 Althea	

Vines on the wall must not cover more than 10% of the wall surface:
6 English Ivy

———

Trees which are existing 1942 and which are to [be] maintained by perpetual care and by re-planting when the tree dies or is destroyed, are indicated thus: – – – – – – – – – – – – – – – o

Trees which are existing 1942 but which are not to be perpetuated as above by replanting when a tree dies or is destroyed are indicated thus:– ✕

Trees which are not existing 1942 (three altheas and one hawthorn) are to be planted and maintained by perpetual care and are indicated thus: – – – – – – – – – – – – – – – – – – △

All self-sown trees, shrubbery or vines which may spring up from time to time are to be eradicated. No vines are to be allowed to strangle any tree.

Roses of the 18th century kinds are to be perpetuated at the sites indicated thus: – – – – – OR

––––––––

Planting Around Walls of Church Immediately
Inside and Outside the Circuit of Brick Walks:

1. No vines of any kind are to be allowed to climb on the walls of the Church.

2. Live oak north of tower as shown.

3. Ground cover of periwinkle as shown, to be maintained.

4. Altheas and a weeping willow as shown.

5. All trees, roses, vines and periwinkle are to be authentic kinds as of 16th century Williamsburg.

Maintenance of Construction

1. Gravestones, monuments and slabs are to [be] kept plumb and are to be repaired when necessary, such repairs to be referred to the Williamsburg Restoration for the best methods and appropriate to the period of the stone.

2. Marginal brick walls, footpath, pavements, steps, lights and seats to be maintained in good condition. If relaying or reconstruction becomes necessary, such matters are to be referred to the Williamsburg Restoration for the best methods and appropriate to the period.

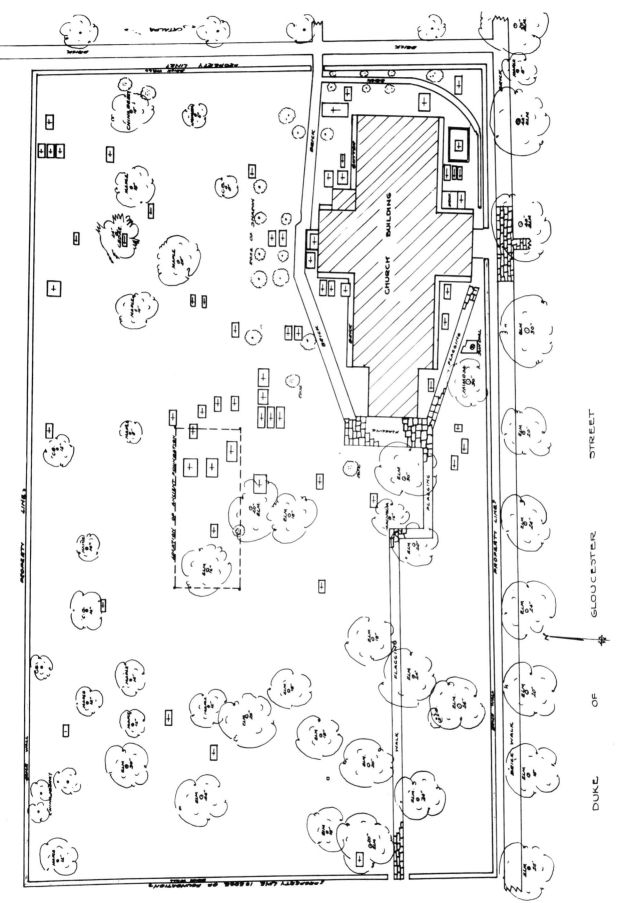

Bruton Parish churchyard as it was in 1939, Williamsburg Restoration, Inc.

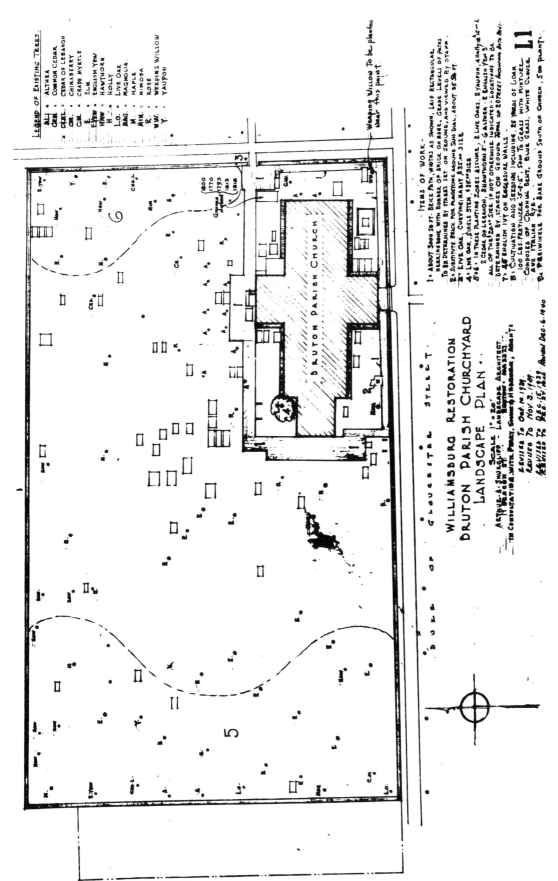

Landscape plan of the Bruton Parish churchyard, Arthur A. Shurcliff, landscape architect, 1940

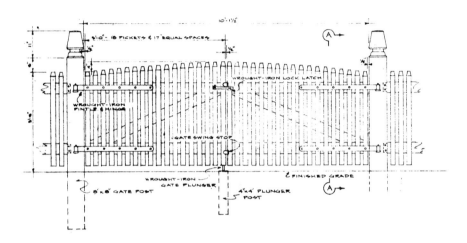

Mary Washington Monument

MARY WASHINGTON DIED only a few months after her son had become the first president of the United States. The monument that marks her grave stands on part of the original Kenmore estate. At the time of her death this estate was the property of her daughter Betty Washington and her son-in-law, Col. Fielding Lewis. Now the property is within the city limits of Fredericksburg.

Mary chose the site for her grave herself. It is a spot to which she came frequently, walking from her nearby cottage. Here a large boulder in the shade of great oak trees provided—and still provides—a restful retreat for reading and meditation.

On his first visit to Fredericksburg after his mother's death, Washington ordered a stone erected over her grave. Through the years this stone was diminished and eventually destroyed by souvenir hunters. In 1826 a movement was begun to raise funds to erect a proper monument. Interest continued in the endeavor for eight years, and on May 7, 1833, the cornerstone of the monument was laid. Ceremonies marking this event were gay and filled with anticipation of success. President Andrew Jackson was the speaker. Anticipation soon faded, for the monument was never completed. The base was ten feet square and fifteen feet high, surmounted by eight pillars. But the shaft was left lying on the ground. During the Civil War intense fighting around Fredericksburg left this partially erected monument an irreparable ruin.

Through the years, in New York, Boston, and Washington, there were women who continued to keep a spark of interest alive in the erection of a monument, and within the immediate area of Fredericksburg there was always such interest. It was the advertisement of a date of sale of the property on which the grave and unfinished monument were located that brought this interest to a head. In awakened consternation at the prospect of a sale, the National Mary Washington Memorial Association and the Mary Washington Monument Association of Fredericksburg were both chartered in 1889. Culmination of the contributions of time and money of these two groups eventually led to successful erection of a monument.

Work was begun on the present structure in September 1893. Remains of the old monument were broken up and used in the foundation of its replacement. The cornerstone of the new monument was laid on October 21, 1893, by the Mary Washington Monument Association of Fredericksburg. The cornerstone of the old monument, with its contents, was placed in the foundation of the present structure. Once again a celebra-

Boxwood bordered entrance walk

tion was held, this time with President Cleveland as the principal speaker. Attendance of the president's cabinet and other dignitaries made the occasion an event of national note.

In 1937 the National Mary Washington Memorial Association of Fredericksburg asked The Garden Club of Virginia to landscape the grounds around the monument. This project was assumed and completed in 1939. Alden Hopkins, who had recently returned from the American Academy in Rome, was engaged to draw plans for landscaping the grave site and its attendant seven acres.

Two major problems had to be resolved in creating the landscape plan. The first was the necessity of establishing a satisfying relationship between the grade of the city street on which the property fronts and the site itself. This difficulty was solved by close cooperation between the city and the architect, both making concessions to effect a pleasing grade. The second major problem was that the monument was not parallel to the cemetery wall, a fact particularly in evidence in winter's exposure. Hopkins lessened this imbalance by extending the wall at the west end of the graveyard.

It was necessary to unite the monument with its surrounding property. This was accomplished by constructing a brick wall. This wall is similar in design to the one at Kenmore and, like that at Kenmore, is a cross section of the old wall around Ware Church yard in Gloucester County. The Ware Church yard wall curved the coping and stepped the beveled water table where there was a change of grade. This was the precedent for the curving top of the wall Hopkins designed. The wall is laid in Flemish bond. From the street steps and a walk lead through the wall directly to the monument. Brick paving surrounds the actual monument enclosure.

With a strong design by a framework of brick established, judicious planting was done. At the entrance steps a low planting of boxwood, white azaleas, and dwarf holly was established. Specimen boxwood were planted as accents along the approach walk and, again, were used in defining the paved area surrounding the monument. The eight boxwood on either side of the entering path were underplanted with periwinkle. At the northwest corner of the old cemetery wall, where the path leads to the ledge of rock behind the monument, a few shrubs soften the design. Here below the shaded boulder lie fields to the north and west. These are enclosed with a post-and-rail fence that joins the brick wall. Along this fence were planted flowering trees and shrubs. The fence and shrubs suggest the simple barriers of the old farms of this area.

To the north, where the land falls off steeply, trees were planted on the hillside to broaden the base of the monument visually from this awkward perspective. The total effect of this planting expressed a dignity that would be lost in an involved, landscaped setting.

On May 15, 1939, the National Mary Washington Memorial Association dedicated this memorial planting executed by The Garden Club of Virginia. This date was appropriate, for it was the one hundred and fiftieth anniversary of the death of Mary, George Washington's mother.

TREES

Cornus florida, Flowering Dogwood
Gleditsia triacanthos, Honey Locust
Halesia carolina (Tetraptera), Snowdrop-Tree, Silver-Bell
Ilex opaca, American Holly
Liriodendron Tulipifera, Tulip-Tree
Pinus resinosa, Resinous Pine
Quercus rubra, Red Oak

SHRUBS

Buxus sempervirens, Common Boxwood (true tree)
Buxus sempervirens suffruticosa, Dwarf Boxwood (true dwarf)
Chionanthus virginicus, Fringe-Tree
Cotoneaster horizontalis, Rock Spray
Fothergilla major, American Witch-Elder
Ilex glabra, Inkberry
Kalmia latifolia, Mountain-Laurel
Lagerstroemia indica, Crape-Myrtle
Leucothoë Catesbaei, Drooping Leucothoë
Ligustrum vulgare, Common Privet
Lonicera pileata, Evergreen Honeysuckle
Rhododendron ferrugineum, Alpine Rose Rhododendron
Rhododendron nudiflorum, Pinxter-Flower
Symphoricarpos vulgaris, Indian Currant
Syringa vulgaris, Common Lilac

HERBACEOUS PLANTS—ANNUALS AND PERENNIALS

Dictamnus albus, Fraxinella, Gas-Plant
Hemerocallis flava, Yellow Day-Lily
Hypericum aureum, St. Johns-Wort
Iris germanica florentina, Orris-Root Iris
Vinca minor, Periwinkle

Entrance on Charles Street (photo by Frackleton)

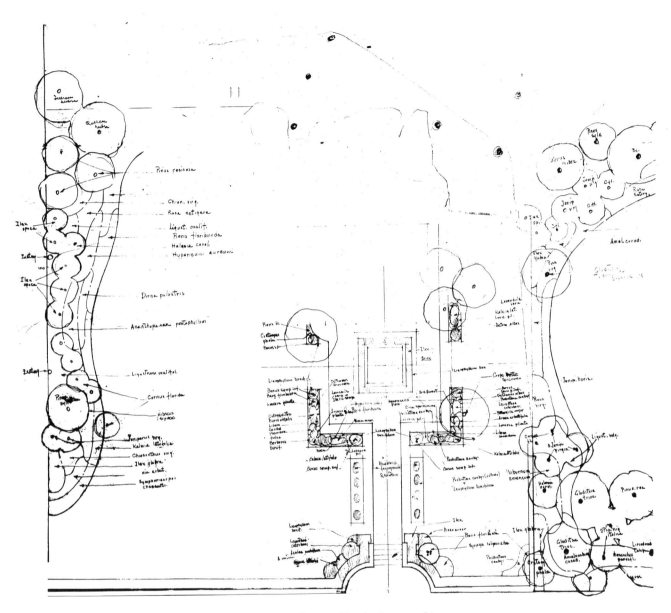

Planting plan for the Mary Washington Monument, Alden Hopkins, landscape architect

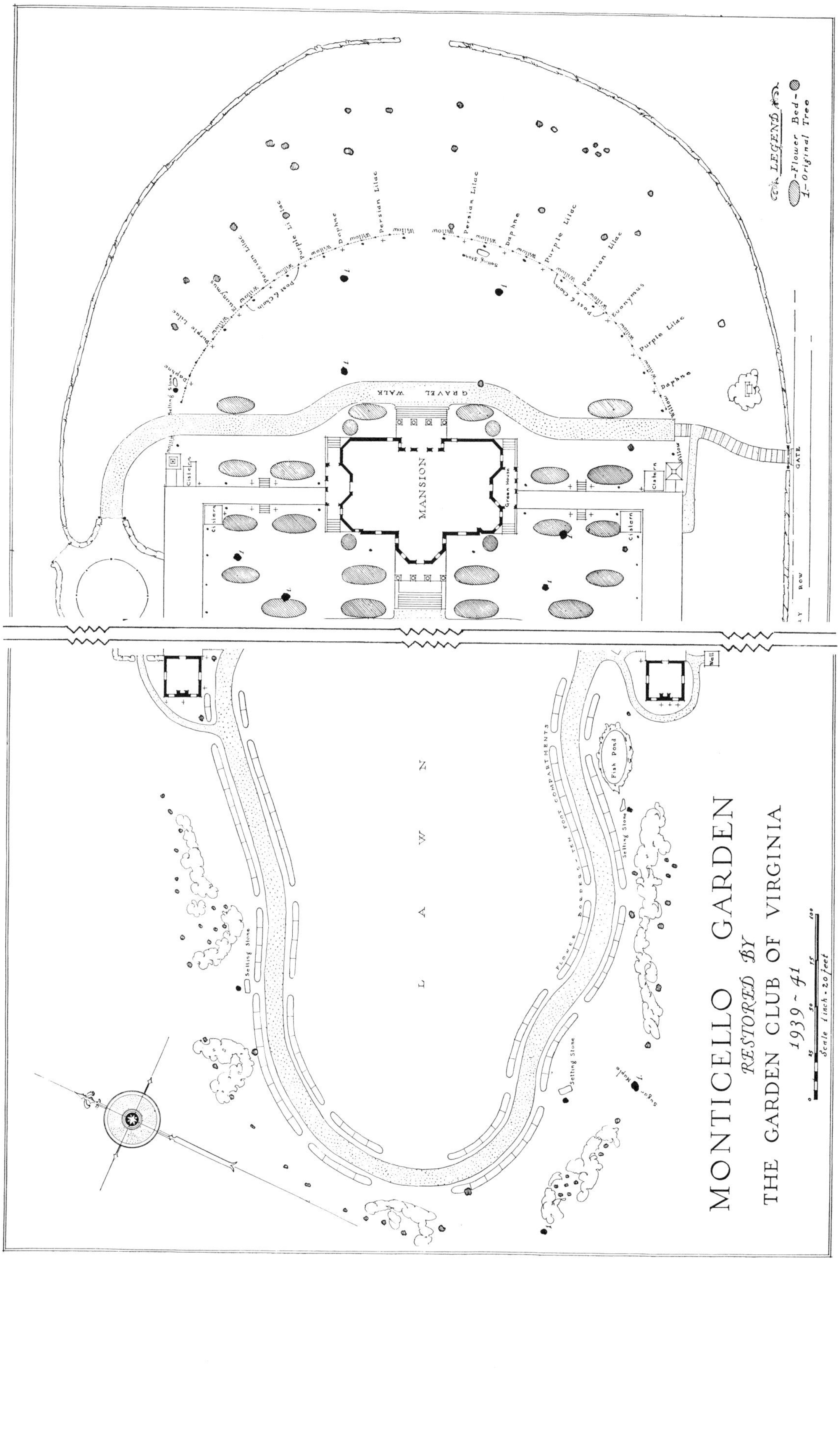

MONTICELLO GARDEN
RESTORED BY
THE GARDEN CLUB OF VIRGINIA
1939 ~ 41

Scale 1 inch = 20 feet

Monticello Garden, 1939–1941

Monticello

THE GARDENS OF
THOMAS JEFFERSON
WERE RESTORED AND PRESENTED TO
MONTICELLO
BY THE
GARDEN CLUB OF VIRGINIA
1940

HIGH ON A MOUNTAIN TOP overlooking Charlottesville stands Monticello. For over fifty years this was the beloved home of Thomas Jefferson. Here he returned at every opportunity his demanding public life would allow.

In 1757 Jefferson inherited from his father the acreage that he later named Monticello. The holding embraced slightly over 1,000 acres. To this initial acreage, other lands were added until, in 1794, Jefferson's total holding in Albemarle County was over 5,000 acres.

Having acquired Monticello, Jefferson began the task of leveling the top of his mountain as preparation for establishing his dwelling and garden. This undertaking was a three-year endeavor that was completed in 1772. He dreamed of designing a garden of his own and began sketching plans while still living with his mother at Shadwell. While making these early sketches, he was intrigued by the new and informal English landscape style as illustrated in Shenstone's *Collected Works* and Thomas Whateley's *Observations on Modern Gardening*. These works set forth the naturalistic approach to garden design, a contrast to the ordered formality of the gardens of a Shirley or a Mount Airy. The evolution of Jefferson's preference in garden design may be clearly traced through the pages of his Garden Book,[1] a horticultural diary he kept from 1766 to 1824.

Jefferson moved to Monticello in 1770 after his mother's house burned. Following his marriage in January 1772, he and his bride lived in a small completed wing of the house. It was not until 1793 that the first planned gardens were actually planted and not until fourteen years later, during the last years of his presidency, that the gardens as we know them today were laid out.

Architectural design was, for Jefferson, a constant challenge. His inherent love of "building and pulling down," as he himself expressed it, accounts for the many and ever-changing sketches he drew for both his house and his grounds. From the titles in his personal library it is evident that he read widely in this field, seeking architectural designs that would please him, but he was not a copyist. It was always his own inventive concept that made the designs he ultimately used entirely his own.

His originality and imagination frequently led him to try the unusual. The decision to establish his home on the top of a mountain was unusual at that time, as heretofore

---

1. Published as *Thomas Jefferson's Garden Book, 1766–1824*, ed. Edwin Morris Betts (Philadelphia: n.p., 1944).

the great plantation houses were situated on rivers that provided ready transportation. Another major departure was in the architectural design of his house. Georgian dwellings were the norm for the period, being much in favor in Williamsburg and Annapolis. But Monticello, as initially planned by Jefferson, was inspired by his study of Palladian design.

In 1784, two years after the death of his wife, Jefferson was appointed minister to France. During his five years in France he had ample opportunity to study outstanding architectural designs on the Continent. He found he was particularly responsive to French Roman classicism, as exemplified in the Hotel de Salm in Paris, a one-story house with a dome. Upon returning home, Jefferson added to, and refined, the design of Monticello to reflect the influences of his European observations.

Jefferson's propensity for change to satisfy new ideas was as much a dominating force in his garden design as in his residence. Here, also, he departed from the conven-

The garden loggia, the lombardy poplar, and the tulip poplars are all authentic restorations.

The oval flower beds are maintained as laid out by Jefferson.

tional style of the period. The evolution of his garden covered a period of many years. The combination of Jefferson's English travels and Thomas Whateley's writings most strongly influenced the design. Other Virginia gardens of the period were characterized by formality of design outlined by boxwood. At Monticello the composition was in curvilinear paths and oval beds planted informally. The Monticello plan introduced to American the revolutionary naturalistic garden.

Jefferson's life was one of unstinting service to his country. As a result his own personal affairs were often neglected. Shortly after his death, on July 4, 1826, Monticello was sold in partial payment of debts accrued. The new owner, a former apothecary from Staunton, bought the property in the hope of establishing a profitable business in silkworm culture. Some mulberry trees, both paper mulberries and silkworm mulberries, had been planted by Jefferson. To further the new enterprise, many established trees of other varities were cut down and the grounds planted with silkworm mulberries. This venture soon failed and the property was resold. In 1836 Uriah Phillips Levy, an officer in the United States Navy, became the new owner. The years from the end of the Civil War to 1875 marked the low period of the physical condition of the property. These were years of absentee ownership.

On Jefferson's 180th birthday, April 13, 1923, the Thomas Jefferson Memorial Foundation was established. This nonprofit group was headed by Stuart Gibboney, a New York lawyer of Virginia ancestry. Concerted efforts of this organization raised the funds to purchase Monticello, then a holding of slightly more than six hundred acres, from the Levy estate. Control of the property was transferred December 1, 1923. Under the guidance of Sidney Fiske Kimball, chairman of the Monticello Restoration Committee and Edwin Morris Betts, professor of biology at the University of Virginia, renovation and restoration were undertaken. There was a discouraging amount to be done, but there were quantities of old plans, planting lists, and views of what had been to urge the project on.

The Garden Club of Virginia had had a sustained interest in the restoration of the gardens and grounds at Monticello over a period of many years. In 1927 the president of The Garden Club of Virginia lived nearby and was vitally interested in the restoration of Monticello. She was distressed by the deterioration of the trees, some of which had been planted by Jefferson. Because of her interest, The Garden Club of Virginia organized and held a colorful three-day fair at Monticello. Blessed by assurance from the weather bureau, Hill's Almanac, and the Birthday Book, two beautiful days were selected and a successful gala raised $7,000. This was used to preserve the few remaining trees on the lawn of the estate.

In May 1938 Stuart Gibboney formally requested The Garden Club of Virginia to restore the gardens at Monticello, following the original designs and planting lists delineated by Jefferson. This request was presented to the Board of Governors in October 1938, and approval was given to designate funds accruing from the 1939 Garden Week to this project.

Through the years of his garden's development, Jefferson kept such meticulous notes and drawings that a real problem of selection was posed in restoration. Which of the many designs were actually executed? Which were merely experimental sketches? Though the first planting plan considered by The Garden Club of Virginia was one contained in the Jefferson manuscripts and selected after careful study, it was abandoned even after blueprints had been made because of a most fortuitous discovery.

While engaged in research at the Philadelphia Historical Society, Edwin Betts found a plan drawn in 1807 on which was written in Jefferson's handwriting, "planted and sowed flower beds as above April 15, 16, 18 and 20." Here was proof positive of a plan executed. It was this plan that was used as basis for restoration. With the exception of minor adjustments, necessary to accommodate present usage of the grounds, this plan was faithfully reproduced. Beyond the noted April planting, further details for planting were contained in a letter to his granddaughter, Anne Cary Randolph, who shared his love of gardening.

On the back of a letter to Anne dated June 7, 1807, is a rough sketch of the entire design of the landscape around the dwelling. It shows the round and oval beds set in the four angles made by the intersection of the terrace walks and the house; each angle contained four oval beds and a shrub circle. The serpentine walk of the West Lawn is shown, as were the beds bordering this walk. It is interesting to note that though the beds in the corners of the house were planted in 1807, the serpentine walk and its accompanying beds were not established until about five years later.

Not only was there a large collection of documents and contemporary prints and paintings, but many traces of the original garden features still remained in the ground. The roundabout walk of the West Lawn was the first of these discoveries. With the plan as a guide the outline of the walk was clearly indicated by an oval mound of grass extending around the West Lawn. There were even occasional bulbs, hyacinths, iris, and daffodils that sprang up along the edge of the grassy mound. The rediscovered walk coincided in curves and width exactly with the plan.

The second find was the fish pond, located from a description in one of Jefferson's letters, which gave the distance of the pond from the South Pavilion. At this point there was a depression in the ground thought to have been an abandoned flower bed. But digging at the indicated spot disclosed the bottom of the pond with many of the original bricks, verifying the size and shape of the pond. It is known that this pond served not

Jefferson imported and planted many tulips.

only as an ornament and a reservoir for rainwater from the pavilion roof but chiefly as a holding basin for keeping fish alive until they were needed for the table.

With these two features located, attention was focused on establishing the beds in the corners of the house. These were laid out according to the plans sent to Anne and were planted according to the list of seeds and plants that Jefferson noted he planted "1807 April 15, 16, 18, 20."

A gravel walk at the East Front was reestablished according to a drawing found in the Jefferson-Coolidge collection in Boston. On the same plan was shown a design for the Ellipse. Here again verification was found in surviving plant material. In the area shown on the Jefferson plan the semicircle was still marked by a few surviving golden willows alternating with lilacs and other shrubs. The Ellipse was restored and the surviving planting augmented by new material as specified. In restoration, after the Ellipse was planted with willows, it was found that half of its distance was 182 feet, which exactly corresponded to notes in Jefferson's Garden Book.

Because of the survival of Jefferson's meticulous records, it was possible to produce at Monticello accuracy in restoration seldom achieved. True, there is no surviving planting plan for the roundabout of the West Lawn. However, Jefferson's extensive records include the many plants that interested him. The plant material to fill the beds and borders was originally gathered from the mountainside. But Jefferson was a horticultural experimentalist, and he added to the native growth many seeds and plants from abroad. Some of these survived, some failed to become acclimated. He brought the empress tree from China and Japan, the Osage orange, the goldenrain tree, the snowberry, the Scotch broom, and many other plants from abroad. As president he encouraged the collection of western plants through the Lewis and Clark expedition to the northwest. Many of these plants successfully naturalized at Monticello. In restoration the challenge was to recreate the same mass effect and varied bloom succession that Jefferson had produced through horticultural experimentation.

About halfway up the Monticello mountainside, Jefferson laid out a family cemetery of approximately an acre. This graveyard has always been used by Jefferson's descendants. In 1944 the Thomas Jefferson Memorial Foundation requested The Garden Club of Virginia to undertake the rebuilding of the approach and steps to this graveyard, the then existing approach being considered of inappropriate character. The request was granted. Steps leading from the driveway to the cemetery were reconstructed, a necessary wall was laid up, and an adjustment was made in the entrance driveway. The resulting design was one of simple dignity, befitting the man who directed that his tombstone should bear this brief inscription:

Here Was Buried Thomas Jefferson
Author of The Declaration of American Independence
Of the Statute of Virginia for Religious Freedom
And Father of the University of Virginia

The perimeter of the original roundabout is still intact.

TREES

Abies alba, Silver Fir
Abies balsamea, Balsam
Abies sp., Norway Fir
Acer Negundo, Box-Elder
Acer rubrum, Red Maple
Acer saccharum, Sugar Maple
Acer tataricum, Tatarian Maple
Aesculus alba, White Horse-Chestnut
Aesculus Hippocastanum, Horse-Chestnut
Aesculus hybrida, Hybrid Buckeye
Aesculus pavia, Red Buckeye
Aesculus virginica, Yellow Horse-
  Chestnut
Albizzia Julibrissin, Mimosa, Silk-Tree
Amerlanchier canadensis, Shad-Bush,
  Service-Berry
Arbutus unedo, Strawberry-Tree
Broussonetia papyrifera, Paper Mulberry
Carpinus caroliniana, Hornbeam
Carya, Hickory
Carya alba, Mockernut
Castanea dentata, American Chestnut
Castanea pumila, Chinquapin
Castanea sativa, French or Spanish
  Chestnut
Catalpa bignonioides, Eastern or Common
  Catalpa
Catalpa speciosa, Western Catalpa
Cedrus libani, Cedar-of-Lebanon
Cercis canadensis, Eastern Redbud
Chamaecyparis thyoides, White Cedar
Chionanthus virginica, Fringe-Tree
Citrus sinensis, Orange
Cornus florida, Flowering Dogwood
Corylus americana, Hazelnut
Cytisus scoparius, Scotch Broom
Diospyros virginiana, Persimmon
Fagus americana, American Beech
Fagus sylvatica var. *purpurea*, Copper
  Beech
Fraxinus americana, White Ash
Gleditsia triacanthos, Honey Locust
Gymnocladus dioeca, Kentucky Coffee-
  Tree
Halesia carolina, Snowdrop-Tree,
  Silver-Bell
Ilex aquifolium, English Holly

Ilex opaca, American Holly
Juglans nigra, Black Walnut
Juglans regia, English Walnut, Madeira-
  Nut
Juniperus sp., Juniper
Juniperus virginiana, Eastern Red Cedar
Koelreuteria paniculata aurea, Goldenrain-
  Tree, Varnish-Tree
Larix decidua, Larch
Larix sp., Italian Larch
Liriodendron Tulipifera, Tulip-Tree
Maclura pomifera, Osage Orange
Magnolia acuminata, Cucumber-Tree
Magnolia grandiflora, Southern Magnolia
Magnolia tripetala, Umbrella-Tree
Magnolia virginiana, Swamp Bay,
  Sweet Bay Magnolia
Melia Azedarach, Pride-of-India-Tree
Morus alba, White Mulberry
Morus rubra, Red Mulberry
Olea europaea, Olive
Paulownia tomentosa, Empress-Tree
Picea sp., Newfoundland Spruce
Picea sp., Spruce
Pinus Strobus, White Pine
Pinus sylvestris, Scotch Pine
Platanus occidentalis, Sycamore, Plane-
  Tree, Buttonwood
Populus candicans, Balm-of-Gilead
Populus nigra var. *italica*, Lombardy
  Poplar
Populus tacamahaca, Balsam Poplar
Populus tremula, Aspen
Prunus caroliniana, Cherry-Laurel, Wild
  Little Orange
Prunus cerasus, Dwarf Cherry
Prunus serotina, Wild Cherry
Prunus virginiana, Choke Cherry
Pyrus coronaria, Wild Sweet Crab
Quercus ilicifolia, Ground Oak
Quercus phellos, Willow Oak
Quercus robur, English Oak
Robinia viscosa, Clammy Locust
Salix babylonica, Weeping Willow
Salix vitellina, Yellow Willow
Symphoricarpos albus, Snowberry
Taxus baccata, English Yew

Thuja occidentalis, Arborvitae
Thuja orientalis, Chinese Arborvitae
*Tilia americana, American Linden
Tilia sp., Linden
*Tsuga canadensis, Eastern Hemlock

Ulmus americana, American Elm
Viburnum prunifolium, Black-Haw
  Viburnum
Zanthoxylum americanum, Prickly Ash
Zizyphus jujuba, Chinese Jujube

SHRUBS

Acacia Farnesiana, Cassie, Italian Mimosa
Acacia sp., Acacia
Alnus sp., Alder
*Amorpha fruticosa, Bastard Indigo
Artemisia abrotanum, Southernwood
Berberis vulgaris, Common Barberry
Boehneria nivea, Silk Plant
*Buddleja globosa, Butterfly-Bush
*Callicarpa americana, French Callicarpa
*Calycanthus floridus, Bubby-Flower,
  Sweet-Shrub
*Ceanothus americanus, New Jersey Tea
*Chaenomeles lagenaria, Japanese Quince
Clethra alnifolia, Clethra, Summer
  Sweet
*Colutea arborescens, Bladder Senna
Coronilla emurus, Scorpion Senna
*Crataegus Crus-galli, Cockspur Thorn
Crataegus sp., Hawthorn
Daphne Cneorum, Daphne
*Daphne Mezereum, Mezereon
Euonymus americana, Strawberry-Bush
Euonymus japonica, Evergreen Euonymus
Euonymus latifolia, Spindle-Tree
*Hibiscus syriacus, Althea, Rose-of-Sharon
*Ilex verticillata, Common Winterberry
Ilex vomitoria, Yaupon
*Kalmia latifolia, Mountain-Laurel
*Laburnum anagyroides, Goldenchain-Tree
Lavatera thuringica, Tree-Mallow
*Ligustrum vulgare, Common Privet

Mimosa nilotica, Egyptian Acacia
  (Jefferson originally used this name but
  later switched to *Acacia Farnesiana*)
*Mimosa pudica, Sensitive-Plant
*Nerium oleander, Oleander
*Philadelphus coronarius, Mock-Orange
Prunus triloba, Double Blossom Almond
Punica granatum, Pomegranate
*Pyrancantha coccinea, Firethorn
*Rhododendron maximum, Rosebay
  Rhododendron
Rhododendron nudiflorum, Pinxter-Flower
Rhus sp., Venetian Sumac
Ribes odoratum, Yellow Currant
*Robinia hispida, Rose Acacia
Sambucus canadensis, Elder
*Spartium junceum, Spanish Broom
*Symphoricarpus albus, Snowberry
*Syringa persica, Persian Lilac
*Syringa vulgaris, Common Lilac
*Taxus baccata, English Yew
*Taxus canadensis, Dwarf or American
  Yew
*Ulex europaeus, Furze
Viburnum acerifolium, Dockmackie,
  Maple-Leaf Viburnum
Viburnum opulus, European Cranberry-
  Bush
Vitex Agnus-castus, Chaste-Tree, Hemp-
  Tree, Monks Pepper-Tree

VINES

*Campsis radicans, Trumpet-Vine
  Jessamine
Clematis virginiana, Virgins-Bower
*Gelsemium sempervirens, Carolina Yellow
*Hedera Helix, English Ivy
Jasminum sp., Persian Jessamine
Jasminum nudiflorum, Yellow or Winter
  Jessamine

*Jasminum officinale, White Jessamine
Lonicera amoena, Red-Berried Honey-
  suckle
*Lonicera japonica, Climbing Honeysuckle
Rhus toxicodendron, Poison Oak
Trachelospermum jasminoides, Star-
  Jasmine

HERBACEOUS PLANTS—ANNUALS AND PERENNIALS

Althea rosea, Hollyhock
Amaranthus hybridus var. *hypochondriacus*, Princes-Feather
Amaryllis atamasco, Atamascos Lily
Amaryllis Belladonna, Belladonna-Lily
Anemone Pulsatilla, Pasque Flower
Anthemis nobilis, Camomile
Antholyza aethiopica, African Gladiola
Antirrhinum majus, Snapdragon
Aquilegia canadensis, Columbine
Argemone grandiflora, Prickly-Poppy
Artemisia absinthium, Wormwood
Artemisia Dracunculus, Tarragon
Bellis perennis, English Daisy
Campanula persicifolia, Bellflower
Campanula pyramidalis, White Bell-flower and Blue Bellflower
Celosia argentea cristata, Cockscomb
Centaurea macrocephala, Yellow Centaurea
Cheiranthus Cheiri, Wallflower
Clematis virginiana, Virgins-Bower
Colchicum autumnale, Fall Crocus
Convallaria majalis, Lilly-of-the-Valley
Crocus sativus, Saffron Crocus
Crocus susianus, 'Cloth-of-Gold' Crocus
Crocus vernus, Spring Crocus
Cypripedium calceolus, Common Lady-Slipper
Delphinium Ajacis, Larkspur
Delphinium exaltatum, American Larskpur
Dianthus barbatus, Sweet William
Dianthus caryophyllus, Carnation
Dianthus chinensis, China Pink
Dianthus plumarius, Grass Pink
Dictamnus albus, Fraxinella, Gas-Plant
Dionaea muscipula, Venus Fly-Trap
Frasera carolinensis, American Columbo
Fritillaria imperialis, Crown Imperial
Gardenia jasminoides, Cape-Jasmine
Geranium maculatum, Wild Geranium
Gladiolus communis var., Gladioli
Glaucium flavum, Yellow Horned-Poppy
Gomphrena globosa, Globe Amaranth
Helianthus annuus, Sunflower
Hibiscus coccineus, Scarlet Mallow

Hyacinthus, Double Blue
Hyacinthus, Double Pink
Hyacinthus, Double White
Hyacinthus, Double Yellow
Hyacinthus orientalis, Purple Hyacinth
Hyacinthus monstrosus, Feathered Hyacinth
Hyssopus officinalis, Hyssop
Impatiens balsamina, Double Balsam
Iris germanica, German Iris
Iris persica, Persian Iris
Iris pseudacorus, Yellow Flag
Iris xiphium, Spanish Iris
Ixia chinensis, Ixia
Lathyrus latifolius, Everlasting Pea
Lathyrus odoratus, Sweet Pea
Lavandula spica, Lavender
Lavatera trimestris, Mallow
Lilium canadense, Meadow Lilly
Lilium candidum, Madonna Lily
Lilium columbiana, Columbian Lily
Lilium martagon, Canada Martagon, Turks-Cap
Lilium tigrinum, Tiger Lily
Linum perennes, Perennial Flax
Lobelia cardinalis, Cardinal Flower
Lunaria biennis, Honesty
Lupinus polyphyllus, Lupine
Lychnis chalcedonica, Scarlet Lightning, Maltese Cross
Majorana hortensis, Sweet Marjoram
Malva sp., Eastern Mallow
Mathiola incana, Gilliflower, Stock
Mentha piperita, Mint
Mertensia virginica, Virginia Bluebell
Mesembryanthemum crystallinum, Ice Plant
Mirabilis jalapa, Four-O'-Clock
Mirabilis longiflora, Sweet-scented Marvel of Peru
Momordica balsamina, Balsam Apple
Monarda didyma, Oswego-Tea, Bee-Balm
Morea flexuosa, African Herb
Muscari comosum monstrosum, Feathered Hyacinth
Narcissus, Emperor
Narcissus, Golden Spur
Narcissus, King Alfred

Narcissus bulbocoduim, Petticoat Daffodil
Narcissus incomparabilis, Narcissus from
  the Mediterranean
Narcissus Jonquilla simplex, Jonquil
Narcissus var., Daffodil
Nigella sativa, Fennel-Flower
Paeonia albiflora, White Peony
Paeonia Moutan banksii, Tree Peony, first
  grown in England (Kew Gardens) in
  1789
Papaver nudicaule, White Poppy
Papaver sp., Poppy
Pelargonium graveolens, Rose Geranium
Primula auricula, Auricula
Primula vulgaris, Common Primrose
Ranunculus asiaticus, Persian Ranunculus
Ranunculus repens, Double Buttercup
Reseda odorata, Mignonette
Ricinus communis, Castor-Oil-Plant,
  Palma Christi
Rosmarinus officinalis, Rosemary
Ruta graveolens, Rue
Salvia officinalis, Sage
Sanguinaria canadensis, Bloodroot

Sanguisorba minor, Burnet
Scabiosa japonica, Pincushion-Flower
Silene schafta, Autumn Catchfly
Tagetes erecta, African Marigold
Tagetes sp., Marigold
Tanacetum vulgare, Tansy
Thymus vulgaris, Thyme
Tritonia fenetrata, Montbretia
Trollius sp., Goldy-Lock Trollius
Tropaeolum majus, Nasturtium
Tulipa Clusiana, Lady Tulip
Tulipa florentina, Tulip
Tulipa fulgens, Tulip
Tulipa Gesneriana, Common Tulip
Tulipa Gesneriana var. *dracontia*, Parrot
  Tulip
Tulipa sp., Tulip in varieties
Vinca minor, Periwinkle
Viola odorata, Double Violet
Viola sp., Violet
Watsonia, Meriana
Ximenesia encelioides, Verbesina
Yucca filamentosa, Adams-Needle

ROSES

Rosa, 'The Monthly'
Rosa, Thornless Rose
Rosa centifolia, Rose of Provence, Cabbage
  Rose, described by Theophrastus before
  300 B.C.
Rosa cinnamomea, Cinnamon Rose
Rosa damascena, White Damask
Rosa gallica officinalis, Rose of Lancaster
Rosa gallica, 'Tricolor'
Rosa laevigata, Cherokee Rose intro-
  duced into America before 1759

Rosa lutea, Yellow Rose
Rosa moschata, Sweet-Smelling Musk Rose
Rosa Mundi [*Rosa gallica versicolor*], a
  bud sport of the ancient Rose of
  Provins (*Rosa gallica officinalis*) men-
  tioned in Clusius in 1683
Rosa rubiginosa, Sweet Briar
Rosa spinosissima, Scotch Hedge Rose

This list was compiled by Edwin M. Betts and Hazlehurst Bolton Perkins for their book
Thomas Jefferson's Flower Garden at Monticello. Flowers marked with an asterisk were planted in
the restored garden. Slight changes have been made for clarity.

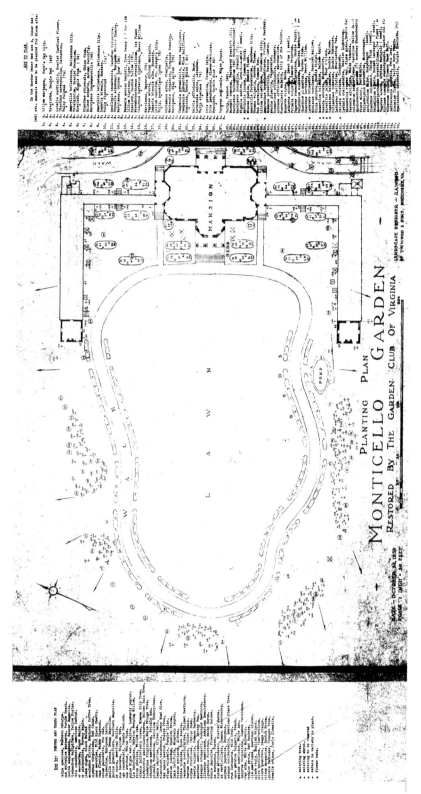

Monticello planting plan, Garland A. Wood, landscape designer, 1939

The enclosing wall has Flemish bond on the front, English bond on the sides.

Christ Church: Middlesex

CHRIST CHURCH, in Middlesex County, gave its name to the village of Christ-church in which it stands. The village and nearby Christchurch School are located just off route 33, south of the Rappahannock River.

The first parish church at this location was built in 1666–67. The walls of the present church, built upon the same site, were erected in 1714, as attested by three dated bricks from the church wall, now preserved in the tympanum of the vestibule. Architecturally, the church has suffered so many changes that little of the 1714 building remains. Despite these alterations, this church is an architectural delight and a valuable historic monument.

The parish's vestry book is the only one in existence that antedates Bacon's Rebellion of 1676. The ancient documents and the parish register of 1653–1812 are in safe-keeping in the State Library at Richmond. The cemetery surrounding the church is outstanding among the cemeteries of Tidewater Virginia, containing graves of many noted colonial families. Here too is the grave of Sir Henry Chicheley, former governor of the colony. Family tombs of the Grymeses and Yateses are considered among the most magnificent in America.

In October 1940 the vestry of Christchurch Parish requested The Garden Club of Virginia to assist in restoring order to the churchyard, which had fallen into a discouraging state. With this request the senior warden submitted a pencil sketch of the churchyard (see replica). Though not drawn to absolute scale, the dimensions were accurate enough to be used for the project. The sketch showed the yard surrounded by a wire fence.

The Garden Club agreed to this project and built a handsome brick wall on the north and west sides facing the two roadways. Existing sample bricks for the wall and perfect coping bricks were found on the site. Bricks to match these samples were made in Urbanna in the fall of 1941. The new wall was located twenty feet from the existing wire fence, giving a little more depth in front of the church itself. The northern line of the wall angles off to follow the right-of-way along the road leading to the river.

On the two unenclosed sides of the property the forest comes to the edge of the churchyard, creating a wall of green in the spring. Dogwood and other native flowering trees are equally lovely in all seasons of the year.

Descendants of the families buried in the churchyard restored the monuments and tombs in 1967.

Churchyard wall

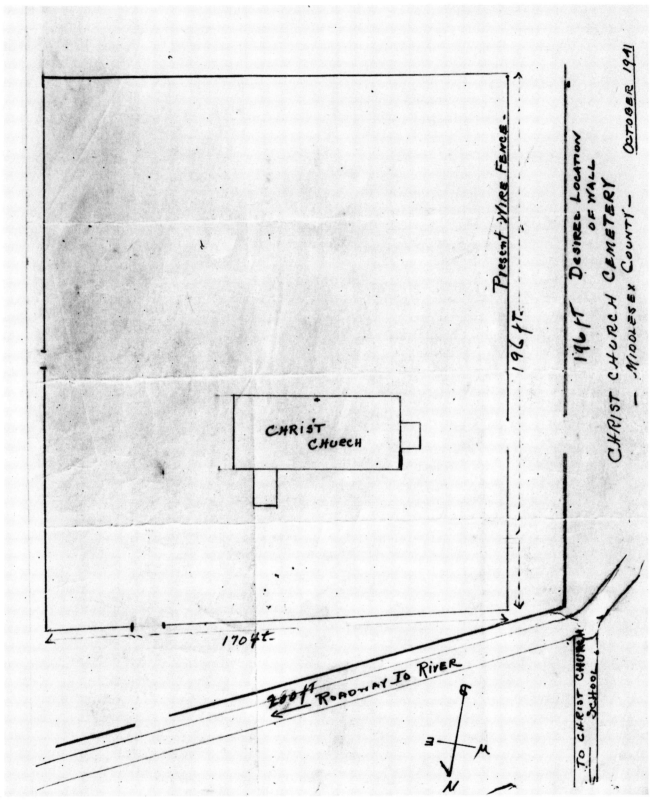

Christ Church: Middlesex, sketch plan by the Rector, 1941

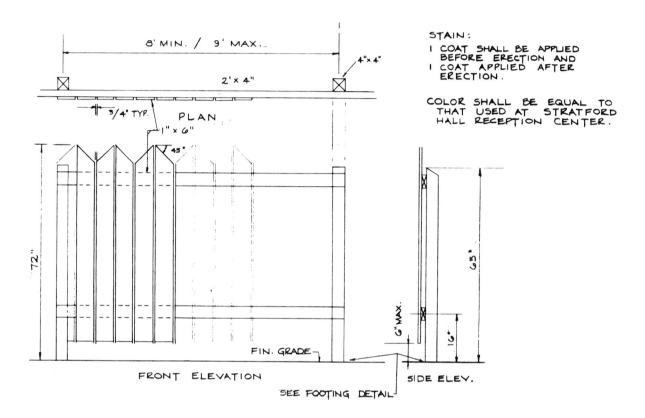

8' MIN. / 9' MAX.

4" x 4"

2' x 4"

3/4" TYP.

PLAN

1" x 6"

45°

72"

FIN. GRADE

FRONT ELEVATION

SEE FOOTING DETAIL

6" MAX.

65"

16"

SIDE ELEV.

STAIN:

1 COAT SHALL BE APPLIED
BEFORE ERECTION AND
1 COAT APPLIED AFTER
ERECTION.

COLOR SHALL BE EQUAL TO
THAT USED AT STRATFORD
HALL RECEPTION CENTER.

Christ Church: Fincastle

T HE QUAINT AND HISTORIC TOWN of Fincastle nestles in the Blue Ridge Mountains in Botetourt County. This county seat was formerly the gateway to all the territory stretching west to the Mississippi. Here lived pioneers who, as framers and signers of the famous Fincastle Declaration (which antedated the Declaration of Independence), strongly influenced the cause of national liberty.

On a hilltop overlooking the village is Christ Church. Built about 1770, it was first the property of the Church of England. In 1785, after the Revolution, with the dissolution of the Church of England in the United States, Christ Church was closed. During the postwar period many large families of Presbyterians who had come from Scotland, via Ireland and Pennsylvania, settled in the vicinity. In 1795 the church property was transferred, by act of the legislature, to the Presbyterians. Repairs and alterations were made to the structure in 1813 and again in 1849, when the church was enlarged. At that time the entrance was moved from the east to the south facade, and a Doric-columned recessed porch and a tall steeple were added.

In the years before 1940 the active congregation shrank to two or three families and there was no regular pastor. The property became neglected through lack of sufficient funds for its upkeep. Locust trees sprang up in the churchyard, which was overgrown with tall grass and weeds.

Realizing the seriousness of the situation, the Roanoke Valley Garden Club proposed the restoration of the churchyard to The Garden Club of Virginia in 1940. The project was favorably received, and restoration followed in 1942 and 1943.

The work to be done was evident on the ground; so no plan was drawn. First, thirty or more truckloads of rubbish had to be removed before the tall grass and locust trees could be cut. The constructive work began with the building of a wall along the west side of the graveyard and the repairing and resetting of the tombstones. Existing iron fence and gates were also repaired.

Immediately in front of the church a brick terrace was built and a brick walk that had been discovered in the cleanup was restored between the entrance to the churchyard and the church. This brick paving provides a practical and pleasant architectural feature. An oil-burning lamp—one of the original town lamps—was repaired, converted to electricity, and mounted at the gateway.

After these structural repairs had been completed only simple planting was needed.

One of the original street lamps was restored and installed at the entrance of the church (Deyerle Studios)

Enclosing fence and wall, restored (Deyerle Studios)

Climbing euonymus was planted on the west wall and on either side of the entrance gate. Virgin's bower was trained over the iron fence of the south wall. Weeping willows, magnolias, holly trees, and crape myrtles were scattered along the iron fence. In the foreground of the west facade boxwood, cedars, and Adam's needle were planted.

The congregation added an education wing at the rear of the property in 1958. To relate this to the historic setting, The Garden Club planted white pine, a catalpa, and boxwood.

Today the Fincastle Presbyterian Church has a congregation numbering more than a hundred. It stands as a living monument to the past and to the men and women whose valiant spirits made the settlement of the West possible.

TREES

Catalpa bignonioides, Catalpa
Ilex opaca, American Holly
Juniperus virginiana, Eastern Red Cedar

Magnolia grandiflora, Southern Magnolia
Pinus Strobus, White Pine
Salix babylonica, Weeping Willow

SHRUBS

Buxus sempervirens, Common Boxwood
 (true tree)

Lagerstroemia indica, Crape-Myrtle

VINES

Clematis virginiana, Virgins-Bower

Euonymus fortunei, Climbing Euonymus

HERBACEOUS PLANTS—ANNUALS AND PERENNIALS

Yucca filamentosa, Adams-Needle

Old Stonewall Jackson College building acquired as headquarters for the Barter Theatre.

Barter Theatre: Abingdon

ABINGDON, VIRGINIA, IS in the southwest corner of the state, in Washington County. It was founded in 1788 and was the center for early pioneering efforts west of the Appalachian range. Here Daniel Boone spent much time.

Situated on a hill above the town was a holding known as Carpet Hill, whose first owner was William Young Conn. The manor house of the estate afforded an unobstructed view of Mount Rogers and White Top Mountain, the two highest points in Virginia. The hillside, steeply descending from the house to the village below, was covered with bluegrass. In the spring violets bloomed through the grass in profusion, carpeting the hillside with color and giving the name to the estate.

The dwelling was a large frame structure of no architectural distinction. The site, however, was one of outstanding beauty as it was surrounded by beautiful old trees and extensive gardens. This house was the center of family gatherings for descendants of Conn for more than a hundred years. In 1915 the property was sold to the Presbyterian Church as the site for Stonewall Jackson College. The college erected five buildings on the property, eventually tearing down the old mansion and replacing it with a brick structure that was designated Montgomery Hall.

In 1929, when the stock market crashed, a young actor named Robert Porterfield, formerly from Washington County, was living in New York City. Along with many other talented people he found it impossible to secure work in the theater. Porterfield, a country boy by birth, conceived the idea of returning to the Virginia countryside and establishing a barter theater where patrons could trade farm produce for an evening of theater, and the actors, in turn, could be fed.

When Porterfield returned to Abingdon to look into the possibilities for furthering his idea, he found that Stonewall Jackson College had been closed as a result of the depression. But he was able to acquire the large rambling building known as Montgomery Hall from the college. From this beginning plans developed until on June 10, 1933, an agreement was signed between Porterfield and twenty-two actors, establishing the Barter Theatre in Abingdon, from which the State Theatre of Virginia developed.

In 1947 The Garden Club of Virginia made a modest planting around the old college building. A severe windstorm had torn away the columns of a porch that extended across the front of Montgomery Hall. A terrace was established in place of the porch, and this was planted with boxwood and espaliered crab apple. Along the driveway leading to the building additional flowering trees were planted; and about the lawn white pine, pin oak, and sugar maple were added. Holly, boxwood, barberry, and yew were used as hedges to define areas of the lawn. This planting remains a living memorial in recognition of the accomplishments of one man, who through imagination and unstinting effort contributed to his state and nation a new approach to an ancient art, the theater.

TREES

Acer saccharum, Sugar Maple
Ilex crenata convexa, Japanese Holly
Malus angustifolia, Southern Crab
Pinus Strobus, White Pine
Quercus palustris, Pin Oak

SHRUBS

Berberis vulgaris, Common Barberry
Buxus sempervirens, Common Boxwood (true tree)
Buxus sempervirens suffruticosa, Dwarf Boxwood (true dwarf)
Taxus cuspidata, Japanese Yew
Taxus media hicksii, Hicks Yew

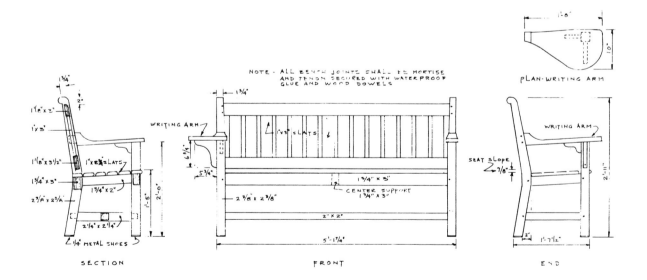

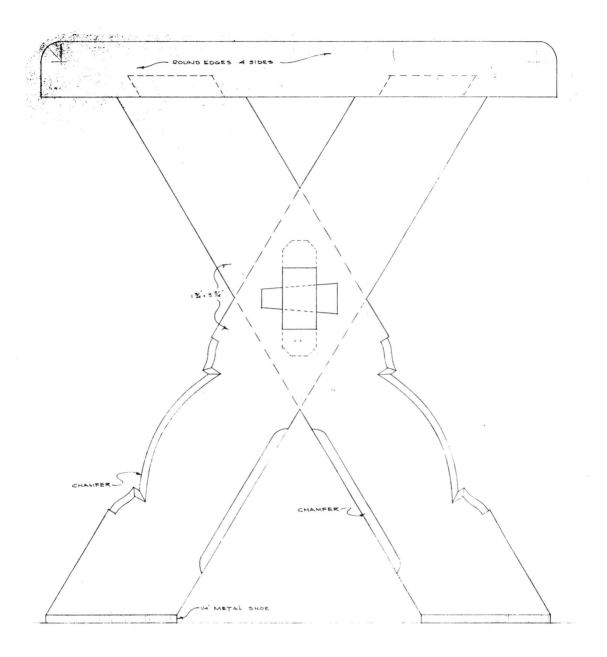

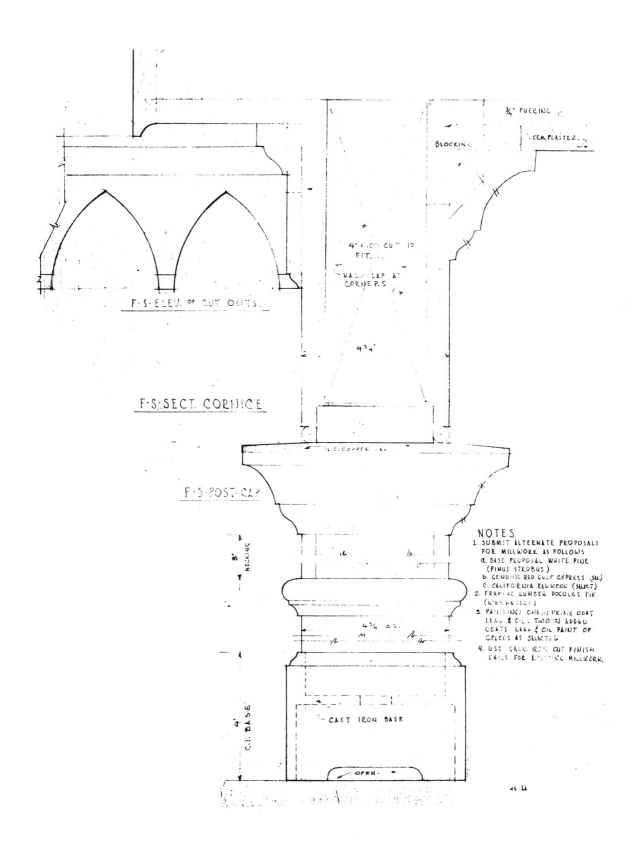

F·S· ELEV. OF CUT OUTS.

F·S· SECT. CORNICE

F·S· POST CAP

NECKING

C.I. BASE

¾" FURRING

BLOCKING

CEM. PLASTER.

4" KILN CUT TO FIT.

HALF LAP AT CORNERS

4³/₄"

L.G. COPPER CAP

CAST IRON BASE

OPEN-

NOTES
1. SUBMIT ALTERNATE PROPOSALS FOR MILLWORK AS FOLLOWS
   a. BASE PROPOSAL WHITE PINE (PINUS STROBUS)
   b. GENUINE RED GULF CYPRESS (SEL)
   c. CALIFORNIA REDWOOD (SELECT)
2. FRAMING LUMBER DOUGLAS FIR (WEYERHAEUSER)
3. PAINTING: ONE (1) PRIME COAT LEAD & OIL. TWO (2) ADDED COATS LEAD & OIL PAINT OF COLORS AS SELECTED
4. USE GALV. IRON CUT FINISH NAILS FOR EXISTING MILLWORK.

Gunston Hall

ONE OF THE FINEST colonial river plantations is Gunston Hall. It stands high above the Potomac River only a few miles below Mount Vernon. The land on which the mansion is located was inherited by George Mason from his father. Originally the tract encompassed 5,000 acres, of which slightly over five hundred now remain.

To this property George Mason moved in 1740, the year of his majority. Four years later he married Ann Eilbeck of Maryland, and together they planned their new home. At Mason's request his brother, then living in England, engaged a young joiner, William Buckland, to come to America under indenture to Mason to design and supervise the architectural details of his new home. So successful were the results of this arrangement that today Buckland's woodcarvings at Gunston are considered unsurpassed in this country. The beauty of the Palladian drawing room, unique with its broken pediments over niches and doors and the delicate porches of Chinese influence, the vogue of the times, shows an architectural perfection seldom seen.

The dwelling, completed in 1758, was followed by development of the gardens. In their design they reflected the elegance of the house. A strong T-shaped motif of dwarf boxwood with the stem of the T extending the central axis of the house binds house and garden together. This kind of unity between house and garden is characteristic of English classical estates but was rare in colonial America. The crosstop of the T parallels the riverside of the house, running east and west from the central axis. The double row of boxwood bordering the long central walk creates the most spectacular feature of the garden—a superb vista of the Potomac.

In 1833 Gunston Hall, by then reduced to an estate of 2,000 acres, was sold out of the Mason family. For the next seventy-nine years the property was held by many owners, one of whom, a lumberman, quartered woodcutters in the house and mules in the basement. Fortunately, it was purchased in 1912 by Louis Hertle of New York, who appreciated the historic and architectural value of this property.

Hertle and his wife spared no expense in restoring the original beauty of the house and their conception of the garden. Except for the magnificent boxwood vista all vestiges of Mason's garden had disappeared. Hertle noticed, however, that halfway down the stem of the T there was a break in the boxwood that seemed to indicate that a cross path had intersected the central path there. This discovery, corroborated by a description written by a member of the Mason family, prompted Hertle to divide the

Willow oaks frame the entrance.

garden area into four major parterres. Two of these were on either side of the central walk and were further subdivided to create a typical eighteenth-century English geometric garden. By patient propagation of cuttings from the original boxwood, he was able to outline the new beds, creating a handsome pattern comparable to the finest formal gardens.

The Hertles imported garden ornaments from Italy, built a pergola and reflecting pool, introduced contemporary bedding plants, shrubs, and hybrid tea roses, and lavished affectionate care on their creation.

When Mrs. Hertle died in 1929, her husband made legal provision that upon his death Gunston Hall would become the property of the Commonwealth under the custodianship of the National Society of the Colonial Dames of America. Thus, in 1949 the wishes of Hertle and the Board of Regents of the Colonial Dames were united in the perpetuation of Gunston Hall as a memorial to George Mason. As soon as the decisions toward this end became the sole responsibility of the Board of Regents, they asked the Garden Club of Virginia to undertake the restoration of this twentieth-century landscape to an eighteenth-century character. Alden Hopkins, resident landscape architect of Colonial Williamsburg, was engaged for this transformation.

Research revealed very little documentary description of the Mason garden. There were, however, notes about some landscape features, such as triple avenues of black-heart cherries converging at the entrance. But this was not within the area of the garden, with which The Garden Club was concerned. It was the problem of restoring as nearly as possible the garden that George Mason laid out on the river side of his house that The Garden Club of Virginia agreed to undertake.

The original boxwood T miraculously survived. No garden restoration has ever been favored with a more auspicious start. The preservation of this glorious green grove, for that is what it appears to be, is a monumental achievement. By comparison, the next obvious step was negative, for the old garden had to be divested of its incongruous twentieth-century ornaments. All pools and fountains had to be deleted; the colonists had no water to spare for garden ornament. The pergola, imported Italian figures, and recent plant importations all had to be cleared away before the simplicity of the Mason garden could be recreated.

The appearance of the four divisions of the parterre was entirely changed by re-arrangement of the beds. In the northeast division a topiary frog of boxwood replaced a central pool. The planting remained substantially the same except for the replacement of unauthentic material.

The northwest division remained unchanged, although some of the inner boxwood hedges had to be removed to prevent crowding by overgrowth. The focal point is a topiary form of boxwood balancing the opposite side. Boxwood-outlined beds are filled with periwinkle interplanted with spring bulbs.

Revisions in the southeastern division resulted in a kind of bowling green surrounded by rectangular flower beds. A similar revision in the southwest division created another central turf panel enclosed by boxwood-edged beds of eighteenth-century roses.

At the south end toward the river there were projecting spurs of land at the far corners of the garden that suggested some sort of overlook. Excavations anticipating the discovery of building foundations revealed nothing. But the existence of pavilions in

Gazebos overlooking the cutting garden with vistas of the Potomac River

Central allée

these spots seemed so obvious that it was assumed that they had been there but set on large corner stones laid on the surface of the ground. Matching Chinese Chippendale pavilions, reflecting the architectural details of the unique porch on the garden facade of the house, were therefore built on these promontories.

Further research indicated a similar but broader promontory at the river end of the green grove, a logical termination for this long path. From here there is a panoramic view of the entire Potomac valley. Below lies the old deer park, spreading out beyond the cut flower terrace that hugs close to the foot of the bank. Sheltered from northern winds, this narrow terrace garden flourishes with varieties of annuals and bulbs to keep the house filled with flowers. The beds, neatly enclosed by dwarf boxwood, form an attractive pattern when seen from the pavilions and central promontory.

The most challenging planting problem was the rehabilitation of the existing dwarf boxwood T, which justified the planting of the entire garden. For most of it proper pruning and feeding were all that was required, but through the attrition of time a large section of the eastern arm had died, and there were also holes in the western arm. To find replacements to fill these holes took almost four years of intense searching before a satisfactory planting of matching boxwood was discovered on a remote farm in Rockbridge County. The row, forty-five feet long, about nine feet high, and from fourteen to eighteen feet wide was available. Transporting it from a remote mountain pasture to the banks of the Potomac was a task to test the most adventurous spirit. Many nurserymen turned down the job as impossible, but finally one agreed to try. He succeeded with the aid of the Virginia State Highway Department, which plotted the route, testing bridges for the weight they would bear and measuring each underpass. The smallest ball moved weighed more than five tons, and that was the load limit for many of the rural bridges. Where necessary, the Highway Department shored up the

Garden as seen from the bedroom floor

bridges to make them safe. It required ten days of concentrated effort by a large crew of men supplied with a bulldozer, tackles, and two underslung trucks to move the box-wood. It was moved at night and required two trips by each truck to transport the entire row.

From the moment it was planted the Rockbridge boxwood seemed at home. It was indistinguishable from the original planting, matching exactly in size and texture. The great T was once more complete. Only the inspired objective to preserve one of the most beautiful boxwood gardens in America could have motivated the Restoration Committee to undertake such a hazardous venture. This living monument is a fitting memorial to George Mason, who wrote the Fairfax Resolves, drafted the Virginia Dec-laration of Rights, helped to frame the Constitution of Virginia and the Constitution of the United States, and advocated the Bill of Rights.

Southwest parterre

TREES

Ilex opaca, American Holly   *Juniperus virginiana*, Eastern Red Cedar
Lagerstroemia indica, Crape-Myrtle

SHRUBS

Buxus sempervirens, Common Boxwood (true tree)

Buxus sempervirens suffruticosa, Dwarf Boxwood (true dwarf)

Chionanthus virginicus, Fringe-Tree

Hibiscus syriacus, Rose-of-Sharon, Shrubby Althea

Syringa vulgaris, Common Lilac

Vitex macrophylla, Chaste-tree, Broad-leaved form of Agnus-castus

HERBACEOUS PLANTS—ANNUALS AND PERENNIALS

Anemone coronaria var., 'de Caen,' 'St. Brigid,' and 'The Bride' Anemones

Hemerocallis flava, Yellow Day-Lily

Muscari botryoides, Grape-Hyacinth

Narcissus Jonquilla campernella, Campernelle Jonquil

Narcissus Jonquilla simplex, Jonquil

Paeonia officinalis, Common Peony

Papaver orientale, Oriental Poppy

Phlox paniculata, Summer Perennial Phlox

Platycodon grandiflorum, Balloon-Flower

Scilla hispanica, Spanish Bluebell

Veronica maritima, Speedwell

Vinca minor, Periwinkle

ROSES

Rosa centifolia, Rose of Provence, Cabbage Rose, described by Theophrastus before 300 B.C.

Rosa centifolia 'des Peintres,' a Provence or Cabbage Rose

Rosa chinensis 'Old Blush,' a China Rose introduced into England before 1759

Rosa damascena, Damask Rose

Rosa damascena versicolor, the Rose of York and Lancaster; contrary to tradition this rose was not known before the early seventeenth century

Rosa gallica, a Provence Rose or French Rose. French roses were cultivated in England prior to 1500

Rosa damascena trigintipetala, the Kazanlik Rose grown for 'attar' in Bulgaria

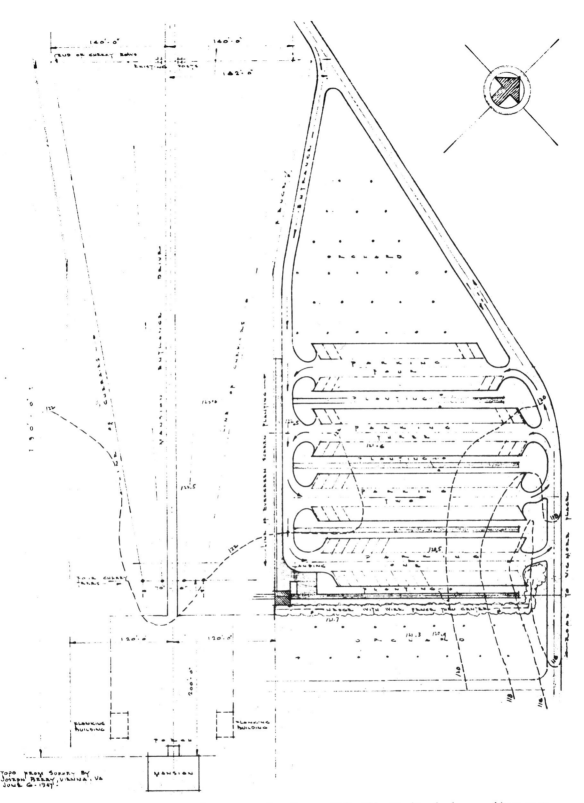

Sketch layout of the parking plan and entrance roads at Gunston Hall, Alden Hopkins, landscape architect, 1930

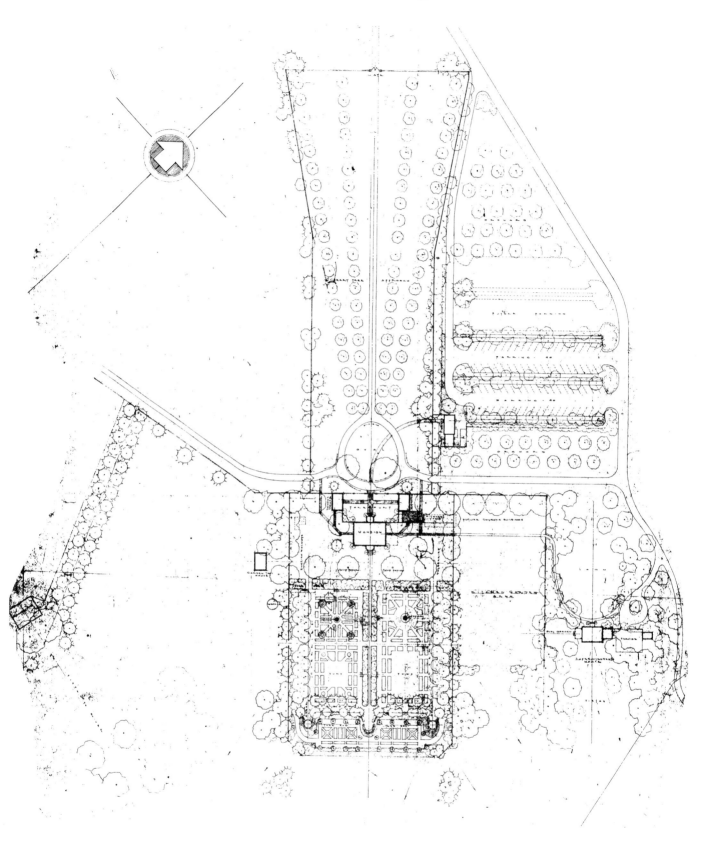

Presentation plan, Gunston Hall, Alden Hopkins, landscape architect, 1950

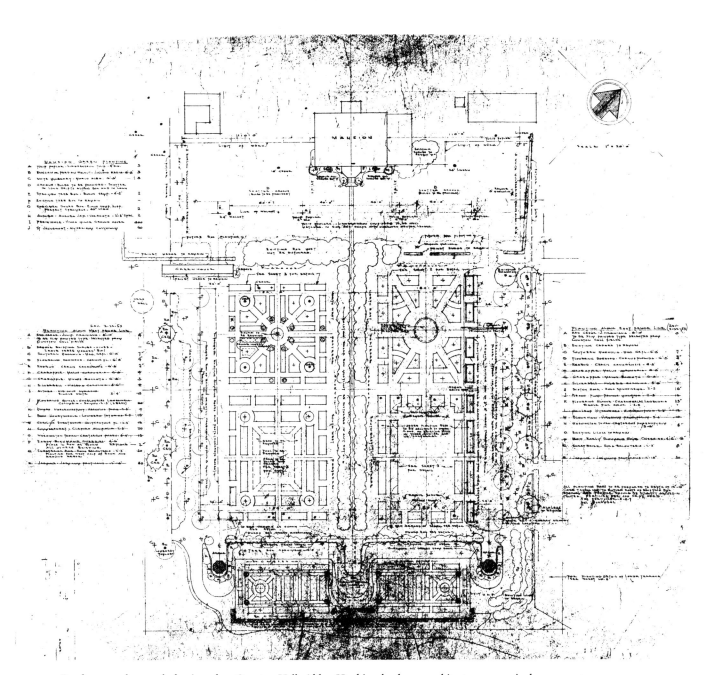

Landscape and general planting plan, Gunston Hall, Alden Hopkins, landscape architect, 1950; revised 1951, 1953

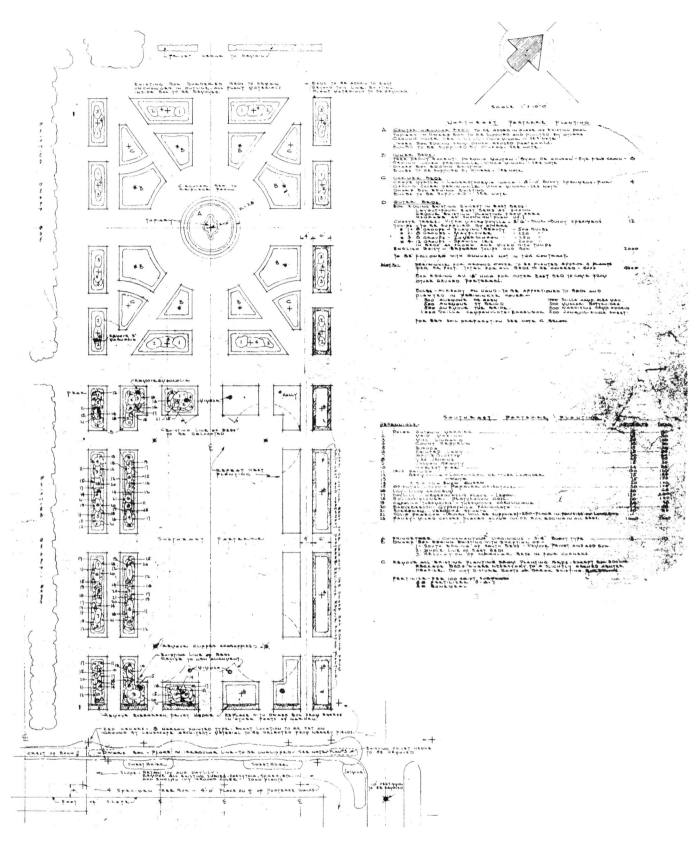

Detailed planting plan and list for the northeast and southeast parterres, Gunston Hall, Alden Hopkins, landscape architect, 1950

Detailed planting plan and list of the northwest and southwest parterres, Gunston Hall, Alden Hopkins, landscape architect, 1950

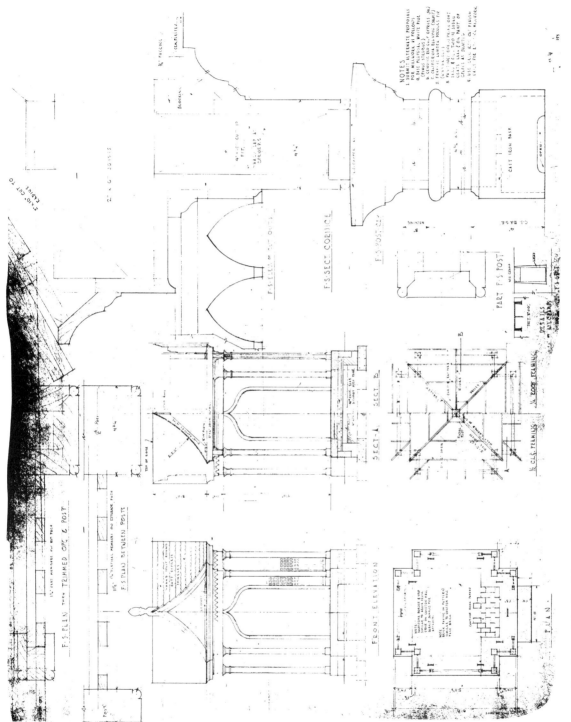

Plans, elevation, and details of the pavilions at Gunston Hall, Alden Hopkins, landscape architect, 1953

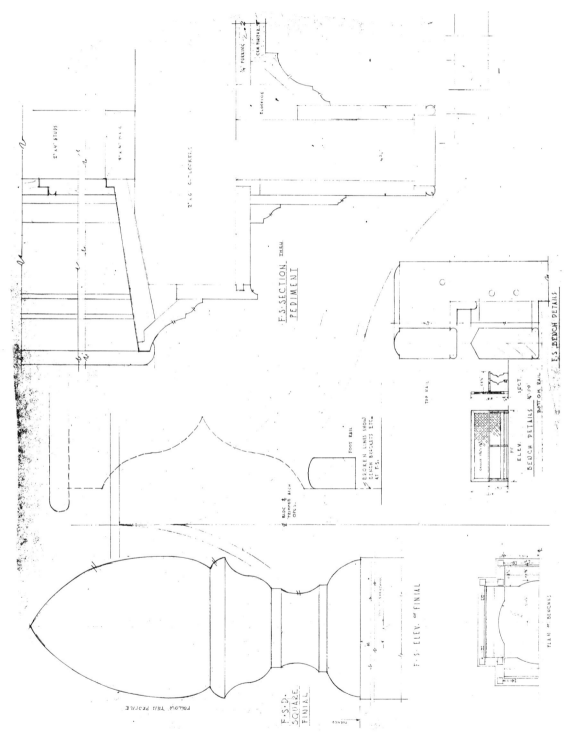

Construction details of the pavilions at Gunston Hall, Alden Hopkins, landscape architect, 1953

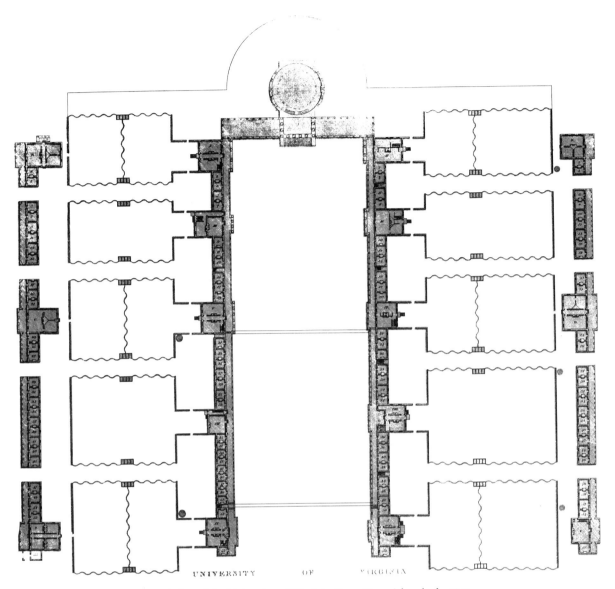

Engraved ground plan of the University of Virginia, Peter Maverick, 2d ed., 1825

The University of Virginia

THOMAS JEFFERSON CONCEIVED, designed, and supervised the construction of what he called an "Academical Village." This was his expression for the type of landscape plan he visualized for the University of Virginia. He chose a site close to Charlottesville, within riding distance of his own home at Monticello. From there he made almost daily visits from the time construction on the pavilions began in 1817 until the mansion and gardens were practically completed in 1824, two years before his death.

His unique conception of what a university ought to be provided ten separate lodges, or pavilions, combining faculty residences with classrooms that were joined "by barracks for a certain portion of the students, opening into a covered way, to give dry communication for all the schools." These alternate "lodges and barracks" were "arranged around an open square of grass and trees." At the high north end of his rectangular composition, Jefferson placed the Rotunda, or library, as the focal point, leaving the opposite end open for a vista of the Piedmont hills.

Unlike all previous American academic institutions, his design did not stop with the buildings but was projected into the landscape by walled gardens. Within the design, the central quadrangle, two hundred feet by six hundred feet, with its pavilions, student rooms, and colonnaded covered way is still known as the Lawn. The outlying hotels, student rooms, and arcaded covered ways are still known as the West Range and East Range, as Jefferson called them. An engraving of his sketch plan for the Lawn was made for him by the New York engraver Peter Maverick in 1822. It is now preserved in the University of Virginia Library, where it was available as reference for the garden wall restoration. This plan shows only the architectural anatomy of his masterful site plan. Nevertheless, Jefferson was as skillful in garden design as he was in architecture, and within the walled gardens he intended "embellishment of grounds by fancy"—his own definition of "gardening as a fine art." Those beautifully proportioned gardens, enclosed by serpentine brick walls, like elegant rooms, were perfection even before they were embellished with planting.

Beyond the gardens were the ranges of dormitories into which hotels for dining-commons were built opposite the two end and center gardens. The gardens opposite the hotels were divided approximately in half by serpentine walls with communicating gates, one part relating to the pavilions and the other to the hotels. The pavilion sections were treated as pleasure gardens; those adjacent to the hotels were planted with fruit

The alleys separating the gardens were as beautiful as the gardens themselves.

The garden walls formed the back walls of the privies.

trees and other food-producing plants. Although differently planted, they seem like single units.

Unfortunately, there is little available information about the planting of the gardens back of the pavilions. Over the years the designs of these gardens had changed with changing residents, and many small buildings had been added. Service roads had been cut through the middle of all ten gardens, and new walls had been built without respect for the original locations on the Jefferson plan. The challenge to restore these original garden walls according to the Maverick engraving was accepted as a project in 1948 by The Garden Club of Virginia. Included in this project was the creation within these walls of gardens that could have been laid out and planted by Jefferson.

Although it was realized that the enclosing walls established decisively the historic character of the gardens, the problem of creating historically sympathetic interior designs required expert professional direction. To assist the Restoration Committee and university historians, Alden Hopkins, landscape architect of Colonial Williamsburg, was retained. For the necessary archaeological excavations and research, James Knight, also of Colonial Williamsburg, was added to the restoration team.

As shown on the Maverick plan and verified by the archaeological excavations, there were in the approximate center of each side wall privies that served both students and faculty. In their adaptation as toolhouses these architecturally attractive little buildings were restored in some of the gardens, where they also serve an important decorative function as garden houses. Not all of them were rebuilt, but the ones that were not rebuilt were marked by a tracery of brick outlining the foundation.

Only from a bird's-eye view is it possible to understand the unique contribution

Jefferson made to the overall plan of the Lawn. From such a vantage point one could see that the width of the gardens increases as the garden location recedes in distance from the Rotunda, from which all pavilions were intended to be viewed. In designing his architectural composition to be so viewed, Jefferson realized that if the pavilions were spaced equidistant they would not appear that way because of foreshortening. In order to correct this optical illusion, he spaced them further apart in proportion to their distance from the focal viewpoint. Not since the Renaissance had this subtlety of design been used so effectively. Naturally the graduated spacing between the pavilions was automatically reflected in the width of the gardens.

All the gardens were separated by lanes leading to courtyards that served the pavilions. This required walls on both sides of the lanes to screen them from the gardens. The extra cost of two walls instead of one to insure privacy in the gardens shows the importance Jefferson attached to their sanctity as retreats.

The designs of all ten pavilion facades were purposely different to furnish examples of fine architecture for students. The architecture of all the original buildings was based upon classic models: the Rotunda from the Roman Pantheon; Pavilions I and VIII from the Baths of Diocletian; Pavilions III, V, and VII after Palladio; Pavilion IV the Doric of Albano; Pavilions II and IX were modeled on the Temple of Fortuna Virilis, and VI and X on the Theater of Marcellus.[1]

This same policy was adopted for the creation of the gardens, making no two alike, despite the temptation to repeat because of the similar enclosures. Cognizant of the dual influences of classical geometrical design, as exemplified in Hampton, near Baltimore, and the trend toward naturalized design, as shown in Jefferson's own Monticello, Hopkins used both styles in his plans for the ten university gardens. Jefferson's preference for English naturalistic gardening was stated in his notes on visiting English gardens and in the choice of books found in his library, such as *James on Gardening*, James's translation of *The Theory and Practice of Gardening* from the French of Dezallier d'Argentville, and *The American Gardner* by Gardiner and Hepburn in 1818.

Hopkins made a comprehensive preliminary plan showing the design of all ten gardens, but because of the more difficult topography of the East Lawn gardens, the West Lawn gardens were undertaken first. They were completed under his direction and presented to the University of Virginia on April 24, 1952.

It was eight years before conditions cleared sufficiently for The Garden Club of Virginia to resume the restoration of the East Lawn gardens. In the meantime the death of Alden Hopkins in September 1960 necessitated the retaining of new professional assistance. The Restoration Committee wished to carry out the Hopkins preliminary plan as nearly as possible. Fortunately, Donald Parker, who succeeded Hopkins as landscape architect for Colonial Williamsburg, was willing to undertake this task. Ralph E. Griswold, landscape architect of Pittsburgh, was retained as consultant, and James Knight continued his work as archaeologist.

For the East Lawn gardens the problem of eliminating the modern road that had been cut through the gardens was much more difficult because another road had to be built to take its place. The removal of the old road and its replacement by a new one

---

1. Sidney Fiske Kimball, *Thomas Jefferson, Architect* (1916; reprint ed., New York: Da Capo Press, 1968).

seemed at first to be an insurmountable expense, but by a gracious gesture of the governor of Virginia, state funds were allocated for its execution. Its relocation was the subject of intensive debate because of the intricate pedestrian traffic patterns. Finally it was resolved by locating the road between the East Range and the east walls of the restored gardens, this being considered the least conspicuous location. The completed East Lawn gardens were presented to the governor of Virginia and the president of the University of Virginia on May 4, 1965. There follows a brief description of the special conditions pertaining to each of the ten gardens.

A great variety of Colonial-style gateways enhance all the gardens.

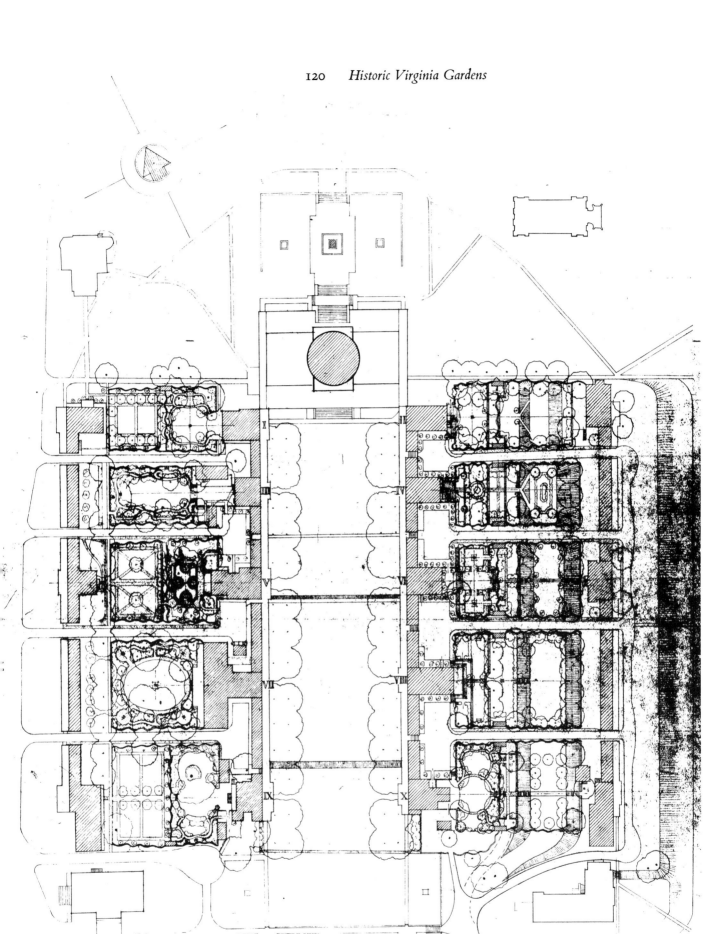

Conjectural designs for the proposed garden restorations at the University of Virginia, Alden Hopkins, landscape architect

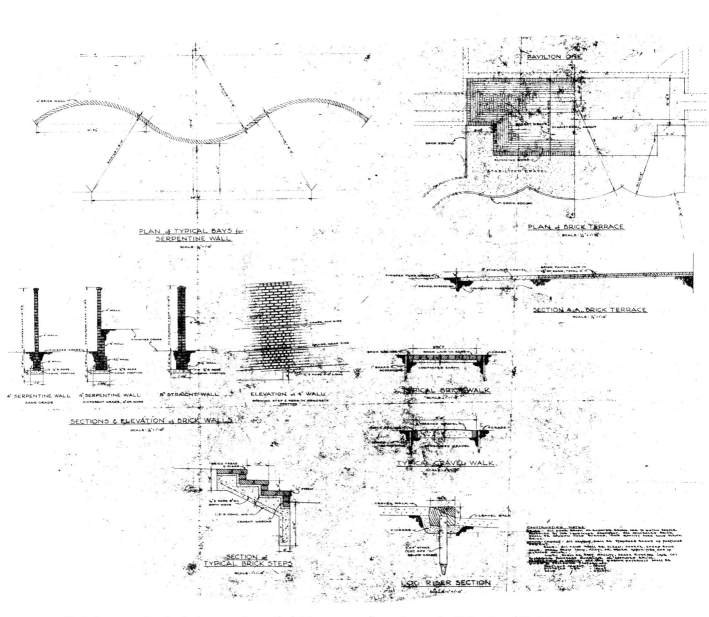

Typical construction details for serpentine walls, brick terrace, walks, and steps, the University of Virginia, 1950

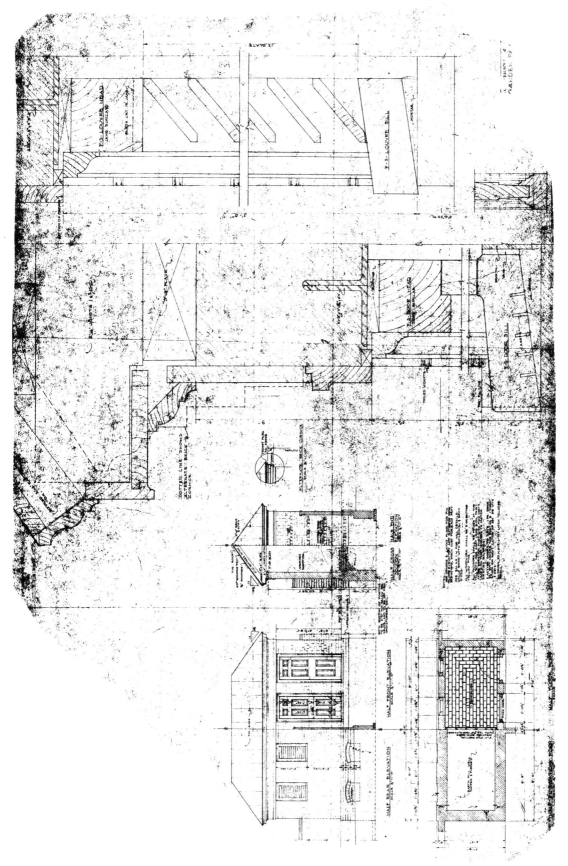

Plan, section, elevation, and details of a typical necessary at the University of Virginia

West Lawn Gardens

The initial conception of the restoration of the Gardens which were a part of the architectural plan of Thomas Jefferson for the University of Virginia took place at a meeting of the Restoration Committee of The Garden Club of Virginia at Stratford, April 15, 1948. From that date until the completion of the gardens in 1952, this work formed the great undertaking of The Garden Club of Virginia. The proceeds from Historic Garden Week from 1948 through 1951 provided approximately $70,000 for this purpose.

Presentation Program, April 24, 1952.

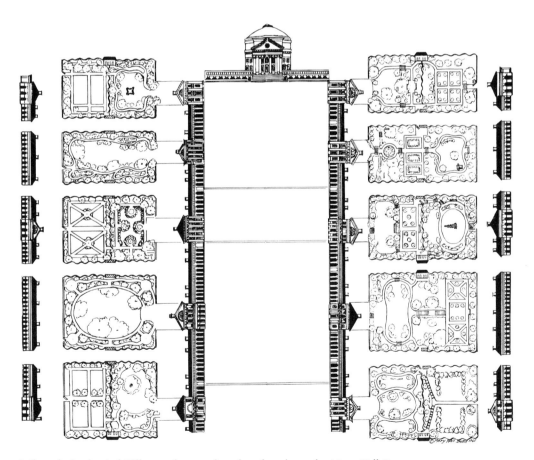

Jefferson's Academical Village and restored garden plans drawn by Mary Hall Betts

Garden of Pavilion I

Pavilion I

All the gardens of the West Lawn are comparatively flat, presenting no serious topographical problems. The garden of Pavilion I is one of the divided areas.[2] Entrance can be had either directly from the pavilion to a brick terrace or from gates on either side of the terrace. On the north side of the garden the alley wall is overhung by a handsome photinia. Gates or benches in the gardens were all carefully designed and constructed in style and workmanship especially for this restoration by Alden Hopkins and his architectural associates at Colonial Williamsburg. They are authentic garden ornaments of the period.

The residential section of this garden is a miniature adaptation of the great terrace at Hampton, near Baltimore. As at Hampton, an ornamental winding walk of white gravel surrounds a green lawn, the four corners of which are softenend by kidney-shaped beds planted with low shrubs interplanted with bulbs and annuals. In the center of the lawn is a partially completed Corinthian capital, one of several cut under Jefferson's direction in the hope of using local stone for the pillars of the Rotunda and the pavilions of his "Academical Village." Having found no stonecutters in this country he considered capable of carving the capitals, he brought from Italy two brothers—Micheli and Giacomo Reggi—and set them to carving the native stone of Albemarle. To his great disappointment this stone proved unsatisfactory, and these unfinished capitals are those left for subsequent garden ornament.

It is of interest that Jefferson ultimately ordered the bases and capitals for the Rotunda columns carved in Italy. Upon completion they were packed in twenty-four crates and sent part to Boston and part to New York. There they were put on other ships and sent to Richmond. From Richmond they came by packet boats up the James to Scottsville, and from there they were hauled by oxcart to Charlottesville. A less determined person than Jefferson would never have attempted to have twenty-four cases, each weighing from three to five tons, transported from Italy to the Virginia countryside.

As in all the gardens, the planting is a combination of native and exotic plants introduced to garden cultivation by Jefferson and his horticultural friends with whom he kept up a constant exchange throughout his adult life. The hotel section of this garden was kept appropriately simple with two central grass panels surrounded by fruit trees. The grass panels might have been vegetable areas but, as such, would have been impractical to maintain in a restoration. Direct access to the hotel is through a gate in the rear wall.

2. West Lawn Pavilions are designated by odd numbers: I, III, V, VII, IX.

Pavilion I, hotel area

Pavilion I, residential area, a discarded local stone capital

TREES

Crataegus Phaenopyrum, Washington Thorn
Magnolia grandiflora, Southern Magnolia
Malus coronaria, Wild Sweet Crab

Prunus cerasifera var., Purple-leaved Plum
Prunus persica var., Peach
Pyrus communis var., Dwarf Pear

SHRUBS

Aucuba japonica variegata, Gold-Dust Tree
Calycanthus floridus, Carolina Sweetshrub
Chionanthus virginica, Fringe-Tree
Hypericum calycinum, St. Johns-Wort
Nandina domestica, Nandina
Photinia serrulata, Photinia
Pieris floribunda, Mountain Andromeda
Potentilla fruticosa, Bush Cinquefoil
Prunus laurocerasus, Cherry Laurel

Pyracantha coccinea, Firethorn
Rhododendron carolinianum, Carolina
   Rhododendron
Rhododendron indicum, Indian Azalea—
   known in Holland before 1680. Brought
   by ships of the Dutch East India Com-
   pany from Japan to Java and then to
   Holland
Sambucus canadensis, Elderberry

Spiraea cantoniensis, Reeves-Spiraea

VINES

Vitis labrusca, Fox Grape

ROSES

Rosa eglanteria, Sweet Briar

Rosa laevigata, Cherokee Rose, introduced
   into America before 1759

Typical garden construction plan and elevations, University of Virginia, West Lawn, Pavilion I. Similar plans were made for all the West Lawn Pavilion gardens but are not reproduced. Alden Hopkins, landscape architect, 1950; revised 1951.

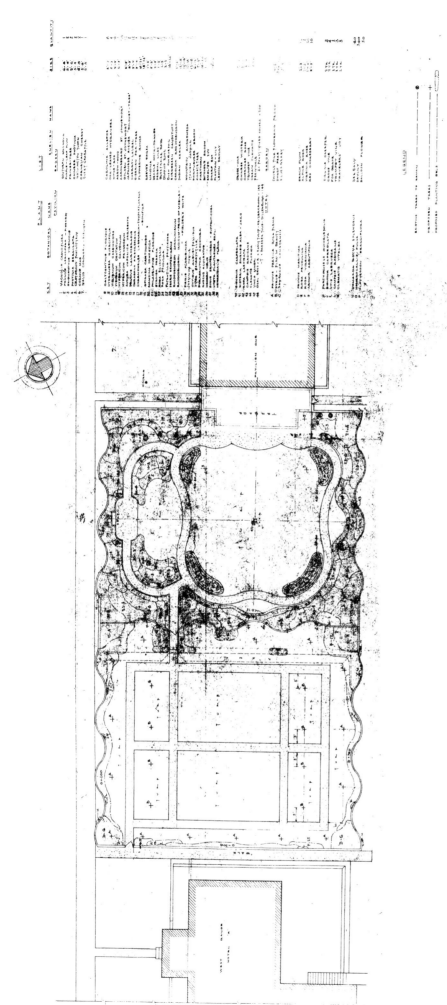

Planting plan and plant list, University of Virginia, Pavilion I garden, Alden Hopkins, landscape architect, 1950

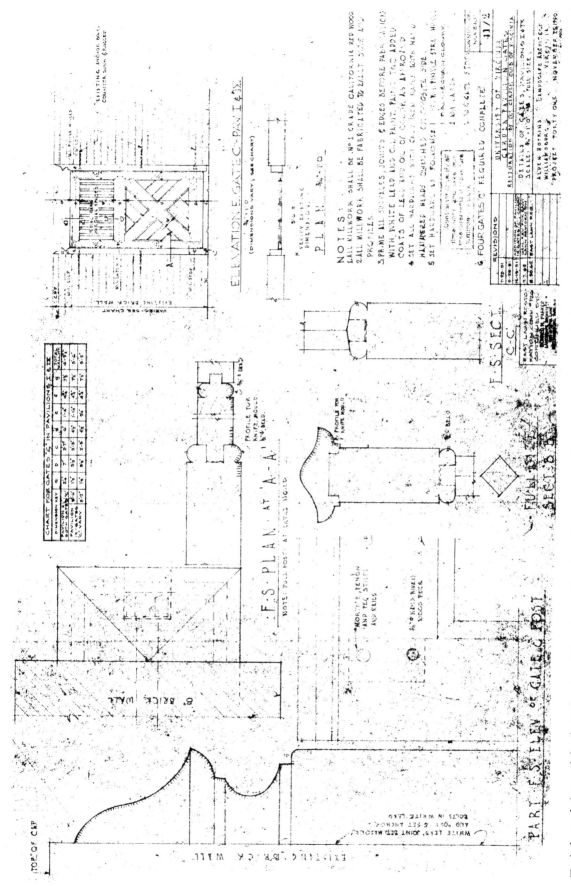

Typical gate designs and details, University of Virginia, Pavilions I and IX, West Lawn Gardens, Alden Hopkins, landscape architect, 1950

Pavilion III. Dogwood and azaleas predominate.

Garden of Pavilion III

Pavilion III

Professors residing in this pavilion did not have to share their garden with a hotel; therefore much greater length was possible. Precedents for this design were the curvilinear lines of Mount Vernon and Monticello. A long, informal oval lawn was outlined by a serpentine gravel walk, weaving its way between planting beds. On the lawn side the planting is low; small shrubs are interspersed with perennials and bulbs. On the outside the trees and shrubs build up to a height that provides privacy. Three minor loops of walks lead to hidden alcoves with sheltered benches. These loops are reminiscent of the gardens of Blenheim, which Jefferson visited in 1786. He wrote of his enjoyment in these gardens, which he described as "small thickets of shrubs in oval raised beds, cultivated and flowers among the shrubs." From the pavilion court there is a vista down a gentle slope, across the lawn to a terminal feature—one of the discarded stone capitals[3] overhung by a wild rose. Spring is the most spectacular time in this garden when pink and white dogwood and azaleas form a picturesque bower around comfortable white benches.

TREES

Cedrus Deodara, Deodar Cedar
Cornus florida, White Flowering Dogwood
Cornus florida rubra, Pink Flowering Dogwood
Cornus mas, Cornelian Cherry
Halesia carolina, Silver-Bell
Koelreuteria paniculata, Goldenrain-Tree
Salix babylonica, Weeping Willow

SHRUBS

Caragana microphylla, Little Leaf Pea-Tree
Clethra alnifolia, Summer Sweet
Cotoneaster microphylla, Small-leaf Cotoneaster
Daphne Cneorum, Rose Daphne
Hypericum, St. Johns-Wort
Ligustrum lucidum, Glossy Privet
Lonicera tatarica, Tatarian Honeysuckle
Neviusia alabamensis, Snow Wreath
Rhododendron indica alba, White Azalea, arrived in England before 1819 from Japan via Java on Dutch trading ships.
Symphoricarpus albus laevigatus, Snowberry
Taxus baccata, English Yew
Viburnum prunifolium, Black-Haw Viburnum

VINES

Campsis radicans, Trumpet-Vine
Clematis Vitalba, Travelers-Joy
Parthenocissus quinquefolia, Virginia Creeper

3. See the description of Pavilion I.

Pavilion III, a full-length garden of informal design

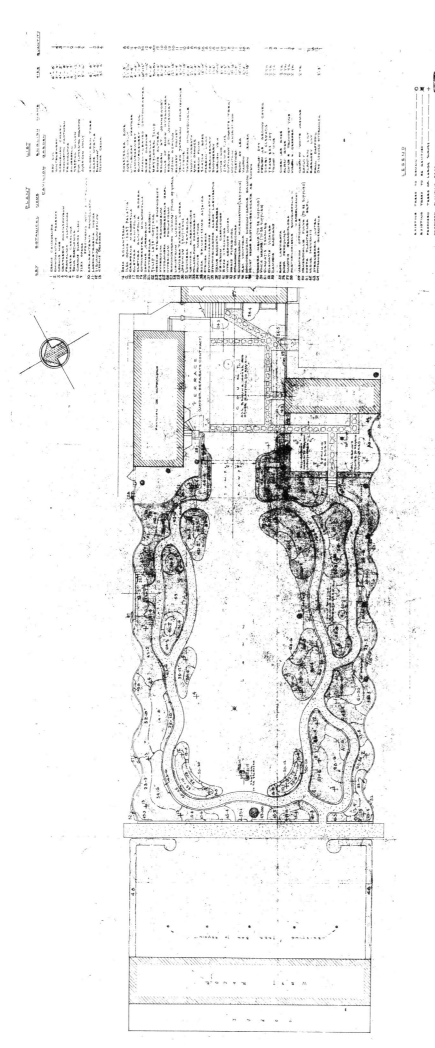

Planting plan and plant list, Pavilion III garden, University of Virginia, Alden Hopkins, landscape architect, 1950

Pavilion V. Service alleys separate the gardens.

Pavilion V. Gravel paths outline a pattern of grass centered on fruit trees.

Pavilion V

Like Pavilion I, this garden also serves a dual purpose: pleasure garden for the residents and kitchen garden for the adjacent hotel. The two areas are separated by a serpentine cross wall with a latticed gate between. Hopkins's design is based upon examples in Loudon's *Encyclopedia of Gardening*, an important garden reference work of the early 1800s. The composition consists of a low boxwood-bordered rectangle intercepted at the corners by four circular paths. This forms a green parterre outlined by white gravel walks, placing the emphasis on pattern more than plants.

Bordering this formal design are beds of bulbs and perennials. Pink crape myrtles with their spectacular summer bloom and suntanned winter trunks add vertical accents. In the corners and along the western wall flowering trees and tall shrubs provide essential screening. Two turf sitting areas are located at the outer sides of the garden on the minor axis.

The hotel garden is divided into two turf rectangles, one on either side of a central walk. Each rectangle is crisscrossed by gravel paths. This is a simple plan of the type advocated by Dezallier in his *Theory and Practice of Gardening*.

TREES

Lagerstroemia indica, Crape-Myrtle
Malus sp., 'Albemarle Pippin' Apple
Oxydendron arboreum, Sourwood
Prunus persica var., Peach

Prunus serrulata var., Flowering Cherry
Quercus Phellos, Willow Oak
Robinia pseudoacacia, Black Acacia, Yellow Locust

SHRUBS

Buxus sempervirens suffruticosa, Dwarf Boxwood (true dwarf)
Chaenomeles lagenaria, Japanese Flowering Quince

Ficus carica, Fig
Rhododendron indica alba, White Azalea, arrived in England before 1819 from Japan via Java on Dutch trading ships

Spiraea cantonensis, Reeves-Spiraea
Vitex Agnus-castus, Chaste-Tree, Hemp-Tree, Monks Pepper-Tree

VINES

Wisteria sinensis, Chinese Wisteria

Wisteria sinensis alba, White Chinese Wisteria

ROSES

Rosa alba, Rose of York

Rosa multiflora var. *platyphylla*, Seven Sisters Rose

Rosa spinosissima, Scotch Hedge Rose

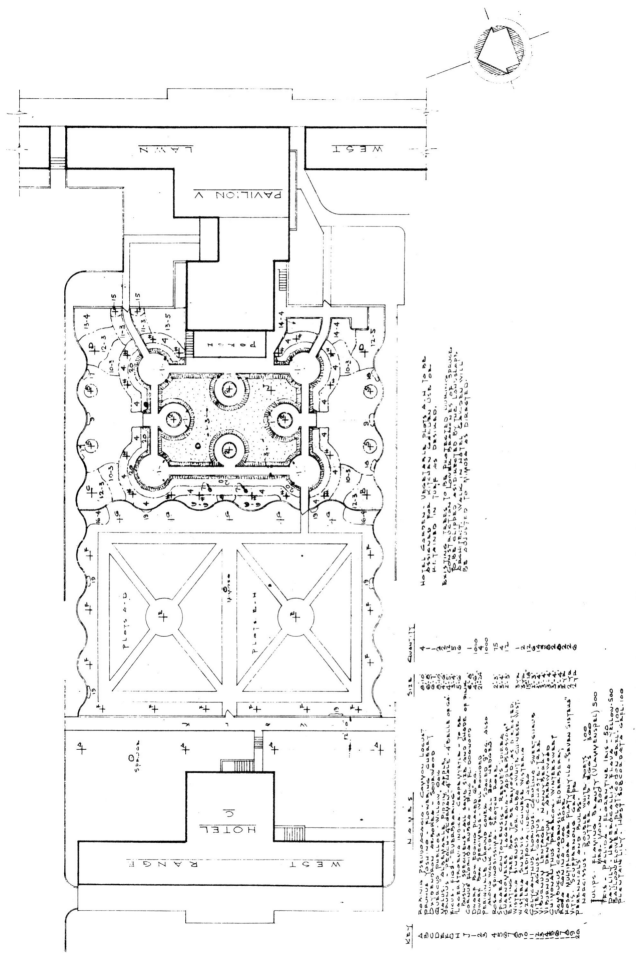

Planting plan and plant list, Pavilion V garden, University of Virginia, Alden Hopkins, landscape architect

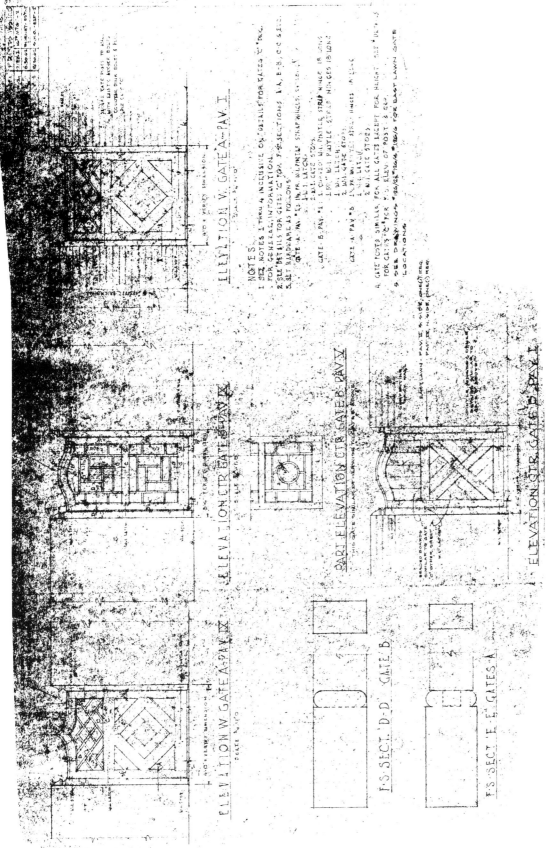

Detail of gates for Pavilions I, V, and IX, University of Virginia, Alden Hopkins, landscape architect, 1950

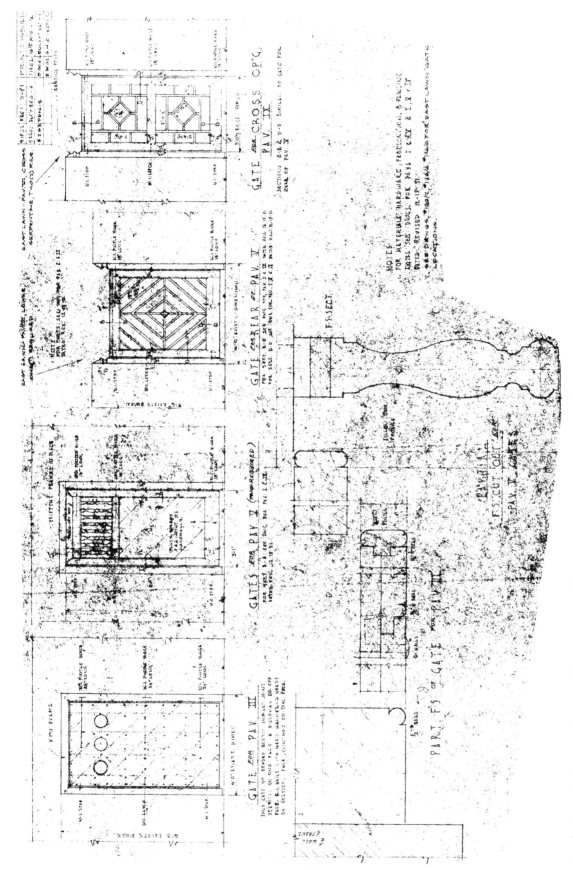

Detail of gates for Pavilions III, V, and IX, University of Virginia, Alden Hopkins, landscape architect, 1951

Pavilion VII

The cornerstone of the university was laid at this pavilion on October 6, 1817. Since 1907 the pavilion and its garden have been used as residence for bachelor professors and by the Colonnade Club, a private club for the faculty, whose special requirements were recognized in the adapted garden design. Precedent for this design was found in Le Rouge's *Jardins Anglo-Chinois*, published in 1785, in which use was made of repeated circular motifs. A large open circular lawn centered on a discarded capital is defined by a white gravel path.

In each of the four corners the path takes a loop secluding circular retreats in which there are comfortable benches for relaxation and conversation. These retreats are connected by an informal path embellished with ornamental planting.

Very old trees already there were incorporated in the design to add shade and seclusion; they spread their shade over the entire garden. Beneath these old trees periwinkle thrives and provides a rich green background for spring-flowering bulbs. Catering as it does to casual strolling by faculty members, this garden is reminiscent of Jefferson's own favorite diversion.

TREES

Cercis canadensis, Eastern Redbud

Ilex opaca, American Holly

Magnolia grandiflora, Southern Magnolia

SHRUBS

Buxus sempervirens, Common Boxwood (true tree)

Chaenomeles lagernaria, Japanese Flowering Quince

Fothergilla Gardeni, Dwarf Fothergilla

Hibiscus syriacus, Rose-of-Sharon, Shrubby Althea

Hydrangea quercifolia, Oak-Leaf Hydrangea

Ilex vomitoria, Yaupon

Ligustrum lucidum, Glossy Privet

Mahonia aquifolium, Oregon Grape

Meratia praecox, Wintersweet

Nandina domestica, Nandina

Syringa chinensis, Chinese Lilac

Syringa vulgaris, Common Lilac

Viburnum dentatum, Arrowwood

Vitex Negundo incisa, Cutleaf Chaste-Tree

VINES

Jasminum nudiflorum, Winter Jessamine

HERBACEOUS PLANTS—ANNUALS AND PERENNIALS

Anemone coronaria var., Anemone

Narcissus odorus, Jonquil

Scilla hispanicus, Spanish Bluebell

Vinca minor, Periwinkle

Yucca filamentosa, Adams-Needle

ROSES

Rosa centifolia, Rose of Provence or Cabbage Rose, described by Theophrastus before 300 B.C.

Rosa spinosissima, Scotch Hedge Rose

Pavilion VII. Secluded niches for study and conversation were typical of the period.

Pavilion VII. Curved paths are bordered with bulbs and perennials. Shrubs have to be controlled.

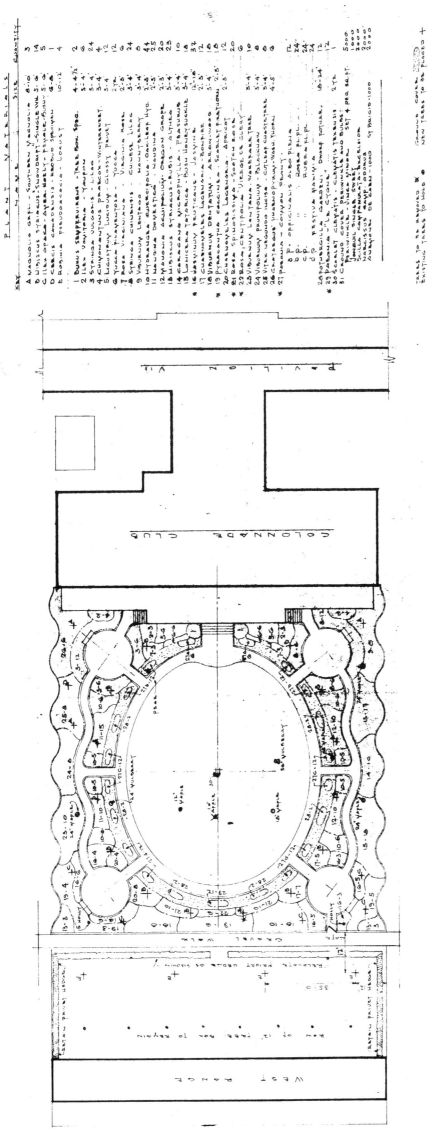

Planting plan and plant list, Pavilion VII garden, University of Virginia, Alden Hopkins, landscape architect, 1951

Pavilion IX

The "McGuffey Ash" (Biltmore Ash) is frequently spoken of as the largest ash tree in the southeastern United States. It was planted about 1826 by George Tucker, the first Professor of Moral Philosophy at the university. Professor Tucker was succeeded in 1845 by William A. McGuffey, famous for his readers.

Tradition says that McGuffey gave up his flower garden for the sake of the handsome young tree. The tree, growing close to the pavilion, is of such enormous trunk size and tremendous branch spread that it had to be recognized as the major factor in Hopkins's garden design. Except for a cluster of azaleas and ground cover around its base, it was left freestanding. Around the edges of an informal lawn an undulating border edged with English ivy and planted with syringa, oakleaf hydrangea, and flowering quince is faced with tulips, iris, phlox, daisies, and asters. On the center line of the pavilion, in the edge of the planting paralleling the serpentine division wall, a white bench marks a focal point.

At the southern end, where sun reaches the planting, a miniature wilderness of blooming plants follows a winding path as a symbol of Jefferson's fancy for naturalistic gardening. From this secluded corner, paths branch off to the privy and to the gate connecting with the kitchen garden. Here, an elemental rectangular path system bisected by a central walk overhung with apple trees demonstrates the effectiveness of a well-executed simple plan.

Pavilion IX.
A comfortable seat terminates an allée of apple trees in the hotel area.

Pavilion IX. A giant ash tree dominates the residential part of this garden.

TREES

Malus sp., Dwarf Apple
Prunus cerasifera var., Purple Leaf Plum
Prunus domestica var., Plum
Prunus glandulosa, Flowering Almond

Prunus persica, Peach
Robinia Pseudoacacia, Black Acacia, Yellow Locust

SHRUBS

Clethra alnifolia, Summer Sweet
Ficus carica, Common Fig
Hypericum prolificum, Shrubby St. Johns-Wort
Ligustrum lucidum, Glossy Privet
Lonicera tatarica alba, White Tatarian Honeysuckle
Rhododendron indicum, Indian Azalea, known in Holland before 1680, brought by ships of the Dutch East India Company from Japan to Java, and then to Holland
Syringa persica, Persian Lilac
Syringa vulgaris, Common Lilac
Syringa vulgaris alba, White Lilac
Viburnum acerfolium, Maple Leaf Viburnum
Viburnum dentatum, Arrowwood
Viburnum lentago, Nanny-Berry

HERBACEOUS PLANTS—ANNUALS AND PERENNIALS

Aster sp., Asters
Fritillaria imperialis, Crown Imperial
Iris, Iris

Narcissus, Daffodil
Phlox sp., Phlox
Tulipa, Tulip

ROSES

Rosa alba suaveolens, Cottage Rose

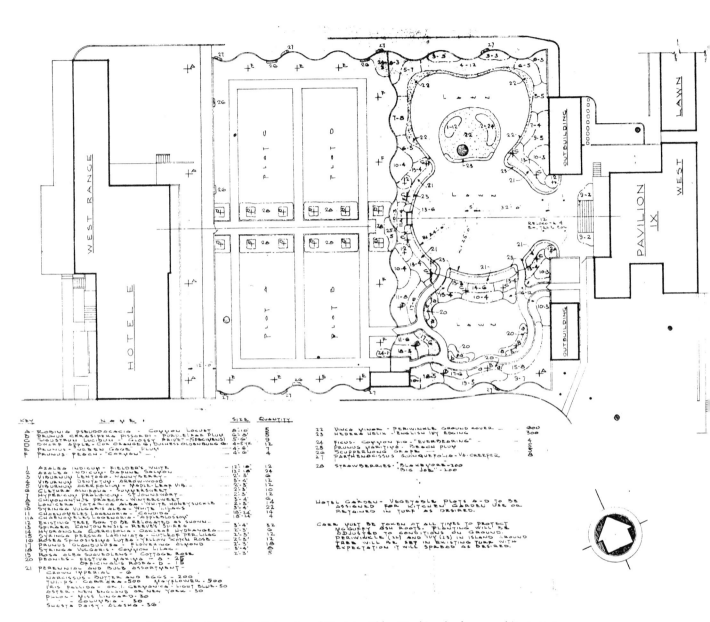

Planting plan and plant list, Pavilion IX garden, University of Virginia, Alden Hopkins, landscape architect, 1951

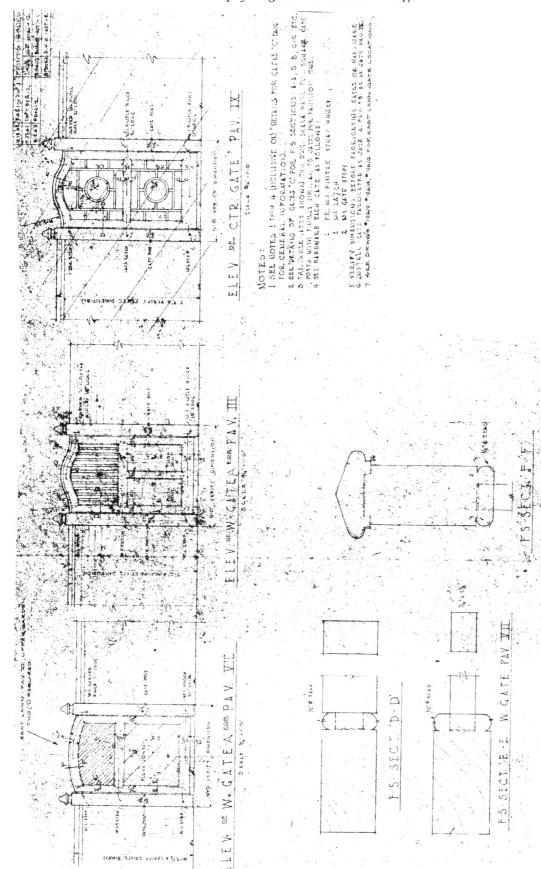

Detail of gates for pavilions III, VII, and IX, University of Virginia, Alden Hopkins, landscape architect

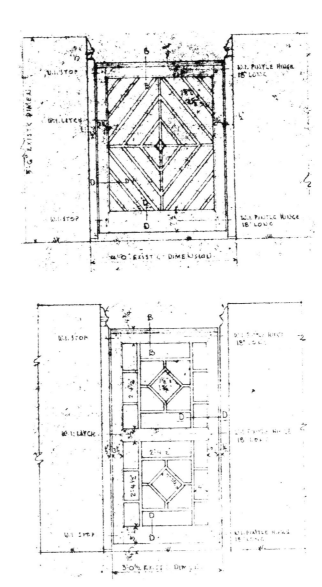

East Lawn Gardens

The Restoration Committee of The Garden Club of Virginia, at its meeting at the home of Alden Hopkins in Williamsburg, September 22, 1959, voted to recommend to the Annual Meeting in May: "The restoration of the gardens between the East Lawn and East Range of the University of Virginia, according to the plans of Mr. Jefferson, as shown in the Peter Maverick engraving, to be executed by Alden Hopkins, Landscape Architect."

This recommendation was accepted by the Garden Club of Virginia at its Fortieth Annual Meeting, May 18–19, 1960, Richmond. A letter from President Shannon said in part: "It would be a source of gratification to me to see completed the companion restoration to the one so generously and beautifully accomplished by the Garden Club of Virginia on the West Side of the Grounds."

From the fall of 1959 until the completion of the gardens in 1964, this work formed a great undertaking for The Garden Club of Virginia. The proceeds from Historic Garden Week from 1960 through 1964 provided approximately $160,000 for this purpose.

Presentation Program, May 4, 1965.

By the time the East Lawn gardens were undertaken in 1960, alterations had wreaked havoc with the original plan of 1822. Concrete-encased utility lines along a new service road through the center of these gardens had destroyed much of the Maverick plan. However, archaeological excavations located foundations for the southeast serpentine wall and fragmentary sections of the northeast and southeast walls, making it possible to rebuild the walls as originally designed. Despite the steepness of the grade on this side, Jefferson's plan showed no difference. His feeling for architectural symmetry here outweighed his preference for asymetrical garden design. It must have been very difficult to construct these serpentine walls with a continuous profile on these steep slopes, but that is the way they were except for the short, level interruptions of the privy walls.

Pavilion II. Two levels of the pavilion connect with the garden terrace.

Pavilion II

The Pavilion II garden is the nearest to the Rotunda and, therefore, is the smallest of the East Lawn gardens.[4] It is divided by a serpentine cross wall. A brick terrace constructed next to the pavilion is accessible by gates in the flanking walls. From either side of the terrace curving walks with steps, following the grades, descend to an intermediate lower level. On this upper lawn a decorative bench, set against a hedge of southern wax myrtle, accents the central axis. An existing umbrella tree and a maidenhair tree are reminders of Jefferson's interest in new plant importations. The side paths connect with the privies and gates to the lowest level. Between these a path parallels the serpentine division wall against which fig trees are espaliered. In the center, on either side, are grape trellises underplanted with herbs. Benches provide pleasant places to rest. Below the dividing wall a steep bank with steps on the lateral paths leads to the hotel garden. This level area is laid out in four square panels with four pear trees planted symmetrically in each. At the very foot of this garden another steep bank with steps to a central gate gives access to the terminal platform. From here additional steps lead down to the hotel.

This description indicates the difficult problem of grades which was resolved in this restoration based on Jefferson's seemingly simple, two-dimensional plan. The several levels in all the east gardens could not be determined by the continuous slope of the side walls. They had to be deduced from internal evidence, such as the grade of existing plants and cross walls or steps.

4. East Lawn Pavilions are designated by even numbers: II, IV, VI, VIII, X.

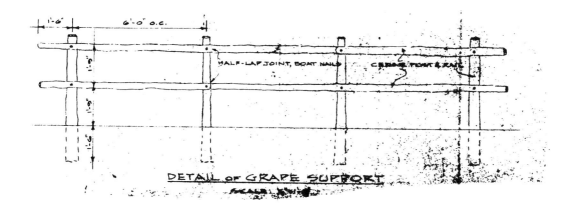

DETAIL OF GRAPE SUPPORT

Pavilion II. An intermediate level leads to the necessary, or privy, and is planted with grapes, huckleberries, figs, and herbs.

Pavilion II. A graceful path leads from the terrace to the lower gardens.

TREES

Albizzia Julibrissin, Mimosa, Silk-Tree
Amelanchier canadensis, Shad-Bush, Service-Berry
Carya pecan, Pecan
Cornus florida, Flowering Dogwood
Ginkgo biloba, Maidenhair Tree
Ilex opaca, American Holly
Juglans nigra, Black Walnut

Lagerstroemia indica, Crape-Myrtle
Magnolia tripetala, Umbrella-Tree
Malus coronaria, Sweet Crab
Malus pumila var., Apple
Prunus domestica var., Plum
Pyrus communis var., Dwarf Pear
Taxus baccata, English Yew
Tsuga canadensis, Canadian Hemlock

SHRUBS

Buxus sempervirens suffruticosa, Dwarf Boxwood (true dwarf)
Chaenomeles speciosa nivalis (*C. lagenaria nivalis*), White Flowering Quince
Cydonia oblonga, Fruiting Quince
Decumaria barbara, Climbing Saxifrage
Ficus carica, Common Fig
Gelsemium sempervirens, Carolina Yellow Jessamine

Hypericum calycinum, St. Johns-Wort
Ilex Cassine, Dahoon Holly
Lonicera tatarica, Tatarian Honeysuckle
Myrica cerifera, Southern Wax Myrtle
Punica granatum, Pomegranate
Rhododendron calendulacea, Flame Azalea
Rhododendron indica var. 'Fielder's White,' Azalea
Sambucus canadensis, Elderberry

Vaccinium corymbosum, Highbush Blueberry
Viburnum Opulus roseum, European Cranberry-Bush
Vitex Agnus-castus, Chaste-Tree, Hemp-Tree, Monks Pepper-Tree

VINES

Hedera helix, English Ivy

Vitis rotundifolia, Muscadine Grape

HERBACEOUS PLANTS—ANNUALS AND PERENNIALS

Aquilegia canadensis, American Columbine
Callistephus chinensis, China Aster
Chrysanthemum peruvianum, Golden Sunflower
Convallaria majalis, Lily-of-the-Valley
Crocus vernus, Common Crocus
Hosta ventriculosa, Plantain Lily
Iris germanica, Blue Flag
Iris sibirica, Siberian Iris

Muscari botryoides, Grape-Hyacinth
Narcissus Jonquilla simplex, Jonquil
Narcissus Poetaz, Poetaz Narcissus
Nerine Sarniense, Guernsey-Lily
Phlox paniculata, Summer Phlox
Ruta graveolens, Rue
Tulipa var., Tulips in variety
Vinca major, Bigleaf Periwinkle
Vinca minor, Periwinkle

FERNS

Adiantum pedatum, Maidenhair Fern

ROSES

Rosa spinosissima, Scotch Hedge Rose

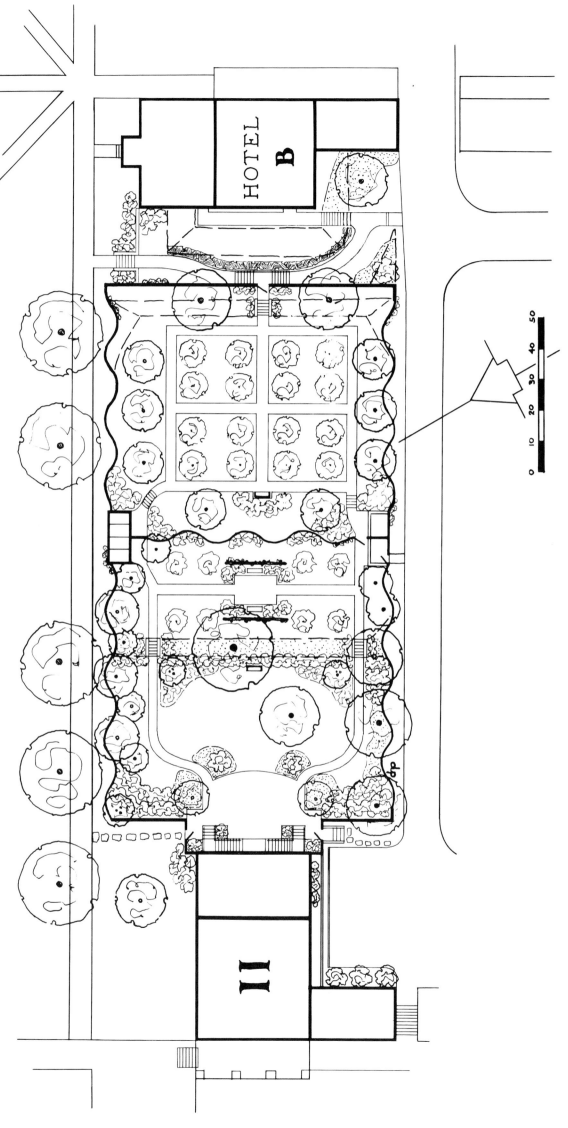

Typical presentation plan, Pavilion II garden, University of Virginia, Donald H. Parker, landscape architect, Ralph E. Griswold, consultant; based on preliminary designs by Alden Hopkins, 1962

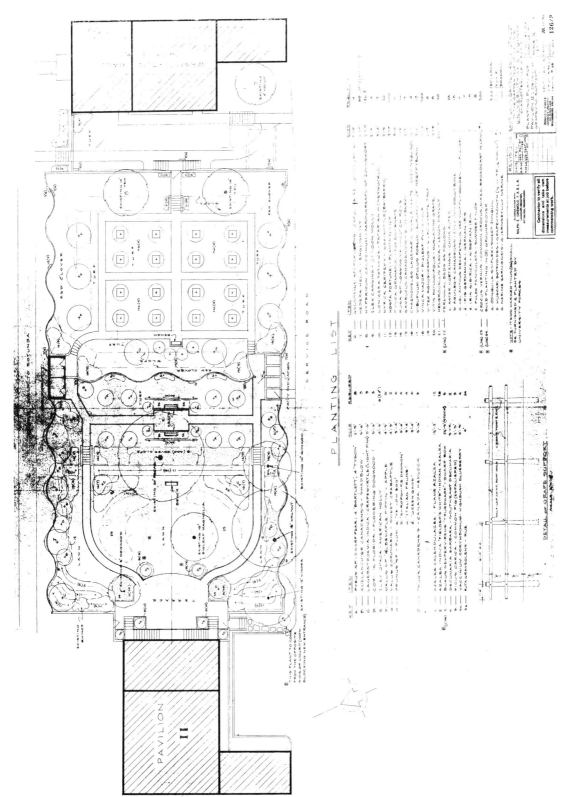

Planting plan and plant list, Pavilion II garden, University of Virginia, Donald H. Parker, landscape architect, 1962; Ralph E. Griswold, consultant

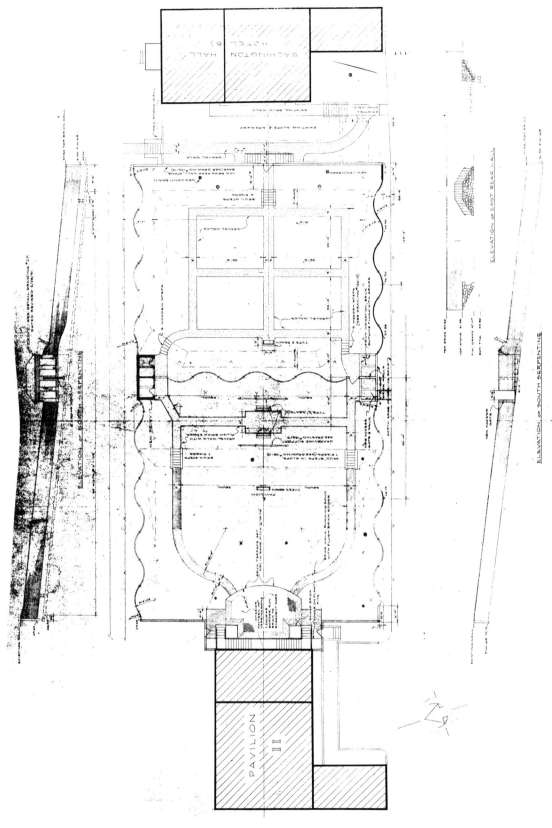

Grading and layout plan, Pavilion II garden, University of Virginia, Donald H. Parker, landscape architect, 1962; Ralph E. Griswold, consultant. Similar plans were made for all the East Lawn pavilion gardens but are not reproduced.

Pavilion IV

The garden of Pavilion IV has enjoyed continuous attention through the years. In 1844 this pavilion was occupied by Schele deVere, Professor of Modern Languages. He loved flowers and developed his garden with care and knowledge.

Several years before The Garden Club of Virginia began its project at the university, the Albemarle Garden Club had done extensive planting here. The trees and shrubs planted at that time flourished and are now outstanding specimens in the new plan.

With no interrupting cross walls, the various levels had to be connected by monumental brick steps that were centered on the pavilion. The pavilion was not centered between the side walls; therefore, the garden axis is off center of the area.

Next to the pavilion is a brick terrace with box-edged walks and a perennial border. Separating this level from the lawn below is a low brick retaining wall and steps. The lawn, outlined by dwarf boxwood, is embellished at both ends by southern magnolias and in the center by a circle of dwarf boxwood grown handsome with age. Below this, approximately where the modern service road was cut through, Parker laid out a sort of kitchen garden patterned after a design from Dezallier's *Theory and Practice of Gardening*. Though the Dezallier planting would have included a variety of fruit trees and vegetables, these were not reproduced for the sake of maintenance economy. The rectangular beds were outlined with ornamental herbs, such as santolina. From this kitchen garden level more steps lead to a rambling informal garden—a bow to Jefferson's preference for naturalistic gardening. Picturesque groupings of English hawthorn, with contrasting foliage of deodar cedar and catalpas are interspersed with shrubs that provide seasonal displays of bloom and berries.

A Chippendale bench, located on a secluded bypath at the north end, balances a Corinthian cast-iron capital casually placed in the bend of the path at the south end. It was one of the capitals made for the modern annex to the Rotunda, an 1853 desecration of Jefferson's design. In 1895 the annex burned and was never replaced. Use of one of the capitals as an ornament in this garden provides a nostalgic note.

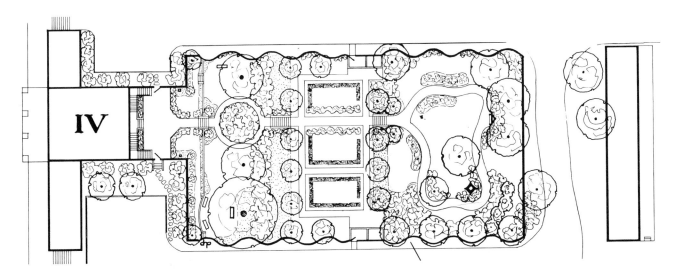

Presentation plan, Pavilion IV, University of Virginia

Pavilion IV. A straight central axis from the pavilion leads to a meandering walk at the lower level.

Pavilion IV. One of the cast-iron capitals used on the annex to the Rotunda, which burned in 1895. Placed here as an incidental garden ornament.

TREES

Catalpa speciosa, Western Catalpa
Cedrus deodara, Deodar Cedar
Crataegus oxyacantha, English Hawthorn
Halesia carolina, Carolina Silver-Bell
Liquidambar Styraciflua, Sweet Gum
Liriodendron Tulipifera, Tulip-Tree
Magnolia grandiflora, Southern Magnolia
Melia Azedarach, Pride-of-India Tree

Prunus cerasus var., Sour Cherry
Prunus persica nectarina var., Nectarine
Prunus persica var., Peach
Quercus coccinea, Scarlet Oak
Robinia pseudoacacia, Black Acacia, Yellow Locust
Tilia americana, American Linden
Stewartia Malacodendron, Virginia Stewartia

SHRUBS

Aesculus parviflora, Bottlebrush Buckeye
Buxus sempervirens suffruticosa, Dwarf Boxwood (true dwarf)
Callicarpa americana, American Beauty Berry
Calycanthus floridus, Sweet Shrub
Clethra alnifolia, Summer Sweet
Cotoneaster microphylla, Small-leaf Cotoneaster
Crataegus Crus-galli, Cockspur Thorn
Hibiscus syriacus, Rose-of-Sharon, Shrubby Althea
Ilex verticillata, Winterberry

Ilex vomitoria, Yaupon
Lagerstroemia indica alba, White Crape-Myrtle
Philadelphus coronarius, Mock-Orange
Pyrus communis, Pear (Espalier)
Rhododendron indica alba, White Azalea, arrived in England before 1819 from Japan and Java on Dutch Trading Ships
Rhododendron nudiflora, Pinxter-Flower
Rubus odoratus, Flowering Raspberry
Staphylea Trifolia, Eastern Bladder-Nut
Syringa vulgaris, Common Lilac

Syringa vulgaris alba, White Lilac

VINES

Celastrus scandens, Shrubby Bitter-Sweet
Hedera helix, English Ivy

Jasminum nudiflorum, Winter Jessamine
Lonicera japonica, Japanese Honeysuckle

Lycium halimifolium, Matrimony Vine

HERBACEOUS PLANTS—ANNUALS AND PERENNIALS

Bellis perennis, English Daisy
Chrysanthemum Parthenium, Feverfew
Comphrena globosa, Globe Amaranth, Everlastings
Dicentra eximia, Bleeding Heart
Iris xiphium, Dutch Iris
Lantana camara, Lantana
Lavandula spica, Lavender
Mertensia virginica, Virginia Bluebells
Monarda dydima, Oswego-Tea, Bee-Balm

Paeonia Moutan banksii, Tree Peony, first grown in England (Kew Gardens) in 1789
Santolina chamaecyparissus var., Green and Grey-Leaved Santolina
Stokesia laevis, Stokes Aster
Tagetes patula, French Marigold
Tradescantia virginiana, Spiderwort
Tulipa var., Tulip
Vinca minor, Periwinkle

FERNS

Dryopteris marginalis, Leatherwood Fern

ROSES

Rosa damascena, Damask Rose
Rosa laevigata, Cherokee Rose, introduced

into America before 1759
Rosa moschata, Musk Rose

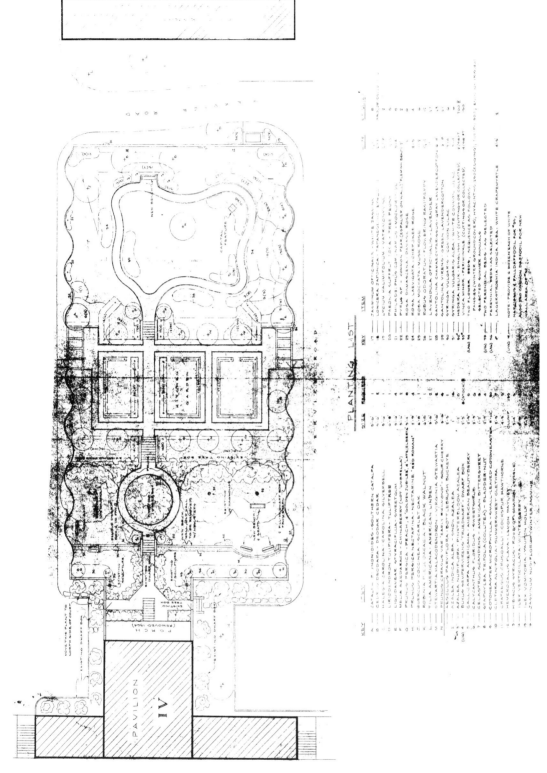

Planting plan and plant list, Pavilion IV garden, University of Virginia, Donald H. Parker, landscape architect; Ralph E. Griswold, consultant

Pavilion VI

The two upper levels of this garden had already been carefully developed before The Garden Club of Virginia began work. The only changes necessary were for access. The brick terrace now has gates at either end as well as an entrance directly from the house. It overlooks a lawn, sometimes referred to as a bowling green, which is reached by central steps on axis with the pavilion. A bench, placed directly across the lawn from the steps, terminates the axis. Surrounding this green is an informal shrub border with benches at each end but no bordering path.

To the east, at the top of a bank, a boxwood hedge divides the green from the orchard below. The orchard is reached by steps at the extremities of the hedge. Beyond the orchard a serpentine cross wall separates it from the hotel garden below. Espaliered fruit trees were planted in the curves of this wall.

Through connecting gates next to the privies, rustic steps run down the slope to a refined wilderness garden. Existing large white pines and Norway spruces were evidence that this hotel area had long been used for something other than a kitchen garden. This adapted use was augmented by planting native shrubs and trees to create woodland thickets at the ends. Through these thickets curved ear-shaped paths carved out shaded retreats with benches. In contrast to these miniature wildernesses, an open oval lawn is ornamented by a stone Gothic spire presented by Merton College of Oxford to the University of Virginia in 1927. This is the architectural touch that creates the typical eighteenth-century, seminaturalistic atmosphere of an English garden such as Jefferson admired at Blenheim.

Pavilion VI. An original stone spire from Merton College, Oxford, England, was made the central motif of the lower garden.

TREES

Acer rubrum, Red Maple
Albizzia Julibrissin, Mimosa, Silk-Tree
Amelanchier canadensis, Shad-Bush, Service-Berry
Carpinus caroliniana, American Hornbeam
Cercis canadensis, Eastern Redbud
Cornus florida, Flowering Dogwood
Cornus mas, Cornelian Cherry
Franklinia alatamaha, Franklinia
Gymnocladus dioicus, Kentucky Coffee-Tree
Hamamelis vernalis, Vernal Witch-Hazel
Ilex opaca, American Holly
Laburnum anagyroides, Goldenchain-Tree
Malus pumila var., Apple
Nyssa sylvatica, Tupelo, Black Gum

Oxydendron arboreum, Sourwood
Picea Abies, Norway Spruce
Pinus resinosa, Red Pine
Pinus Strobus, White Pine
Pinus sylvestris, Scotch Pine
Pinus Taeda, Loblolly Pine
Prunus armeniaca, Apricot (Espalier)
Prunus domestica var., Plum
Prunus Padus, European Bird Cherry
Prunus persica var., Peach
Pyrus communis var., Pear
Quercus falcata, Southern Red Oak
Sassafras albidum, Sassafras
Tsuga caroliniana, Carolina Hemlock

SHRUBS

Alnus incana, Speckled Alder
Chaenomeles lagenaria nivalis, Winter Flowering Quince
Hibiscus syriacus, Rose-of-Sharon, Shrubby Althea
Hypericum calycinum, St. Johns-Wort
Hypericum prolificum, Shrubby St. Johns-Wort
Ilex glabra, Inkberry
Ilex monticola, Mountain Winterberry
Ilex verticillata, Winterberry
Kalmia latifolia, Mountain Laurel
Lindera benzoin, Spicebush
Magnolia virginiana, Swamp Bay, Sweet Bay Magnolia
Myrica pennsylvanica, Northern Bayberry
Pieris floribunda, Mountain Andromeda

Pyracantha coccinea, Scarlet Firethorn
Rhododendron arborescens, Sweet Azalea
Rhododendron calendulacea, Flame Azalea
Rhododendron carolinianum, Carolina Rhododendron
Rhododendron maximum, Rosebay Rhododendron
Rhus aromatica, Fragrant Sumac
Rhus typhina, Staghorn Sumac
Spiraea cantoniensis, Reeves-Spiraea
Symphoricarpus albus, Snowberry
Viburnum acerifolium, Dockmakcie, Maple-Leaf Viburnum
Viburnum lantana, Wayfaring-Tree
Viburnum Lentago, Nanny-Berry
Viburnum prunifolium, Black-Haw Viburnum

VINES

Bignonia capreolata, Cross-Vine
Campsis radicans, Trumpet-Vine
Euonymus obovata, Running Strawberry Bush

Lonicera sempervirens, Trumpet Honeysuckle
Parthenocissus quinquefolia, Virginia Creeper

HERBACEOUS PLANTS—ANNUALS AND PERENNIALS

Anemone coronaria, Poppy Anemone
Brodiaea uniflora, Spring Starflower
Convallaria majalis, Lily-of-the-Valley
Crocus susianus, 'Cloth-of-Gold' Crocus
Erythronium dens-canis, Dogs-Tooth Violet
Iris cristata, Crested Iris

Narcissus Campernelli, Campernelle Jonquil
Nerine sarniensis, Guernsey-Lily
Sanguinaria canadensis, Bloodroot
Smilacina racemosa, False Solomons-Seal
Trillium grandiflorum, Great Trillium
Tulipa var., Tulip

Viola tricolor hortensis, Pansy

FERNS

Comptonia asplenifolia, Sweet Fern

Pavilion VI. The intersection of the serpentine walls of the alleys with the straight end walls was a tricky masonry problem.

Presentation plan, Pavilion VI, University of Virginia

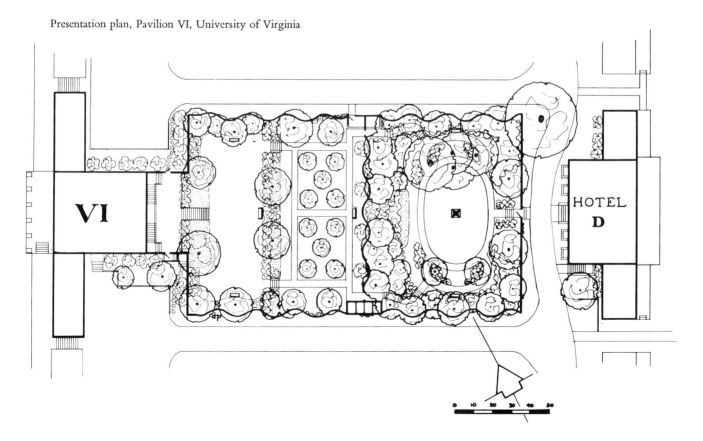

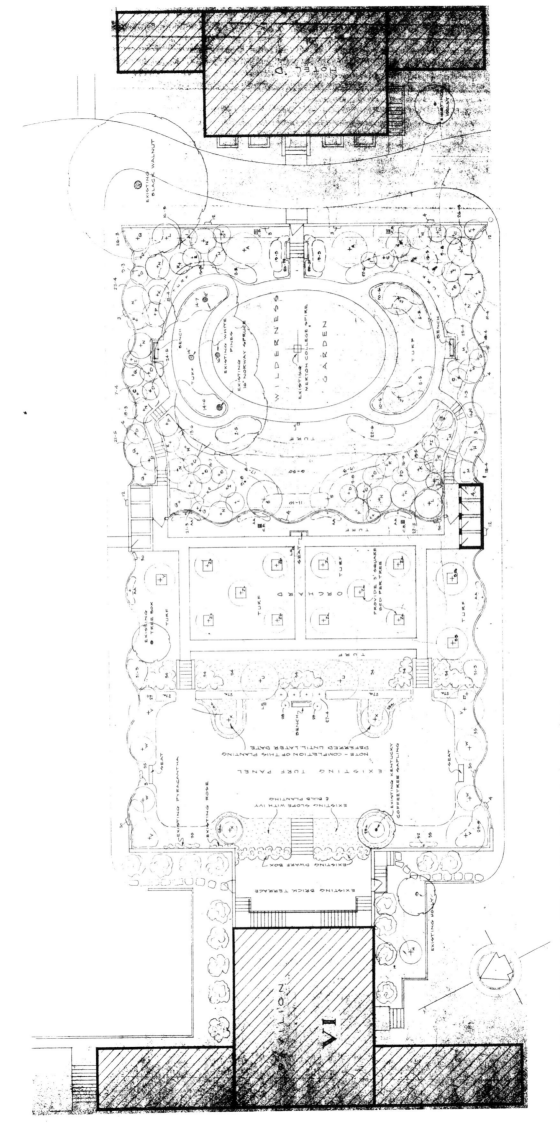

Planting plan, Pavilion VI, University of Virginia, Alden Hopkins, landscape architect

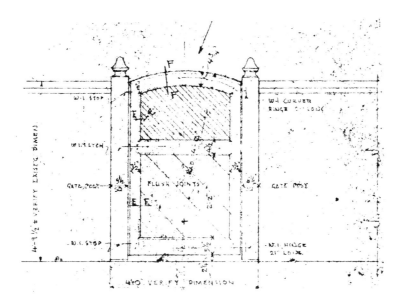

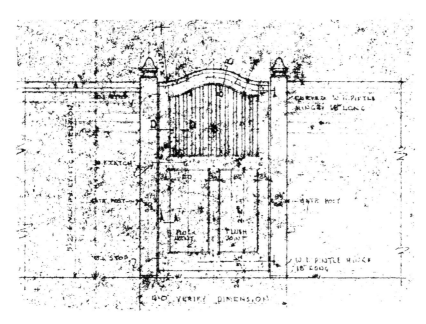

Pavilion VIII. The garden connection from every pavilion was different.

Pavilion VIII

At present the pavilion served by this garden is used as the office of the president of the university. This use suggested a type of design that provided for small gatherings, conferences, and private conversations. Its divisions were only those required by the steep grades. A central hourglass composition is the major theme. Though this theme extends over two levels, its shape is carried through by a continuous gravel path. Visual connection between the two levels is maintained by a central grass ramp, but brick steps are required for the paths at either side.

Designed primarily for spring and summer use, the planting accentuates blooming trees and shrubs, bulbs and summer-blooming perennials. "Setting stones" are placed at the ends of the grass walks, an adoption of Jefferson's idea at Monticello.

From the hourglass area a wide brick stairway leads to an orchard on a lower level. At the top of the slope on either side of this stairway a row of goldenrain trees may be considered a memorial to Jefferson, who is reputed to have introduced this beautiful tree to Albemarle County.

In this orchard, Parker used designs from Dezallier, adapting them to Jefferson's taste for informality. Two balancing panels with diagonal gravel paths are planted with fruit trees; through their center a row of pear trees forms an allée terminated by a white bench set against dark green southern magnolias. This creates a striking climax to the long vista extending the full length of the garden from the pavilion.

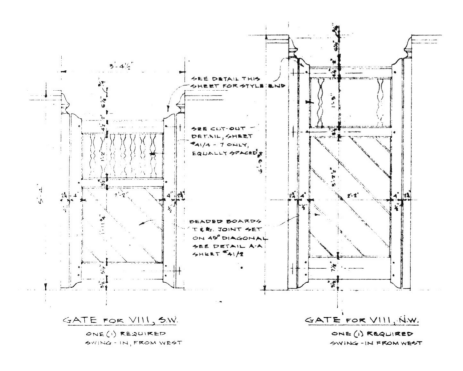

GATE FOR VIII, S.W.
ONE (1) REQUIRED
SWING - IN, FROM WEST

GATE FOR VIII, N.W.
ONE (1) REQUIRED
SWING - IN FROM WEST

TREES

Acer saccharum, Sugar Maple
Amelanchier canadensis, Shad-Bush
Cornus florida, Flowering Dogwood
Cornus florida rubra, Pink Flowering
  Dogwood
Fagus americana, American Beech
Ilex aquifolium, English Holly
Ilex opaca, American Holly
Juglans regia, English Walnut

Koelreuteria paniculata, Goldenrain-Tree
Lagerstroemia indica, Crape-Myrtle
Lagerstroemia indica alba, White Crape-
  Myrtle
Magnolia grandiflora, Southern Magnolia
Malus pumila var., Apple
Picea Abies, Norway Spruce
Prunus cerasus var., Sweet and Sour Cherry
Pyrus communis var., Pear

Salix babylonica, Weeping Willow

SHRUBS

Aesculus parviflora, Bottlebrush Buckeye
Camellia japonica, Japanese Camellia
Cydonia oblongata, Fruiting Quince
Cytisus scoparius, Scotch Broom
Decumaria barbara, Southeast Decumaria

Hibiscus syriacus, Rose-of-Sharon, Shrubby
  Althea
Hydrangea quercifolia, Oak-Leaf Hydrangea
Hypericum frondosum, Golden St. Johns-
  Wort

Robinia hispida, Rose Acacia
Syringa vulgaris alba, White Lilac
Taxua baccata, English Yew

VINES

Campsis radicans, Trumpet-Vine
Celastrus scandens, Srhubby Bitter-Sweet

Hedera helix, English Ivy
Wisteria sinensis, Chinese Wisteria

HERBACEOUS PLANTS—ANNUALS AND PERENNIALS

Althea rosea, Hollyhock
Anemone coronaria, Poppy Anemone
Anthemis tinctoria, Golden Camomile
Aquilegia canadensis, American Columbine
Artemisia absinthium, Wormwood
Asclepias tuberosa, Butterflyweed
Campanula medium, Canterbury Bell
Celosia plumosa, Feather Cockscomb
Crocus susianus, 'Cloth-of-Gold' Crocus
Crocus vernus, Spring Crocus
Dianthus barbatus, Sweet William
Dianthus sinensis, Japanese Pink
Dictamnus alba, Fraxinella, Gas-Plant
Digitalis purpurea, Foxglove
Gypsophila paniculata, Babys-Breath

Helianthus decapetalus, Thinleaf Sunflower
Hemerocallis fulva, Tawny Day-Lily
Hibiscus Moscheutos, Rose Mallow, Hardy
  Hibiscus
Iris xiphioides, English Iris
Narcissus bulbocodium, Petticoat Daffodil
Narcissus poetaz var., Poetaz Narcissus
Nerine sarniensis, Guernsey-Lily
Paeonia tenuifolia flore plena, Peony
Papaver orientale, Oriental Poppy
Phlox paniculata, Summer Phlox
Thermopsis caroliniana, Carolina Thermop-
  sis
Tulipa Clusiana, Tulip
Tulip Gesneria var. *dracontia*, Parrot Tulip

Vinca major, Bigleaf Periwinkle

ROSES

Rosa alba regalis, Maiden's Blush Rose,
  England (Kew Gardens) 1797

Rosa damascena bifera, Autumn Damask
  Rose

Rosa virginiana, Virginia Rose

Pavilion VIII. The necessaries, or privies, had the appearance of ornamental garden houses.

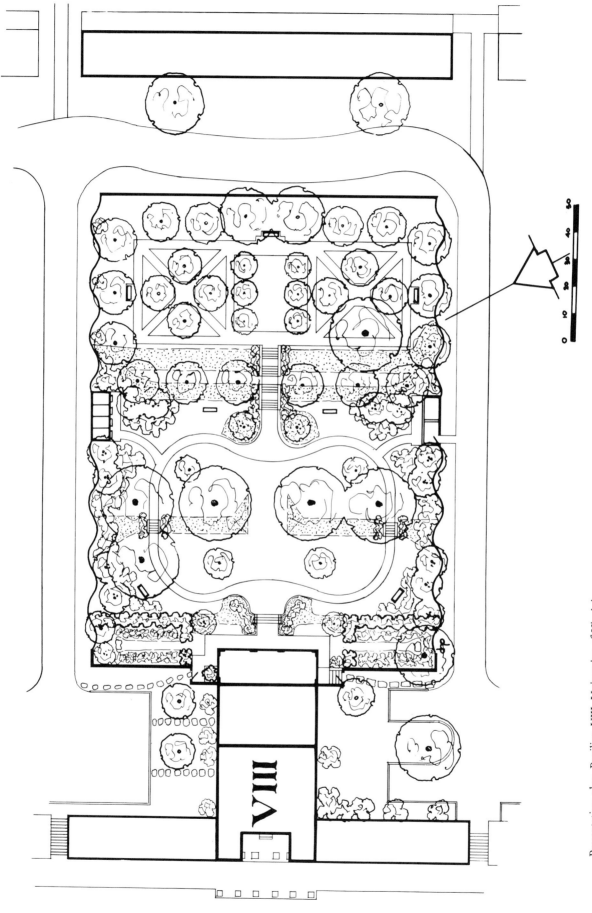

Presentation plan, Pavilion VIII, University of Virginia

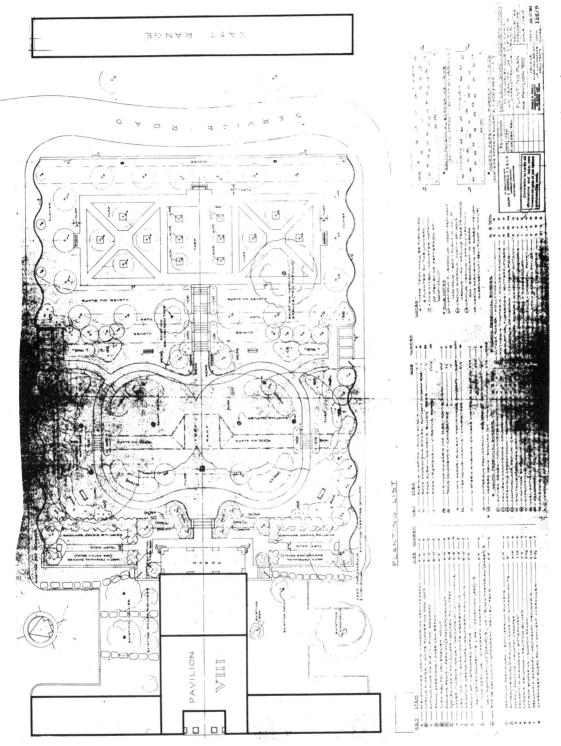

Planting plan and plant list, Pavilion VIII, University of Virginia, Donald H. Parker, landscape architect, 1963; Ralph E. Griswold, consultant

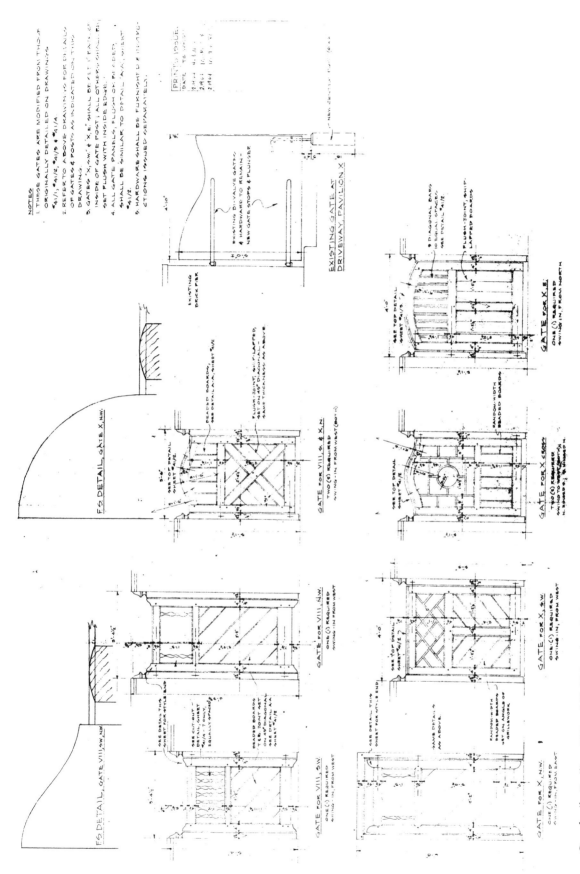

Gate details, Pavilions VIII and X, University of Virginia

Pavilion X

The upper level of this garden is dominated by a pair of monumental American hollies. The ground layout has a resemblance to the ears of an elephant. Perhaps this is caused by the extra width of this last in the row of East Lawn gardens. It is ninety feet wide.

In the center is a circular grass plot surrounded by a brick walk. The ear shapes on either side, as laid out by Parker, create a total pattern reminiscent of those frequently shown in Le Rouge's *Jardins Anglo-Chinois*. Only a few new trees were needed to supplement the existing hollies, magnolias, and weeping willow. In the outer beds small lozenge-shaped herb plantings parallel the inner edges of the paths. It is all curvilinear.

Against the serpentine cross wall evergreens were introduced, and in the center is a bench backed by attractive planting. At either end of the cross wall, privies are reached by inconspicuous paths. From these paths gates open onto long flights of steps that run down the bank, meeting in the center of the lower area. Here enormous tree boxwood create an impressive green room with fifteen-foot-high walls. Although this area had been originally intended as a hotel kitchen garden, it had long been used as a pleasure garden and was, therefore, kept that way.

Within the enclosure Kentucky coffee trees were planted in the center of both sides to provide shade. Around these trees circular wrought-iron benches were erected following the romantic custom of the period.

Pavilion X. The lower level was reached by informal slope steps with wooden risers.

Pavilion X. A pair of extraordinary American holly trees dictated the design of the upper level.

TREES

Acer saccharum, Sugar Maple
Cedrus libani, Cedar-of-Lebanon
Celtis occidentalis, Hackberry
Gymnocladus dioica, Kentucky Coffee-Tree
Ilex opaca var., Red and Yellow Berried
  Holly
Magnolia grandiflora, Southern Magnolia

Magnolia Soulangeana, Saucer Magnolia
Malus baccata, Siberian Crab
Malus pumilia var., Apple
Morus rubra, Red Mulberry
Paulownia tomentosa, Empress-Tree
Quercus Robur, English Oak
Salix babylonica, Weeping Willow

SHRUBS

Amorpha fruticosa, False Indigo
Buxus sempervirens, Common Boxwood
  (true tree)
Buxus sempervirens suffruticosa, Dwarf
  Boxwood (true dwarf)
Callicarpa americana, American Beauty
  Berry
Calycanthus floridus, Sweet Shrub
Chaenomeles lagenaria, Japanese Flowering
  Quince
Clethra alnifolia, Summer Sweet
Cotinus coggyria, Smoke-Tree
Euonymus americana, Strawberry-Bush
Gelsemium sempervirens, Carolina Yellow
  Jessamine

Ilex glabra, Inkberry
Kalmia latifolia, Mountain Laurel
Philadelphus coronarius, Mock-Orange
Punica granatum, Pomegranate
Rhododendron maximum, Rosebay
  Rhododendron
Rhododendron nudiflorum, Pinxter-Flower
Rhus aromatica, Fragrant Sumac
Sambucus canadensis, Elderberry
Syringa persica, Persian Lilac
Taxus canadensis, Dwarf Yew
Viburnum acerifolium, Dockmackie, Maple-
  Leaf Viburnum
Viburnum opulus roseum, European Cran-
  berry-Bush

VINES

Clematis virginiana, Virgins-Bower
Hedera helix, English Ivy

Lonicera japonica, Japanese Honeysuckle
Parthenocissus quinquefolia, Virginia Creeper

HERBACEOUS PLANTS—ANNUALS AND PERENNIALS

Ajuga reptans, Bugle-Weed
Allium Schoenoprasum, Chives
Anethum graneolens, Dill
Anthemis tinctoria, Golden Chamomile
Artemidis Absinthium, Wormwood
Artemisis Dracunculus, Tarragon
Borago officinalis, Borage
Brodiaea uniflora, Spring Star-Flower
Chrysanthemum balsamita, Costmary
Convallaria majalis, Lilly-of-the-Valley
Crocus susianus, 'Cloth-of-Gold' Crocus
Crocus vernus, Spring Crocus
Lavandula Spica, Lavender
Marrubium vulgare, Hoarhound
Mentha peperita, Peppermint
Mentha Pulegium, Pennyroyal Mint

Mentha spicata, Spearmint
Monarda didyma, Oswego-Tea, Bee-Balm
Muscari botryoides, Grape-Hyacinth
Muscari comosum monstrosum, Tassel or
  Feathered Grape Hyacinth
Narcissus, Daffodil
Narcissus Jonquilla simplex, Jonquil
Nerine sarniensis, Guernsey-Lily
Nigella damascena, Love-in-a-Mist
Ocium basilicum, Sweet Basil
Petroselimun hortense, Parsley
Pimpernella anisum, Anise
Rosemarinus officinalis, Rosemary
Salvia officinalis, Sage
Santolina chamaecyparissus, Green and
  Grey-Leaved Santolina

Sternbergia lutea, Fall Daffodil
Tanacetum vulgare, Tansy
Thymus vulgaris, Common Thyme

Vinca major, Bigleaf Periwinkle
Vinca minor, Periwinkle
Yucca filamentosa, Adams-Needle

ROSES

Rosa gallica officinalis, Rose of Lancaster
Rosa laevigata, Cherokee Rose, introduced
into America before 1759

Pavilion X. The main approach to the garden was from the upper level.

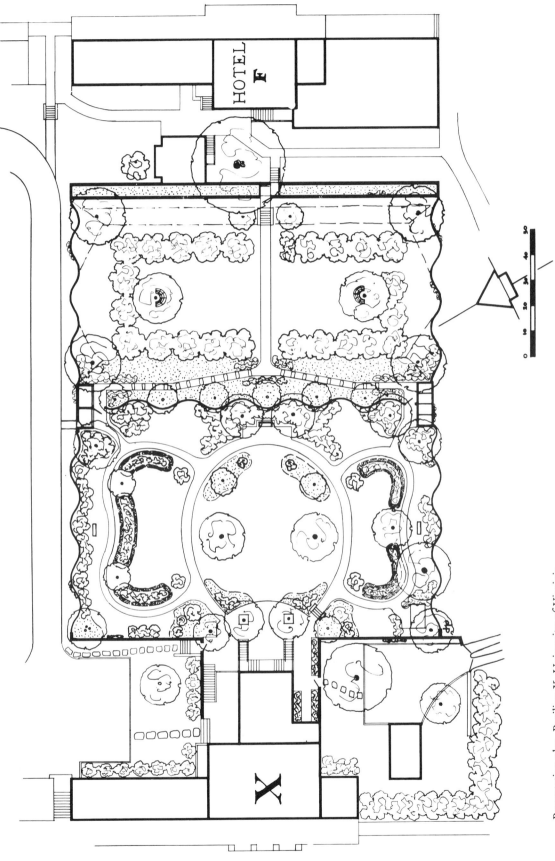

Presentation plan, Pavilion X, University of Virginia

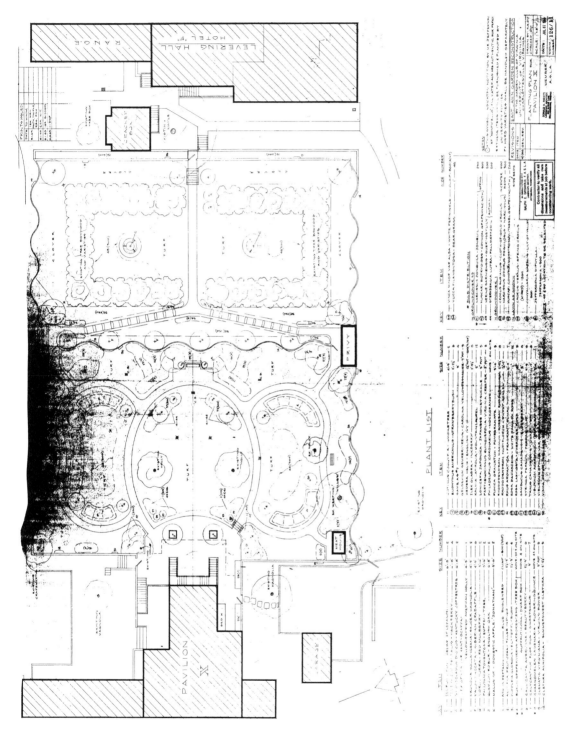

Planting plan and plant list, Pavilion X, University of Virginia, Donald H. Parker, landscape architect, 1963; Ralph E. Griswold, consultant

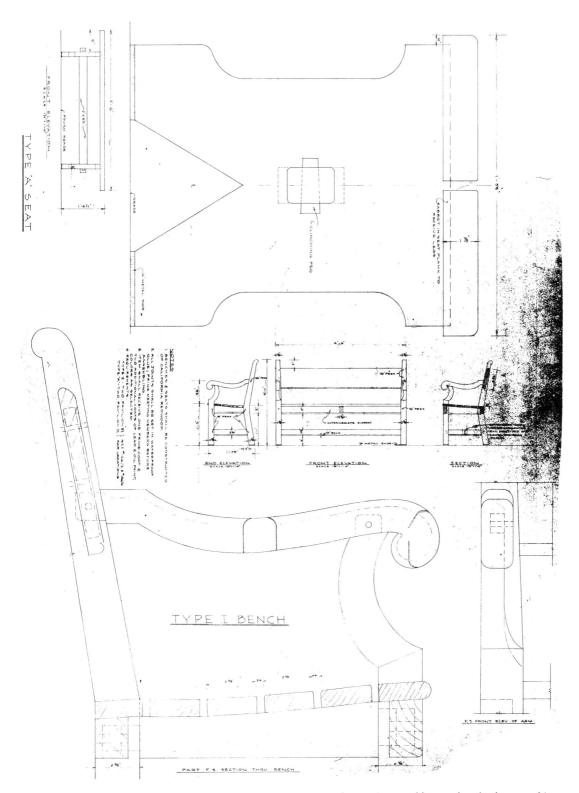

Bench, type I and Seat, type A, East Lawn gardens, University of Virginia, Donald H. Parker, landscape architect; Ralph E. Griswold, consultant

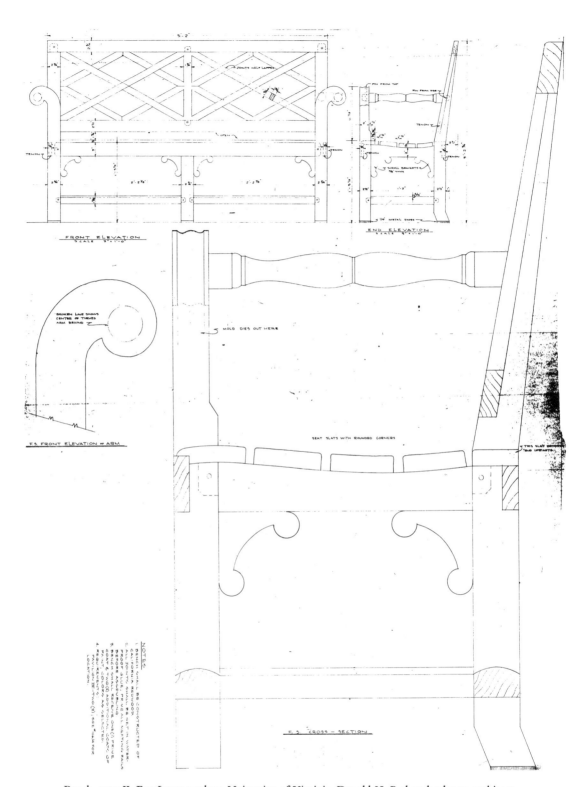

Bench, type II, East Lawn gardens, University of Virginia, Donald H. Parker, landscape architect

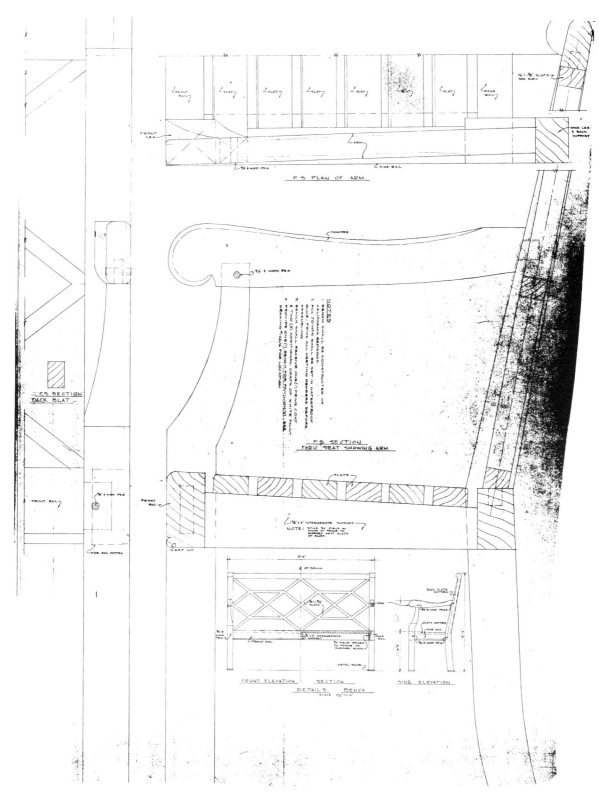

Bench, type III, East Lawn gardens, University of Virginia, Donald H. Parker, landscape architect;
Ralph E. Griswold, consultant

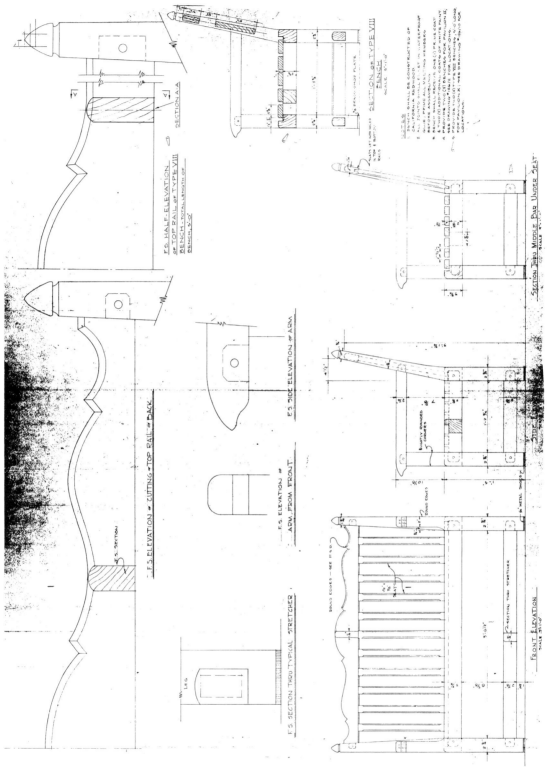

Benches, type IV and VIII, East Lawn gardens, University of Virginia, Donald H. Parker, landscape architect; Ralph E. Griswold, consutant

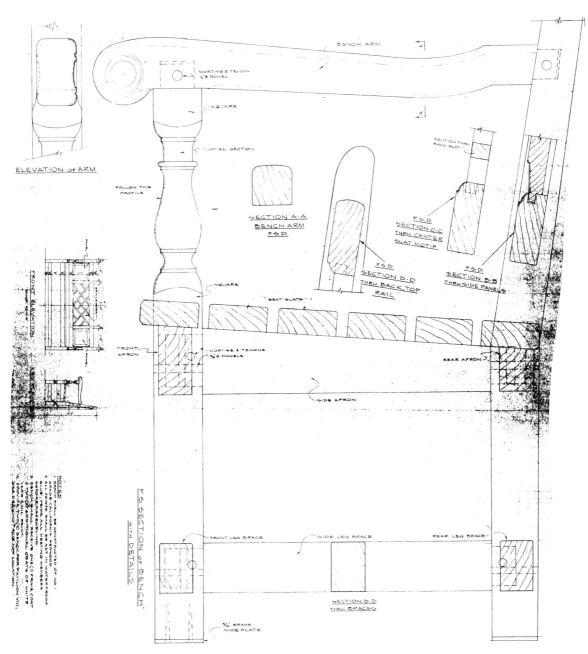

Bench, type V, East Lawn gardens, University of Virginia, Donald H. Parker, landscape architect; Ralph E. Griswold, consultant

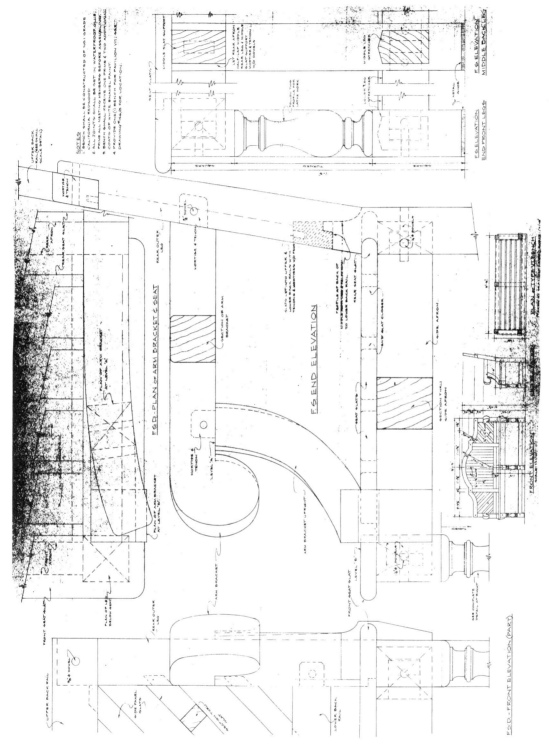

Bench, type VI, East Lawn gardens, University of Virginia, Donald H. Parker, landscape architect; Ralph E. Griswold, consultant

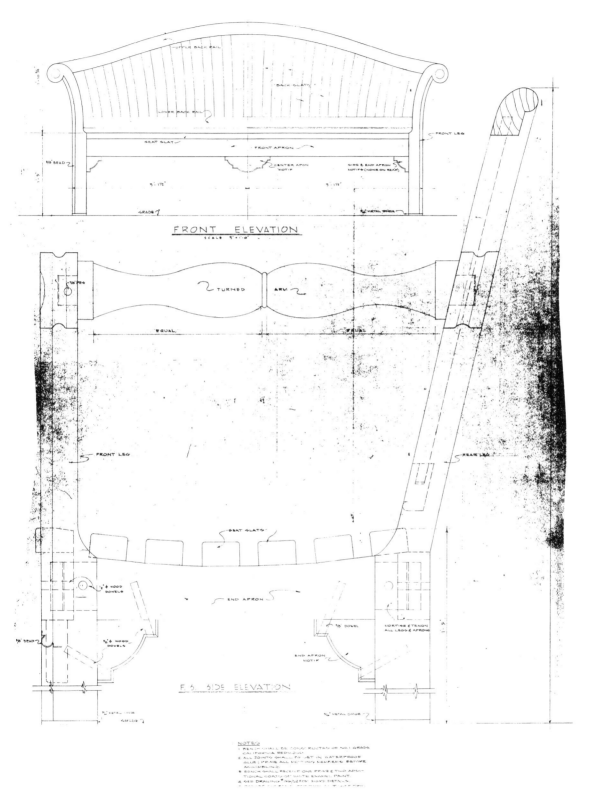

FRONT ELEVATION

F.S. SIDE ELEVATION

Bench, type VII, front and side elevations, East Lawn gardens, University of Virginia, Donald H. Parker, landscape architect; Ralph E. Griswold, consultant

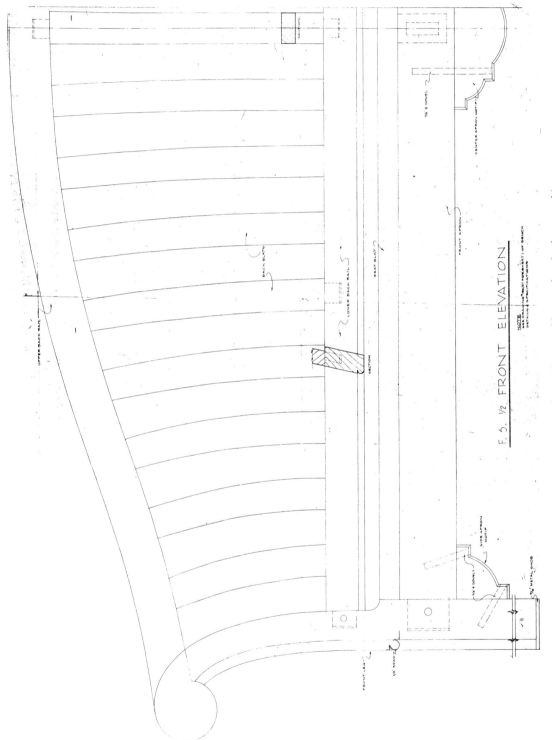

Bench, type VII, half front elevation, East Lawn gardens, University of Virginia, Donald H. Parker, landscape architect, 1964; Ralph E. Griswold, consultant

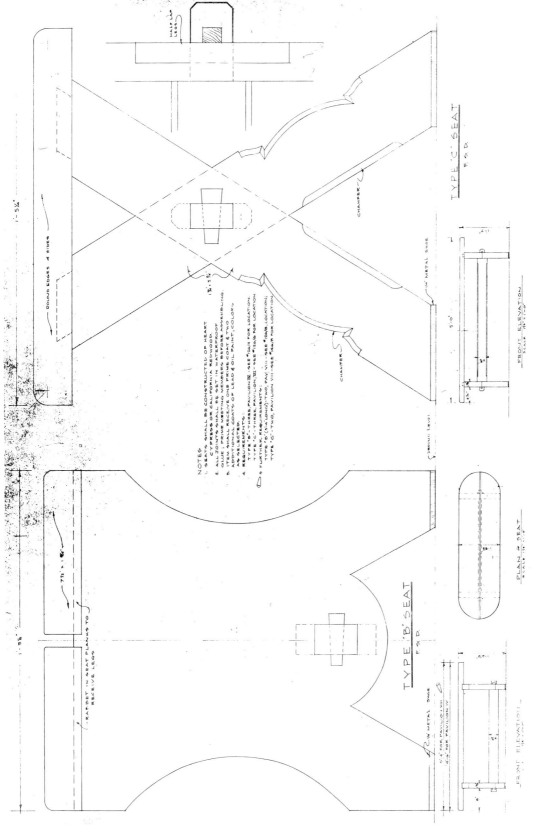

Seat, types B and C, East Lawn gardens, University of Virginia, Donald H. Parker, landscape architect; Ralph E. Griswold, consultant

Entrance court

Woodlawn

U.S. ROUTE 1, which runs from Falmouth on the Rappahannock to Alexandria on the Potomac, follows the route traveled by George Washington, George Mason, and all the Southern statesmen who influenced the affairs of this nation in the years before the American Revolution. This was the link between North and South, and along this road were situated homes of many men of political influence. Of these great homes only three remain—Gunston Hall, Mount Vernon, and Woodlawn. Gunston Hall and Mount Vernon are situated on bluffs above the Potomac. Woodlawn is located inland on a hill that provides a panoramic view of Mount Vernon, the Potomac, and the distant Maryland shore.

On February 22, 1799, Eleanor Parke (Nelly) Custis, granddaughter of Martha Custis Washington, married Lawrence Lewis, son of Fielding and Betty Washington Lewis of Kenmore. As a wedding gift George Washington gave the young couple a 2,000-acre tract of land upon which they built their home, Woodlawn. This mansion, designed by William Thornton and completed in 1805, is of late Georgian design and consists of a large center unit connected by hyphens. Within this handsome house the Lewises established a center of brilliant cultural and social life.

Woodlawn passed from possession of the Lewis family in 1846. Until 1951 there were six owners and two periods of no occupancy. In 1951 the administration of Woodlawn was assumed by the National Trust for Historic Preservation in the United States. The following year a request was made by the National Trust and the Woodlawn Committee that The Garden Club of Virginia consider restoration of the Woodlawn Plantation garden. This request was approved on February 26, 1958, and Alden Hopkins, landscape architect of Williamsburg, was retained for the restoration.

Though historical research revealed little of the original landscape layout of Woodlawn, there were certain leads. Indication that Woodlawn was well named is found in a letter from Mrs. Thornton written in 1800. "He [Lawrence Lewis] has a fine seat; all in woods from which he will have an extensive and beautiful view." Beyond a doubt the magnificent oaks of the north lawn are part of this woods and are the same ones that were judiciously saved when the site was cleared originally. It is surmised that the trees on the bluff, or south side, were destroyed in a storm in 1827. Of this storm Lawrence Lewis wrote his sister, "We had on the 4th inst. a most severe gale of wind and rain which broke, and tore up by the roots, in and about the house fifty trees."

Garden vista

Garden pavilion

In early letters to friends Nelly made frequent mention of plant materials in her gardens. Roses, woodbine, flowering shrubs, pines, cedars, dogwood, fruit trees, and vegetables all appear repeatedly in correspondence. As late as 1822 we find Nelly interested in improving the landscape. She writes, "I have been busy planting trees, etc. today and planning a bower of woodbine." Though such gleanings from correspondence were studied carefully, all in all, the references provided scanty basis for authentic restoration.

Extensive archaeological research was undertaken. With the assistance of archaeologists of Colonial Williamsburg, the major portion of the grounds was trenched and excavated to undisturbed soil wherever it was thought walks, drives, a garden area, and buildings might have existed. Concurrently, a topographical survey was undertaken. This survey revealed a line of cedars of ancient vintage, extending to the south, at right angles to the mansion. Further along, this line seemed to join a similar line to the west, perhaps indicating a former fence line. As a result of this survey the location of the new fence, enclosing part of the entrance court, was established.

In the same manner a curving line of tulip trees and a huge hemlock in the lawn to the west indicated need for investigation. Archaeological research of the area revealed a serpentine drive beside these trees. Further trenching and scraping-clear showed a balancing north serpentine drive. There, from beneath the green lawn, emerged the

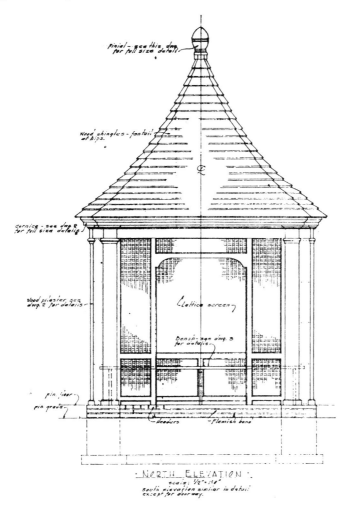

· NORTH ELEVATION ·

original ten-foot-wide drive in remarkably good condition. Traces of gravel indicated extension of the drive near the boxwood circle directly in front of the dwelling. This serpentine drive was considered by Hopkins the most important discovery. Upon its design he based his entire plan.

Familiarity with the custom of garden design for the period led to the assumption that walks would have been associated with the newly discovered serpentine drives. With this in mind, attention was focused on a double row of old cedars, in artificial, curving fashion at the far west end of the lawn. Excavation between the trees revealed the remains of a gravel-marl walk. This serpentine walk extended along both sides of the lawn between the splayed entrance drives. It was apparent that the huge hemlock, mentioned earlier, was located at the spot where, according to the gardening fashion of the day, a dramatic tree would have been placed.

In correspondence Nelly makes frequent mention of a wilderness, and existing hollies gave further indication of this feature. In the Hopkins plan these hollies were augmented by newly planted trees and shrubs to provide enclosing sides for the serpentine lawn.

The original flower garden was located beyond a gravel crossroad to the west, on land now occupied by a housing development of Fort Belvoir. This garden was accessible from the dwelling by way of the serpentine walks and was on axis with the the mansion. Location of this former garden is now indicated by a freestanding gate at the far end of the lawn.

With the reasonable assumption that a level stretch of land near the mansion's kitchen wing would have been used as a kitchen garden, it was decided to locate a new flower garden in this area. Though the plot had been ploughed for many years, certain observations substantiated the decision. An ancient apple tree was still standing at the far end of the area, a sign perhaps that an orchard had been located here. Brick fragments and traces of gravel indicated the existence of former paved and graveled walks that would have been needed for ready access to a garden plot.

For the design of this new and elaborate kitchen garden Hopkins drew heavily from Batty Langley's *Gardening*, and, since Nelly had intimate association with Mount Vernon, certain features of that garden were also used. Two parterres provide introduction to the area. A long axial walk is the central feature. It is shaded by a double row of pollarded locust trees set equidistant in the parallel flower borders. This walk, extending the length of the garden, terminates in a summerhouse. Planting along the walk provides constant bloom.

The flanking parterres were planted predominantly with roses, as it was known that they were a favorite flower of the Lewis family. The varieties used were those authentic for the period before 1840. Since these roses were noted for their brief blooming period, they were supplemented by spring bulbs, summer annuals, and flowering shrubs. The entire garden was bordered by fruit trees.

A necessary parking area was established, its harsh reality softened by the diversion of parking lanes and planting. This area is entirely screened from view of the mansion. A curving walk leads visitors from the parking area, through interesting planting, to a gate in the forecourt fence. Only then is the visitor given a view of the mansion; thus there is no intrusion of modern traffic upon the landscape restoration.

One of the two rose garden parterres

Serpentine paths define the entrance lawn.

TREES

Cornus florida, Flowering Dogwood
Juniperus virginiana, Eastern Red Cedar
Lagerstroemia indica, Crape-Myrtle
Magnolia grandiflora, Southern Magnolia
Morus alba, White Mulberry

Prunus persica, Peach
Prunus virginiana, Chokeberry
Robinia Pseudoacacia, Black Acacia, Yellow
 Locust
Tsuga canadensis, Hemlock

SHRUBS

Gelsemium sempervirens, Carolina Yellow
 Jessamine
Ilex var., Holly
Vitex macrophylla, Chaste-Tree, Broad-
 leaved form of Agnus-Castus

HERBACEOUS PLANTS—ANNUALS AND PERENNIALS

Allium azureum, Blue-Flowered Onion
Althea rosea, Hollyhock
Bellis perennis, English Daisy
Chrysanthemum maximum, Shasta Daisy
Chrysanthemum var., Chrysanthemum

Coreopsis verticillata, Coreopsis
Dahlia Mercki, Bedding Dahlia
Dianthus barbatus, Sweet William
Dianthus var., Pink
Fritillaria imperialis, Crown Imperial

Gaillardia pulchella, Gaillardia
Hyacinthus var., Hyacinth
Iris germanica, Blue Flag
Iris sibirica, Siberian Iris
Iris xiphium, Dutch Iris
Ixia viridiflora, Ixia
Lilium candidum, Madonna Lily
Mirabilis jalopa, Four-o'-Clock
Narcissus Jonquilla Campernelli, Campernelle Jonquil
Narcissus Jonquilla simplex, Jonquil
Narcissus var., Daffodil

Paeonia albaflora, White Peony
Paeonia officinalis, Peony
Papaver orientale, Oriental Poppy
Pelargonium var., Geranium
Phlox var., Phlox
Polianthes tuberosa, Tuberose
Salvia officinalis, Sage
Scilla var., Squill
Stokesia laevis, Stokes Aster
Tulipa var., Tulip
Valeriana officinalis, Heliotrope
Verbena officinalis, Verbena

Viola tricolor hortensis, Pansy

ROSES

Rosa alba 'Celestial,' also called 'Celeste,' known from the end of the eighteenth century

Rosa alba regalis 'Maiden's Blush,' a white Rose recorded in Kew Gardens 1797

Rosa centifolia cristata 'Chapeau de Napoleon' 1827, a crested Moss Rose

Rosa centifolia var. *muscosa*, a Moss Rose, a sport of R. centifolia recorded in southern France before 1700

Rosa centifolia var. *muscosa* 'Comtesse de Murinais,' a Moss Rose known since 1843

Rosa chinensis bourboniana 'Coupe d'Hebe' 1840, a Bourbon Rose

Rosa chinensis bourboniana 'Honorine de Brabant' 1817, a Bourbon Rose

Rosa chinensis bourboniana 'Souvenir de la Malmaison' 1843, a Bourbon Rose

Rosa chinensis, 'Louis Philippe' 1834

Rosa chinensis 'Old Blush,' introduced into England before 1759

Rosa damascena 'Castilian,' a Damask Rose known as the Rose of Castille

Rosa damascena 'Celsiana,' Celsiana Damask Rose prior to 1750

Rosa damascena 'Oeillet Parfait' 1841, a Damask Rose sometimes listed as 'Tour d'Auvergne'

Rosa damascena 'Mme Hardy' 1832, a Damask Rose owing some of its qualities to R. centifolia

Rosa eglanteria [*R. rubiginosa*], the eglantine of Shakespeare, also Sweet Briar; naturalized in North America in pastures etc., and cultivated before 1551

Rosa foetida bicolor [*R. lutea*], introduced into England in 1789, Austrian copper is one of its forms

Rosa francofurtana 'Empress Josephine,' before 1770 probably Rosa Cinnamomea R. Gallica

Rosa gallica 'Cardinal Richelieu' 1840, a French Rose in which the influence of other roses is seen

Rosa gallica 'Cramoisi des Alpes' 1838, a French Rose

Rosa gallica 'Duchesse de Montebello' 1842, a French Rose

Rosa 'Duchess of Sutherland' 1839, a very early hybrid created by Laffay

Rosa 'Larmague' 1830, a yellowish Noisette from R. chinensis, R. moschata and others

Rosa moschata 'Mme d'Arblay' 1835, a Hybrid Musk

Rosa odorata 'Safrano' 1839

Rosa roxburghii, the Chestnut Rose or Chinquapin Rose cultivated before 1814

Rosa spinosissima, Scotch Hedge Rose

Rosa spinosissima, 'Stanwell Perpetual' 1838

Rosa, Tea Rose 'Bon Silene' 1839

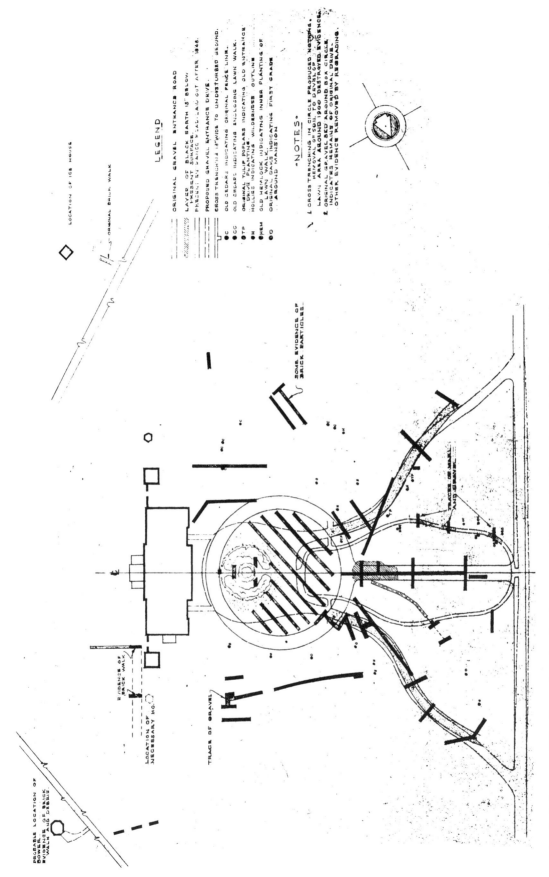

Archaeological survey of Woodlawn plantation showing cross trenching and the discoveries made in April 1954, Alden Hopkins, landscape architect, 1955

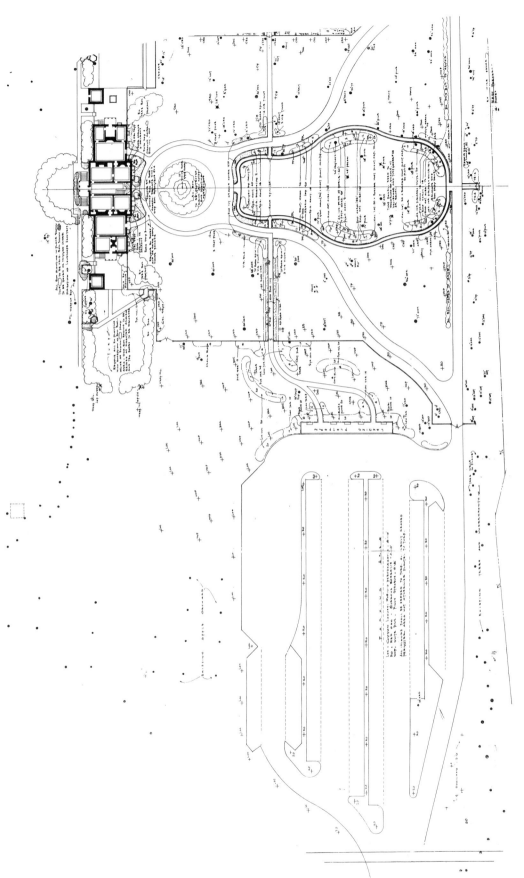

Planting plan of the entrance and parking area of Woodlawn Plantation

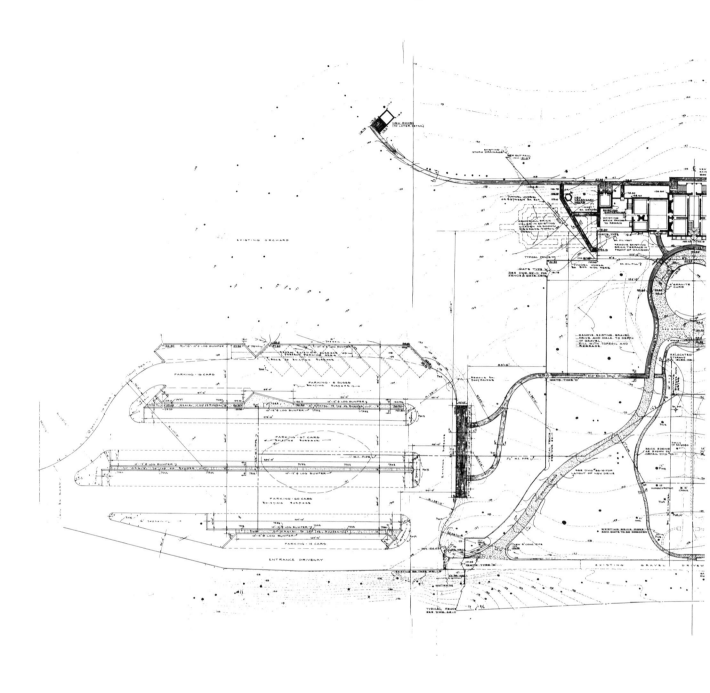

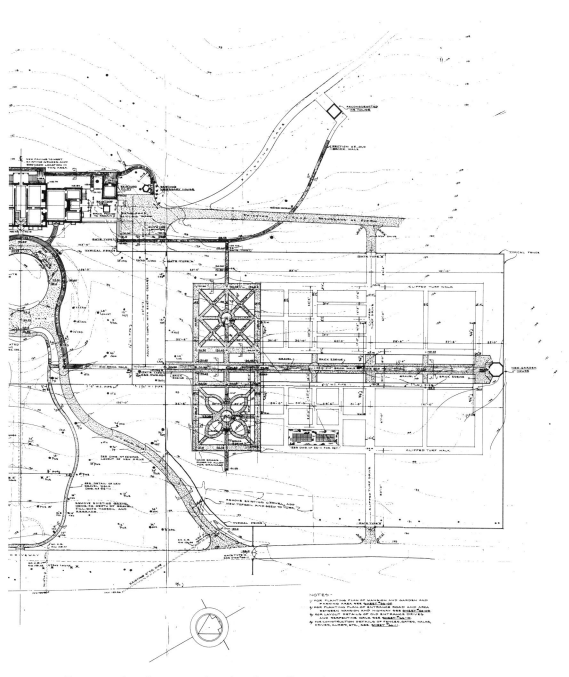

Entrance and garden construction plan of Woodlawn Plantation

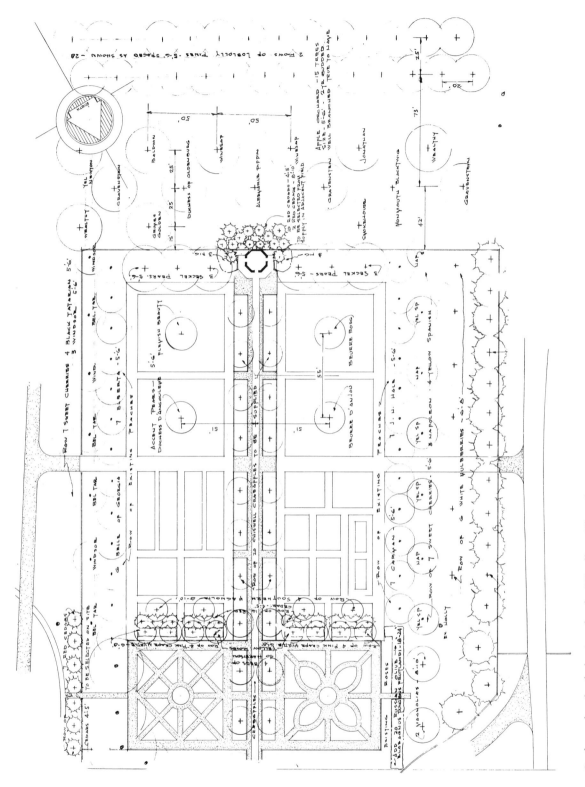

Garden and orchard planting plan for Woodlawn Plantation

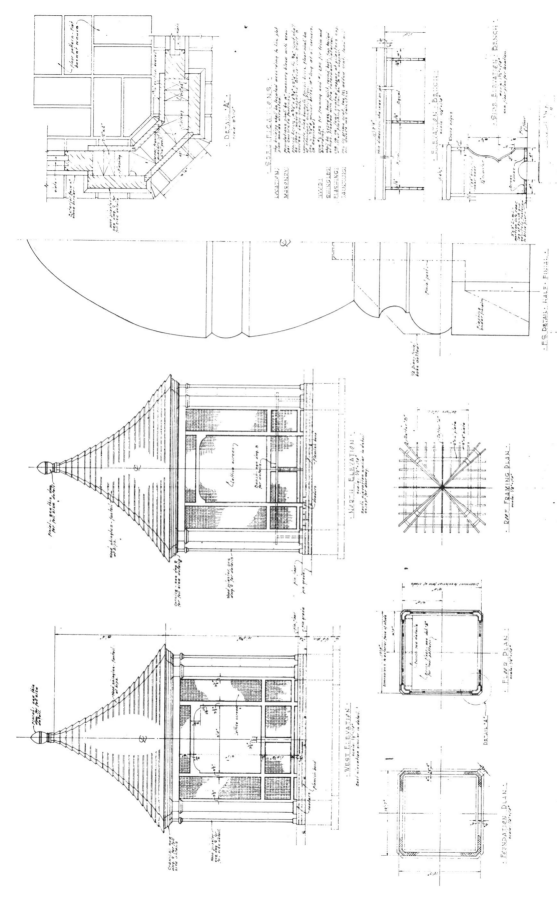

Plans, elevations, and details of the summerhouse at Woodlawn Plantation, Alden Hopkins, landscape architect, 1958

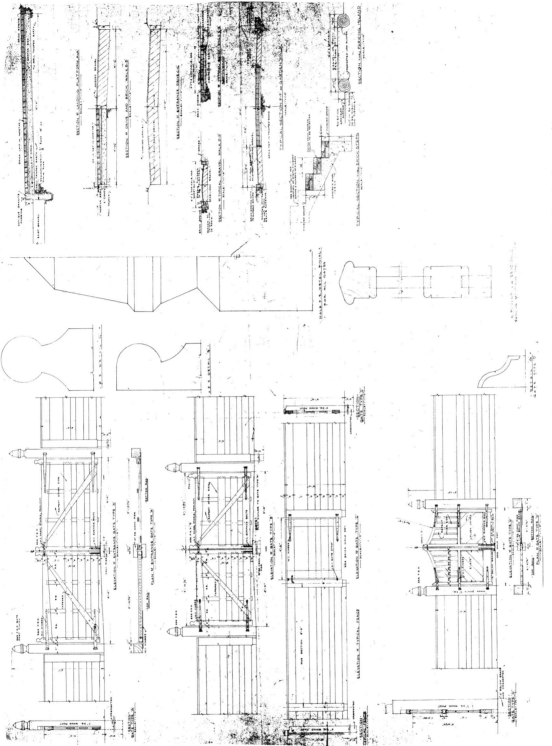

Construction details of fences, gates, walls, drives, parking islands, and steps, Woodlawn Plantation, Alden Hopkins, landscape architect, 1955

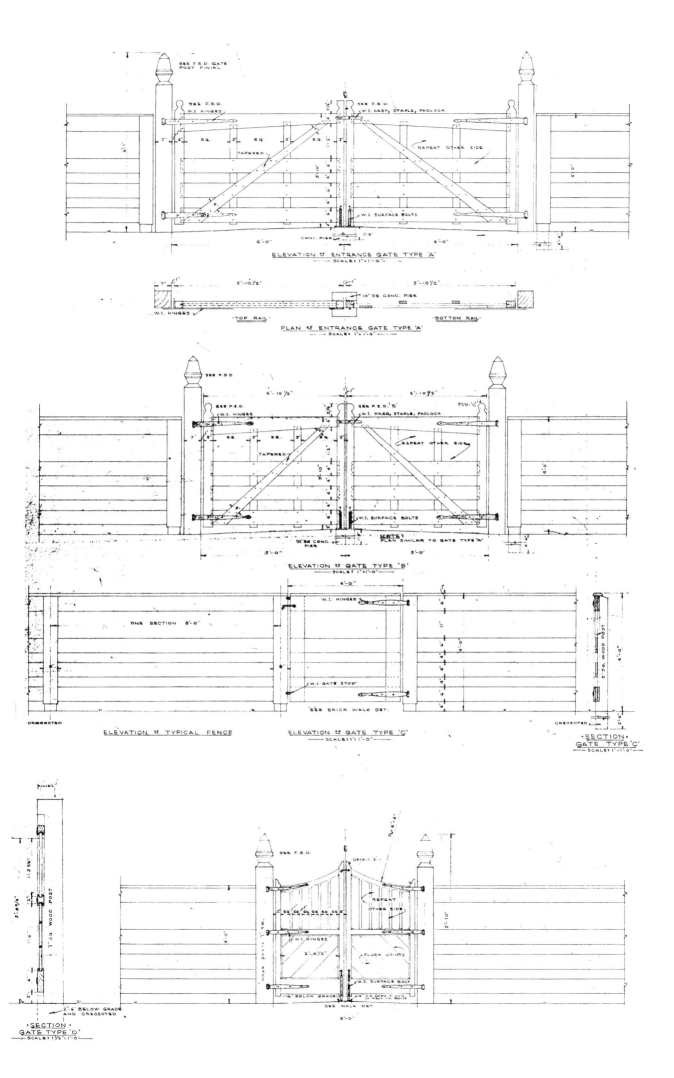

ELEVATION of ENTRANCE GATE TYPE 'A'
SCALE: 1"=1'-0"

PLAN of ENTRANCE GATE TYPE 'A'
SCALE: 1"=1'-0"

ELEVATION of GATE TYPE 'B'
SCALE: 1"=1'-0"

ELEVATION of TYPICAL FENCE

ELEVATION of GATE TYPE 'C'
SCALE: 1"=1'-0"

SECTION
GATE TYPE 'C'
SCALE: 1"=1'-0"

SECTION
GATE TYPE 'D'
SCALE: 1½"=1'-0"

Adam Thoroughgood House

TO THE BEAUTIFULLY RESTORED Adam Thoroughgood House in Princess Anne County a garden was added by The Garden Club of Virginia in 1958-59. The house, unique in structure and history, had been restored by the Adam Thoroughgood House Foundation, an affiliate of The National Trust for Historic Preservation.

The builder of this little house was the son of a pioneer who, true to his name, was of good parentage. He was the seventh child of the Reverend William Thoroughgood of Grinston, England, from whom, by the law of primogeniture, he could expect no in-inheritance. Like many other young Englishmen in his situation, he came to Virginia at age sixteen as an indentured servant. He did well, and within three years, his indenture having been served, he returned to England in 1624 and married Sarah Offly, whose grandfather, Sir Thomas Osborne, had been Lord Mayor of London. On their return to America this young couple brought with them one hundred and five new colonists. For this service they were given 7,000 acres, known as The Grand Patent, on the Lynnhaven River. Here, near Chesapeake Bay, they built a house that has since disappeared.

On another site farther up the river the present house is thought to have been built between 1635 and 1660 by, or for, one of Adam's sons. A brick bearing the initials A. T. does not positively identify the builder, but structural details establish the house as one of the oldest, if not the oldest, brick house standing in America. The exceptional architectural quality of this tiny twenty-two feet by forty-five feet house seems amazing in the wilderness of seventeenth-century America. Here, long before the existence of Williamsburg, Flemish bond with glazed header brick was used on one side of the house and English bond on the other three sides. Here also were a steep A-gabled roof and massive brick chimney, which were as yet unfamiliar architectural features in this country.

Initially Alden Hopkins of Williamsburg had been asked by the Virginia Beach Garden Club to draw plans of a garden for this unusual house. Later, however, the project was taken over by The Garden Club of Virginia and Hopkins was retained as architect.

Creation of this garden presented an unusual challenge, as Hopkins and the Restoration Committee had no Virginia precedent to guide them. They followed contemporary English tradition and balanced two geometric parterres on either side of a central walk leading from the house. Within the beds composing the pattern a ground cover of peri-

Boxwood ties the house and garden together.

Topiary specimens, typical of contemporary English gardens, are here formed of yaupon holly.

winkle was ornamented with topiary specimens of yaupon. These box-bordered beds were enlivened at different seasons by old fashioned snowdrops, iris, and squill. The bordering beds of hardy, low-growing herbs also have seasonal color of day lilies, Adam's needle, peonies, and lilies.

If such a formal garden seems out of place at the edge of the wilderness, it should be remembered that Adam Thoroughgood had become a man of property and importance who would have wished to emulate the English gentry. With them formality still prevailed. The garden is directly related to the lines of the house on the river side. A path from the doorway is terminated at its far end by a bench. On either side cordon pear trees supported by a low wooden rail form a hedge. Paralleling this center path, substantial arbors on the two outer edges of the garden are covered with interwoven yaupon branches to resemble a pleached arbor. Underneath these arches wood seats are pleasant retreats from the sunny parterres. Quaint little wooden animal carvings, known as "beasties," mounted on four-foot oak posts keep a watchful eye on the garden. These heraldic figures so characteristic of the period add whimsical interest to this cottage garden.

To separate this historical scene from the modern subdivision through which it is approached, a red-painted picket and post-and-rail fence was erected around the entire four-acre plot. It is in itself a pleasant picture as seen against the green lawn.

Though both the existence and the design of this garden are founded only on the customs of the times, the garden has the feeling of authenticity because of the magnificent trees that tower above it on the banks of the Lynnhaven River, where dogwood and redbud grow naturally as they probably did when Adam and his wife picked this spot for their home.

An ancient elm towers over the well house.

A substantially designed structure is covered with interwoven yaupon holly branches to resemble a pleached arbor.

Wooden support for cordon pears. The bench terminates the central axis.

TREES

Cercis canadensis, Eastern Redbud

Cornus florida, Flowering Dogwood

Ilex vomitoria, Yaupon (arbor and topiary)

Juniperus virginiana, Eastern Red Cedar

Magnolia grandiflora, Southern Magnolia

Pyrus communis, Seckel Pear (cordon)

Quercus virginiana, Live Oak

SHRUBS

Buxus sempervirens, Common Boxwood
(true tree)

Buxus sempervirens suffruticosa, Dwarf
Boxwood (true dwarf)

Gelsemium sempervirens, Carolina Yellow
Jessamine

Prunus Laurocerasus, Cherry-Laurel

VINES

Campsis radicans, Trumpet-Vine

Hedera helix, English Ivy

Wisteria macrostachys, American Wisteria

HERBACEOUS PLANTS—ANNUALS AND PERENNIALS

Anemone coronaria var., Anemones 'St.
Brigid' and 'de Caen'

Colchicum autumnale, Autumn Crocus

Crocus susianus, 'Cloth-of-Gold' Crocus

Dicentra eximia, Bleeding Heart

Fritillaria imperialis, Crown Imperial

Fritillaria meleagris, Checkered-Lily

Galanthus nivalis, Snowdrop

Galax aphylla, Galax

Hemerocallis fulva, Tawny Day-Lily

Iris florentina, Orris-Root Iris

Iris germanica, Blue Flag

Iris pallida, a bearded species

Iris reticulata, Netted Iris

Lilium longiflorum, White Trumpet Lily

Lilium Martagon album, White Martagon
Lily

Muscari botryoides, Grape-Hyacinth

Narcissus var., Daffodil

Paeonia tenuifolia, Peony

Primula veris, Cowslip

Scilla var., Squill

Sternbergia lutea, Autumn-Flowering
Sternbergia

Tiarella cordifolia, Foam-Flower

Tulipa var., Tulip

Vinca minor, Periwinkle

Yucca filamentosa, Adams-Needle

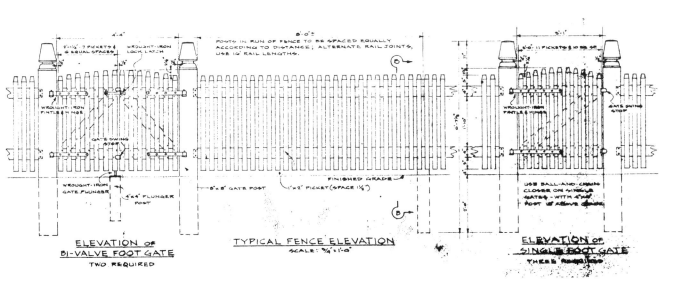

ELEVATION OF
BI-VALVE FOOT GATE
TWO REQUIRED

TYPICAL FENCE ELEVATION
SCALE: ¾"=1'-0"

ELEVATION OF
SINGLE FOOT GATE
THREE REQUIRED

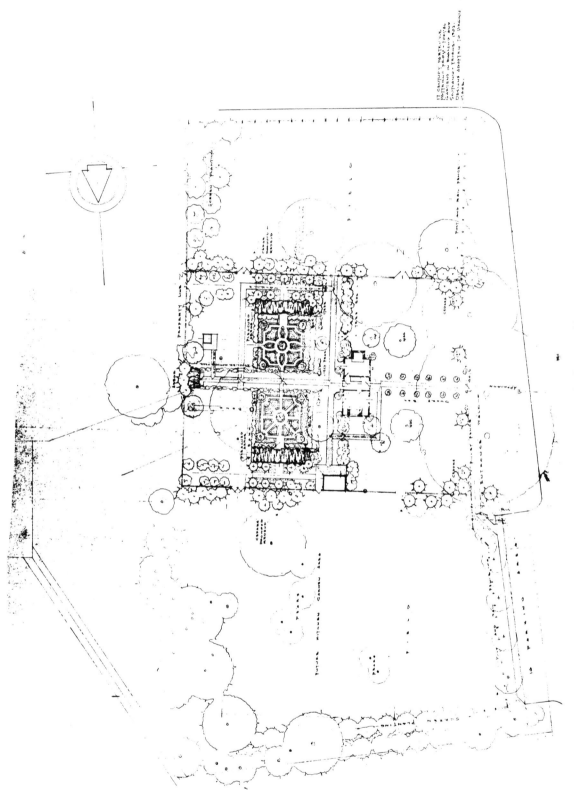

Presentation plan of the Adam Thoroughgood House, Alden Hopkins, landscape architect, 1958

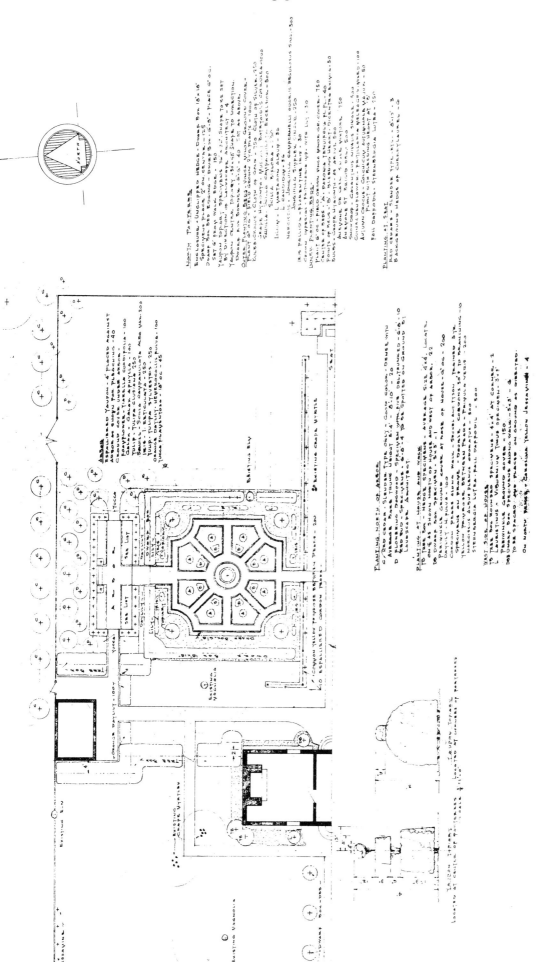

North parterre, Adam Thoroughgood House, Alden Hopkins, landscape architect, 1959

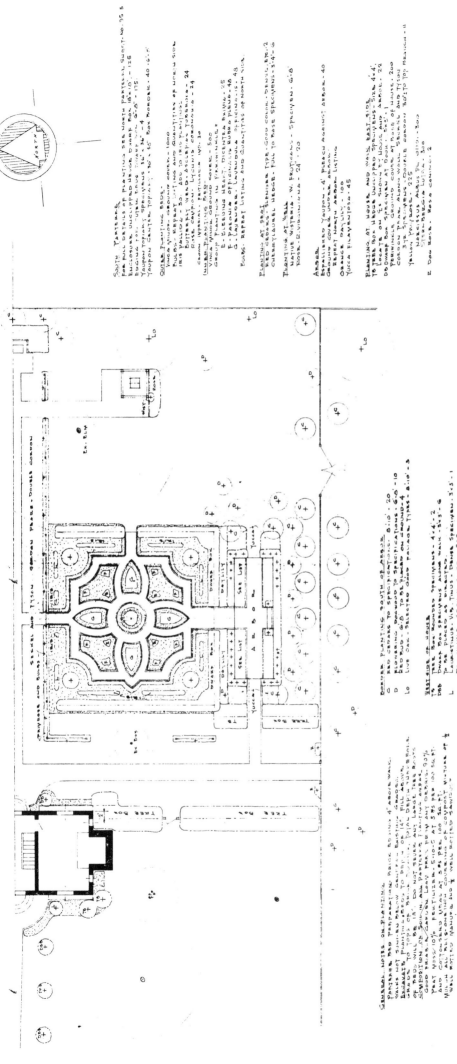

South parterre, Adam Thoroughgood House, Alden Hopkins, landscape architect, 1959

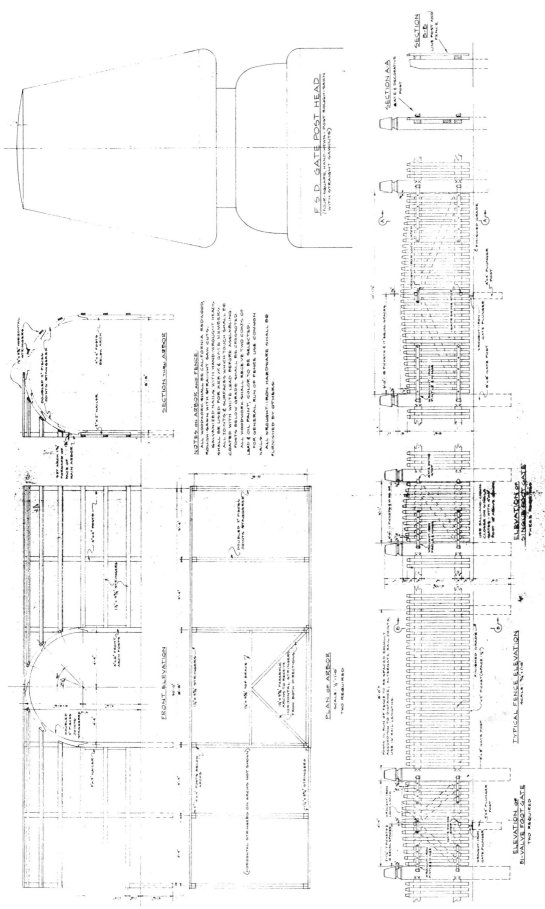

Construction details of the garden arbor, picket fence and gates, Adam Thoroughgood House, Alden Hopkins, landscape architect, 1959

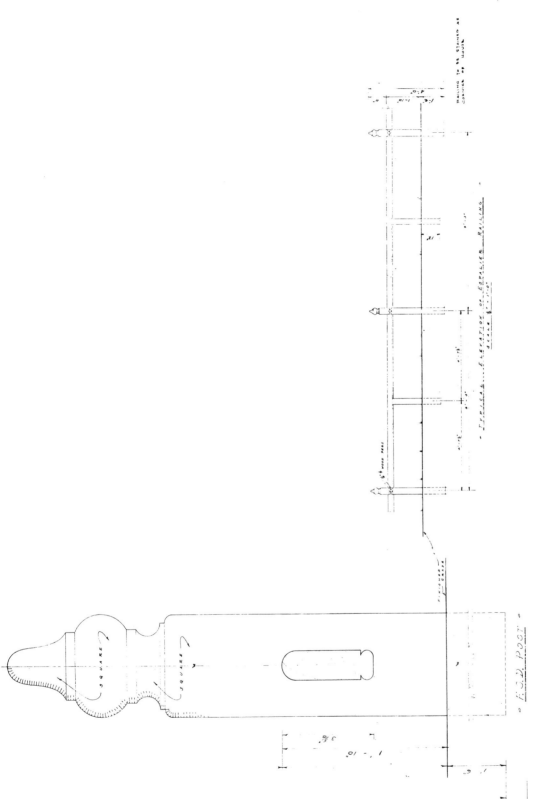

Construction details of the espalier for the cordon pears, Adam Thoroughgood House, Alden Hopkins, landscape architect, 1959

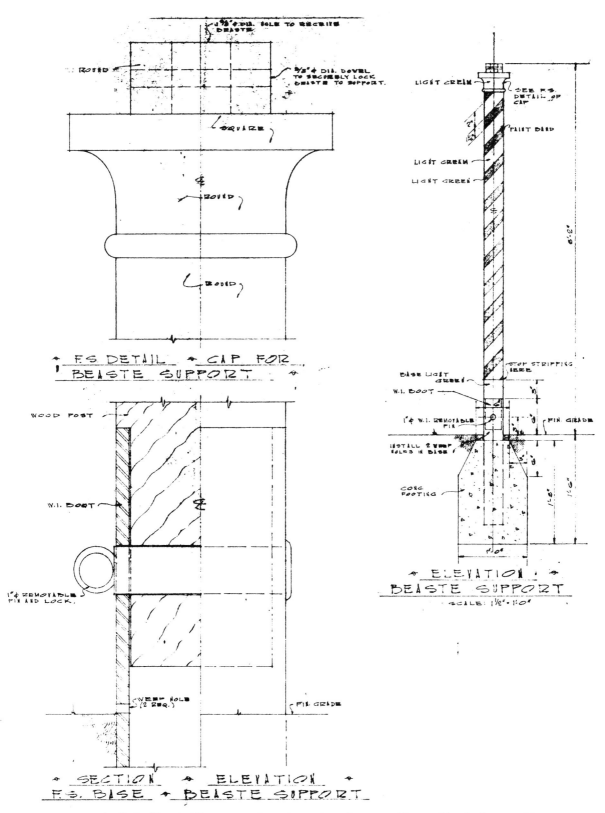

Construction details for "beasties'" support, Adam Thoroughgood House, Alden Hopkins, landscape architect, 1960

Garden pavilion, typical ironwork of historic Richmond

The Mews: Richmond

THE HISTORIC RICHMOND FOUNDATION was organized in 1956 to preserve and restore the Historic Zone on Church Hill where, in Saint John's Church, Patrick Henry uttered his immortal words "Give me liberty or give me death." Symbol of America's struggle for freedom, these words and this spot are of national historic importance. Also, as the site of the original city of Richmond, the area attains further significance. Historic Saint John's Church terminates the vista of the Mews, which is the subject of this restoration.

The entire nineteenth-century area around the Mews is protected by a city code that provides for preservation of buildings or places "commemorative of the events, circumstances and architecture" of historical significance. Adaptive use has been made the policy for restoration in this Church Hill area. Restored buildings are used as offices, apartments, shops, and art galleries; and four adjoining houses have been converted for use as a social club. The Foundation itself uses one house as its headquarters, and imaginative individuals have purchased and restored several old houses for homes.

In the heart of the preserved area is a block bounded by Broad and Grace streets on the north and south sides and 23d and 24th on the east and west. This is Carrington Square, named for the influential Carrington family prominent here in the late nineteenth century. Bisecting this block is a cobbled alleyway once used as a carriageway, hence the adopted restoration designation the Mews. Distinguishing this alleyway from all others was its well-preserved original cobble paving and its vista of Saint John's steeple. This vista was dramatically framed by a huge elm tree that had, by some miracle, escaped the Dutch elm disease.

When in 1964 the Historic Richmond Foundation asked The Garden Club of Virginia to create out of this alleyway a beautiful and useful community garden, it required great imagination to visualize its possibilities. Ralph E. Griswold was retained as landscape architect. Buildings were in ruins, yards strewn with rubbish and grown over with weeds and ailanthus trees, but assurance had been given that the abutting houses on Broad and Grace streets were going to be properly restored and leased or sold to appreciative people.

Some of the houses on Carrington Square had already been restored and sold, and the new owners were showing their interest in maintaining private gardens facing the

Historic cast-iron railings

The ornamental cast-iron preservation wall and tool house

Typical cast-iron bench and gas lamp

Typical cast-iron garden furniture and original paving

Mews. A thirty-foot strip was cut off the back of the Broad Street properties and added to the width of the Mews to make possible some sort of garden.

As a theme for the architectural elements in the proposed design, the world-famous ornamental cast-iron work of Victorian Richmond was adopted. Salvaged iron railings were inserted in panels of the brick wall constructed to separate the garden from the service side of the Broad Street houses. From iron porch colonettes and railings a pavilion was incorporated in the separation wall. The foundation fragments of an old carriage house were used to outline a brick-paved terrace furnished with typical cast-iron chairs and tables. Along the gravel garden walks niches provide spaces for unique cast-iron benches. Vases of various shapes ornament the walls and terraces in nineteenth-century fashion.

Frayed edges of the cobblestone paving were replaced from the city's salvage stock. Paralleling this rather rough surface, a brick walk extends the length of the Mews for the comfort of visitors. An atmosphere of quaintness characteristic of the period prevails, and the cast-iron ornaments preserve examples of the product of nineteenth-century Richmond foundries. It is an outdoor museum of American Victorian garden ornament.

Most of the existing white mulberry trees (not to be confused with silkworm mulberries) were pruned and retained. These provide shade and lend historic authenticity to the planting. A boxwood-bordered bed of Saint-John's-wort and myrtle with bulbs has accent specimens of crape myrtle and mock orange. Liriope, Christmas roses, and plumbago flourish under southern magnolia, azaleas, pomegranates, yaupon and American Holly, Japanese quince, and sasanqua camellias. A willow oak and a white paling fence softened with clematis screen an encroaching yard.

In the space where one Broad Street house was demolished, an entrance from the street was planted with a crape myrtle hanging over the entrance gate, a goldenrain tree silhouetted against one gray house wall, and espaliered pyracantha on the opposite wall. Ground cover of periwinkle and border planting of yucca and cotoneaster are seasonally attractive. One scholar tree casts soft shadows on the adjacent walls.

This community garden in the midst of a former economically depressed area has suffered less vandalism than similar gardens in more fortunate residential areas.

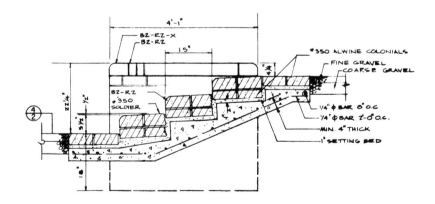

TREES

Ilex Opaca, American Holly
Koelreuteria paniculata, Goldenrain-Tree
Lagerstroemia indica, Crape-Myrtle

Quercus Phellos, Willow Oak
Sophora japonica, Scholar-Tree, Pagoda-Tree

SHRUBS

Abelia grandiflora, Glossy Abelia
Berberis sp., Barberry
Camellia Sasanqua, Camellia
Chaenomeles lagenaria, Japanese Flowering Quince
Clematis var., 'Mrs. Cholmondely,' Clematis introduced in 1870

Clematis paniculata, Sweet Autumn Clematis
Cotoneaster apiculata, Cranberry Cotoneaster
Hypericum, 'Hidcote' St. Johns-Wort
Hypericum calycinum, St. Johns-Wort
Ilex vomitoria, Yaupon
Punica granatum, Pomegranate

Pyracantha sp., Firethorn
Rhododendron macrantha, Late-Blooming Azalea
Syringa japonica, Mockorange

VINES

Hedera hahni, Hahns Ivy
Hedera helix, English Ivy

Parthenocissus tricuspidata 'Lowii,' Boston Ivy (miniature)

Wisteria sinensis, Chinese Wisteria

HERBACEOUS PLANTS—ANNUALS AND PERENNIALS

Ajuga reptans, Bugle-Weed
Aquilegia canadensis, American Columbine
Begonia evansia, Hardy Begonia
Chionodoxa luciliae, Glory-of-the-Snow
Convallaria majalis, Lily-of-the-Valley
Crocus var., Crocus
Digitalis purpurea, Foxglove
Helleborus niger, Christmas-Rose
Hemerocallis var., Day-Lily
Iberis sempervirens, Candytuft
Iris var., Iris
Liriope Muscari, Lily-Turf
Liriope var., Liriope
Mertensia virginica, Virginia Bluebell

Mondo [Ophiopogon] japonicum, Monkey Grass
Muscari botryoides, Grape-Hyacinth
Paeonia Mouton banksii, Tree Peony, first grown in England (Kew Gardens) in 1789
Plumbago larpentae, Leadwort
Primula acaulis, Primrose
Scilla hispanica, Spanish Bluebell
Scilla sibirica, Siberian Squill
Vinca minor, Periwinkle
Viola tricolor hortensis, Pansy
Yucca filamentosa, Adams-Needle

FERNS

Polystichum aristatum, Holly-Fern

Polystichum acrostichoides, Christmas Fern

ROSES

Rosa laevigata, Cherokee Rose introduced into America before 1759

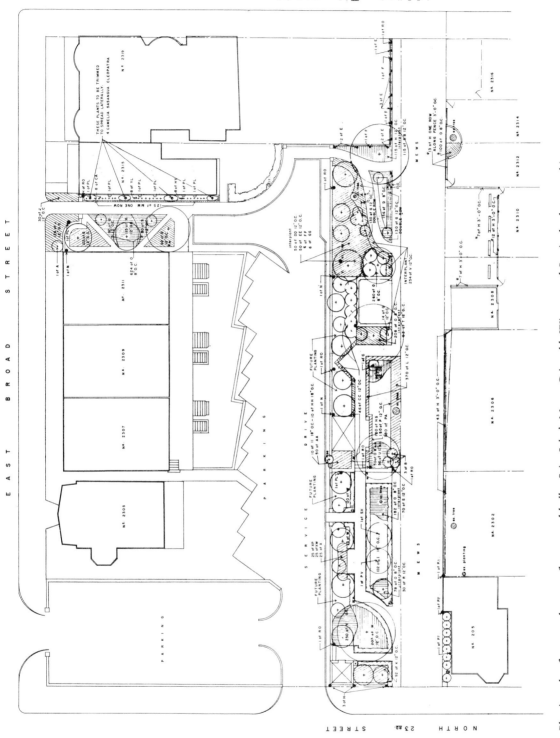

Planting plan for ground covers, flowers, and bulbs. Saint John's Mews, Griswold, Winters, and Swain, landscape architects, 1965

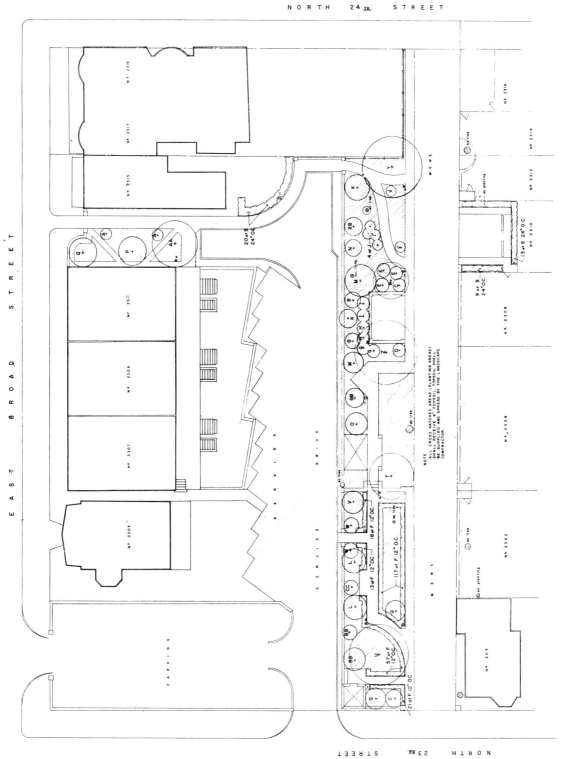

Planting plan for trees and shrubs, Saint John's Mews, Griswold, Winters, and Swain, landscape architects, 1965

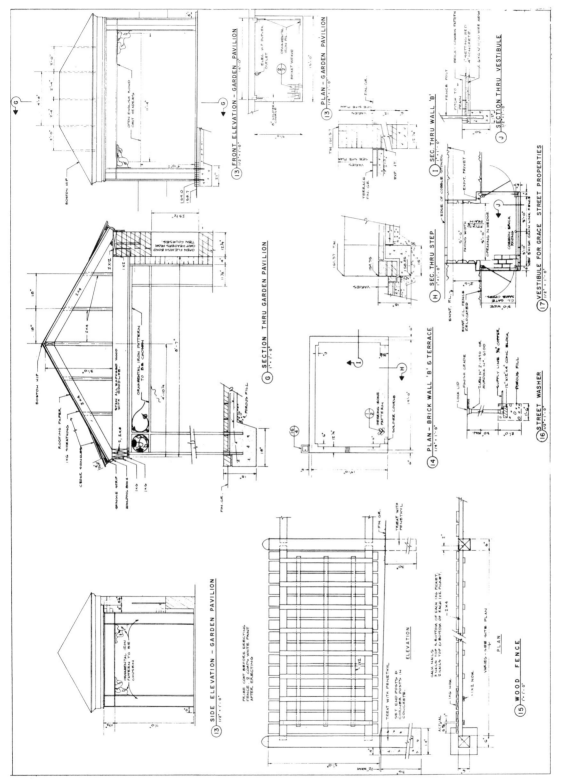

Construction details for garden pavilion, wood fence, and benchwork, Saint John's Mews, Griswold, Winters, and Swain, landscape architects, 1965

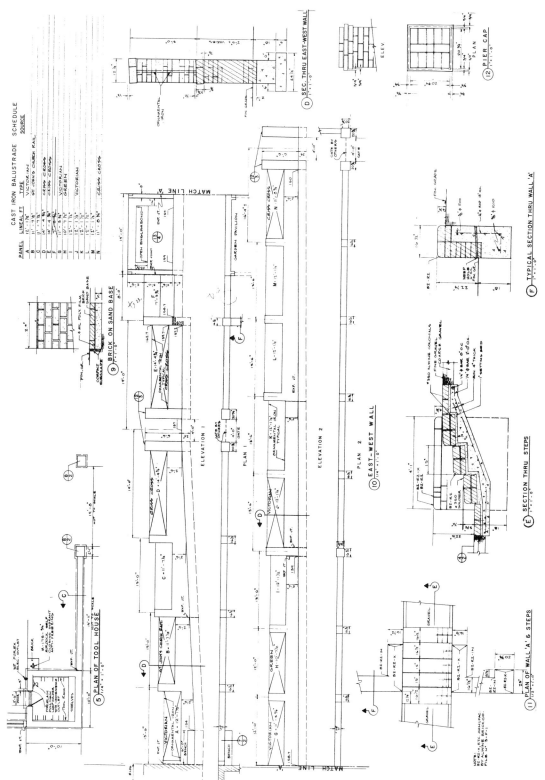

Construction details for brick wall to support the cast-iron panels and steps, Saint John's Mews, Griswold, Winters, and Swain, landscape architects, 1965

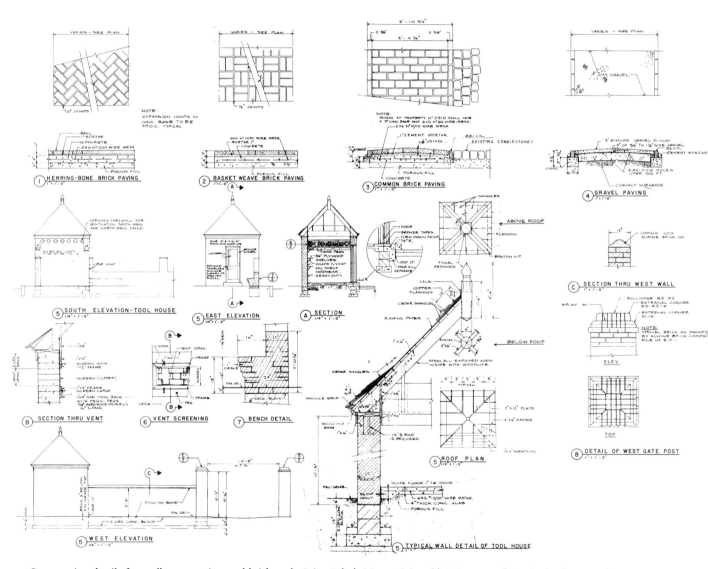

Construction details for toolhouse, paving, and brickwork, Saint John's Mews, Griswold, Winters, and Swain, landscape architects, 1965

Saint John's Church from the Mews

Dogwood planting at Christ Church: Lancaster

Christ Church: Lancaster

A MILE NORTH of Irvington in Lancaster County, Virginia, stands Christ Church; the accepted date of its completion is 1732. Robert "King" Carter, well-known eighteenth-century planter and important figure in the colonial government as well as agent for the Lord Fairfax holdings in the colony, built and endowed the church at his own expense, as his handsome ornate tomb testifies.

Earlier, in 1669, on this same site had been a wooden church built by John Carter, Robert's father. In its chancel were the graves of Robert's parents. When the congregation outgrew the older church a new brick church was proposed, to be built at Kilmarnock, a more convenient location. Robert Carter offered to bear the entire cost of building if the new church was built on the 1669 site, protecting in its chancel the family graves. The offer was quickly accepted.

With the disestablishment of the Anglican Church at the time of the Revolution, the church property became part of Robert Carter's private estate instead of being confiscated and sold by the new government. After a long period of abandonment, the church was leased in the early 1830s to the Episcopalians of the county.

In 1852 the congregation built a new church in Kilmarnock, and Christ Church, without heat or light, was thereafter used only during summer months and on special occasions, as it is today.

In 1958 the Foundation for Historic Christ Church was organized. Ten years of labor on the part of this organization brought about the complete restoration of the handsome Georgian building.

In July 1965 a request to create a landscape setting for the restored church was made by the Foundation to the Restoration Committee of The Garden Club of Virginia. The project was presented to the 1966 Annual Meeting and accepted. Ralph E. Griswold, landscape architect, was commissioned to create an appropriate landscape design.

From the beginning it was recognized that this project required utmost restraint. An unobstructed view of the church itself was the most important consideration. Within the churchyard walls the lawn was regraded and reseeded and a single red oak planted. From the past there remained several huge cedar trees and a red oak. These were retained and pruned. A few vines were planted on the churchyard wall, which had been restored by the Foundation. Brick walks were laid from the three church doors to the corresponding gates, establishing unity of building and churchyard enclosure. A brick

splash course was laid around the base of the building for both practical and historic reasons.

Creating an appropriate landscape setting outside the walls was more complex. Three demands had to be met: provision for automobile access and parking with the minimum intrusion on the landscape; delineation of additional burial area; and recreation of a historic association by reestablishing a token avenue of "goodly cedars" that once, according to legend, extended three miles from Carter's plantation on the Corotoman River to the western entrance of the church.

Cooperation of officials of the Virginia Department of Highways solved the first problem. They arranged the relocation of the existing highway, removing a road of unattractive angles and replacing it with a new road of gentle curves that connected with the proposed access drive.

Automobile parking was placed as far away from the church as the limits of the property allowed. One of the best views of the church is enjoyed while walking from the parking lot to the church through the "row of goodly cedars." However, for those who cannot take this walk, the same view is obtained form the inconspicuous road leading from the parking lot to the main churchyard gate. Having discharged passengers, the driver returns to the parking lot by way of a connecting road. Hollies, willow oaks, and magnolias afford year-round screening of the parking space. Day lilies provide a colorful enclosing ground cover. A few oak trees in the entrance area frame views of the church. The additional burial area, an open lawn, was informally planted with dogwood trees. No monuments or unplanned planting are permitted in this area.

Historical continuity was created by planting the token "row of goodly cedars." The impression of its continuance was achieved by a vista cut through the present grove of trees. The new landscape is unobtrusive, leaving visitors unmindful of its having been thoughtfully designed. Attention is focused on the fine architectural details of the church with its steep hipped roof, turned up at the eaves; its large windows with semicircular arches; and its superb dressing of rubbed brick. The landscape has not been allowed to distract attention from the elegance of this colonial church, second to none in Virginia.

The restoration of the landscape focuses on the church.

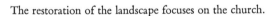

Though far removed from the church, the parking space has been made attractive by its planting.

Restoration of the legendary "row of goodly cedars" unites the interior with the historic landscape.

TREES

Cornus florida, Flowering Dogwood
Ilex opaca, American Holly
Juniperus virginiana, Eastern Red Cedar
Liquidambar Styraciflua, Sweet Gum
Magnolia grandiflora, Southern Magnolia

Pinus Taeda, Loblolly Pine
Quercus falcata, Southern Red Oak
Quercus Phellos, Willow Oak
Viburnum prunifolium, Black-Haw Viburnum

SHRUBS

Hypericum calycinum, St. Johns-Wort

Ilex vomitoria, Yaupon

VINES

Celastris scandens, American Bittersweet
Clematis paniculata, Sweet Autumn Clematis

Clematis virginiana, Virgins-Bower
Hedera helix, English Ivy
Hedera helix baltica, Baltic English Ivy

HERBACEOUS PLANTS—ANNUALS AND PERENNIALS

Hemerocallis var., Day-Lily

Vinca minor, Periwinkle

ROSES

Rosa laevigata, Cherokee Rose introduced
into America before 1759

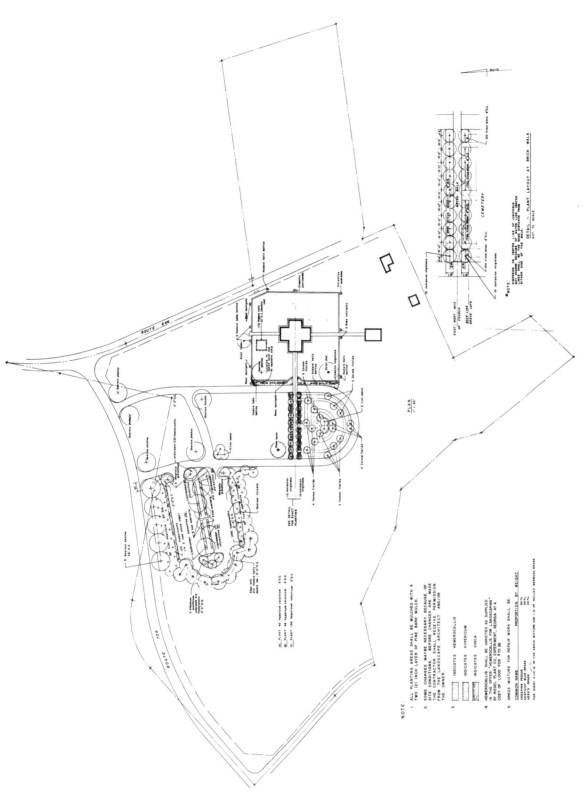

Planting plan, Christ Church: Lancaster, Griswold, Winters, and Swain, landscape architects, 1967

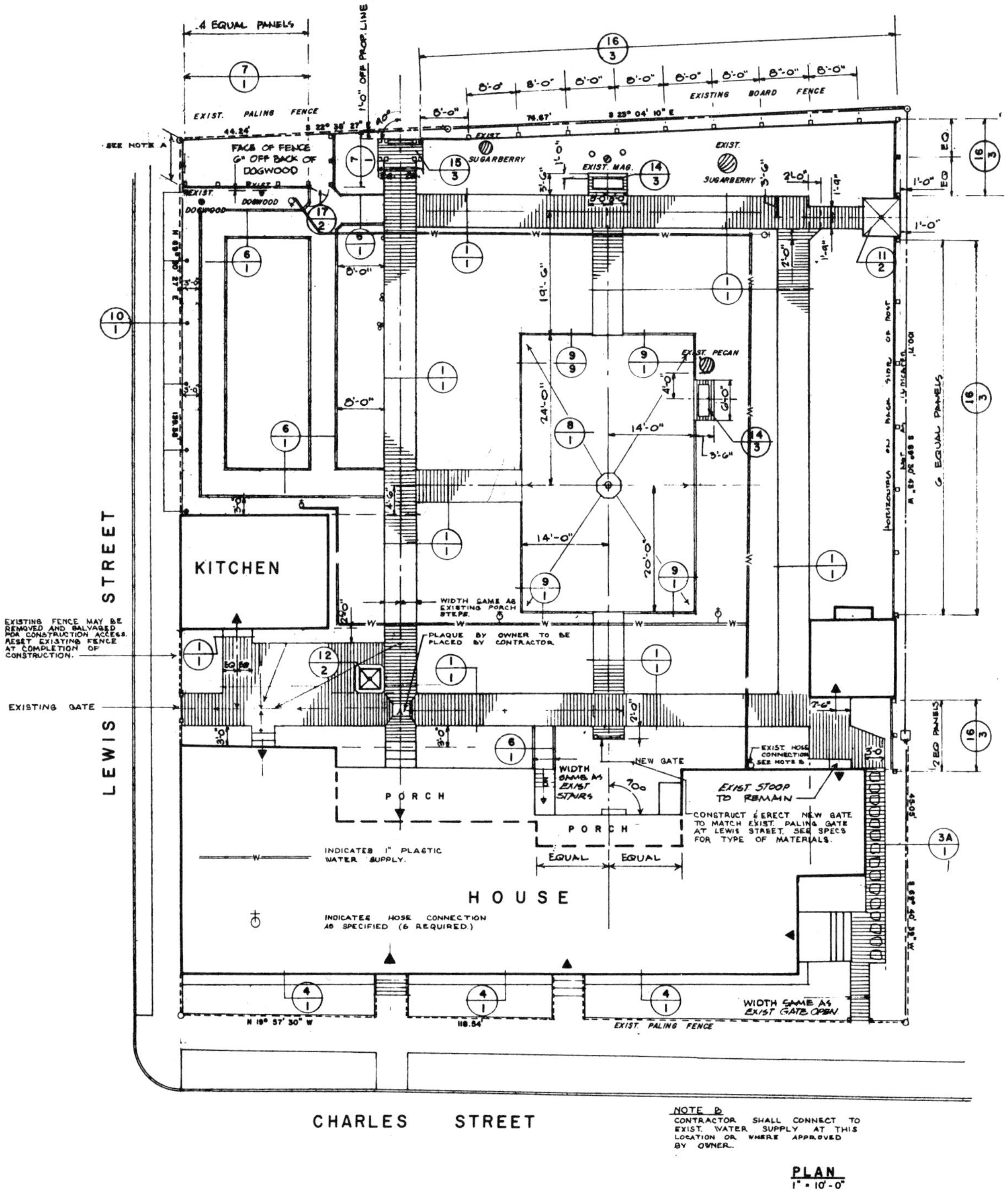

4 EQUAL PANELS

EXIST. PALING FENCE

EXISTING BOARD FENCE

SEE NOTE A

FACE OF FENCE 6" OFF BACK OF DOGWOOD

EXIST. DOGWOOD

EXIST. SUGARBERRY

EXIST. MAG.

EXIST. SUGARBERRY

EXIST. PECAN

KITCHEN

EXISTING FENCE MAY BE REMOVED AND SALVAGED FOR CONSTRUCTION ACCESS. RESET EXISTING FENCE AT COMPLETION OF CONSTRUCTION.

EXISTING GATE

WIDTH SAME AS EXISTING PORCH STEPS.

PLAQUE BY OWNER TO BE PLACED BY CONTRACTOR.

INDICATES 1" PLASTIC WATER SUPPLY.

PORCH

WIDTH SAME AS EXIST STAIRS

NEW GATE

PORCH

EQUAL   EQUAL

EXIST HOSE CONNECTION SEE NOTE B.

EXIST STOOP TO REMAIN

CONSTRUCT & ERECT NEW GATE TO MATCH EXIST. PALING GATE AT LEWIS STREET. SEE SPECS FOR TYPE OF MATERIALS.

HOUSE

INDICATES HOSE CONNECTION AS SPECIFIED (6 REQUIRED.)

WIDTH SAME AS EXIST GATE OPEN

EXIST PALING FENCE

LEWIS STREET

CHARLES STREET

NOTE B
CONTRACTOR SHALL CONNECT TO EXIST. WATER SUPPLY AT THIS LOCATION OR WHERE APPROVED BY OWNER.

PLAN
1" = 10'-0"

Mary Washington House

THE LAST HOME of Mary Ball Washington stands on the corner of Lewis and Charles streets in Fredericksburg. This house was bought by George Washington for his mother on September 18, 1772. It was on an acre of land on the edge of the Kenmore estate. In writing of this transaction to his friend Benjamin Harrison, Washington said, "Before I left Virginia, to make her more comfortable and free from care, I did at her request but at my own expense, purchase a commodious house, garden and lotts, of her own choosing, in Fredericksburg that she might be near my sister Lewis, her only daughter." For thirty-four years before this, Mary had lived on Ferry Farm, across the Rappahannock from Fredericksburg. She had loved the open country life and moved to town reluctantly.

She brought with her as many of her rural possessions as limited space would allow —two horses, a cow, and a dog; and slips and herbs with which she created a miniature country garden in town. Mary lived here seventeen years until her death in 1789.

The property went through a period of private ownerships following her death. In 1890, a proposal was made to buy the cottage and move it for exhibition to the Columbian Exposition in Chicago. Aroused by this offer, the state president of the newly formed Association for the Preservation of Virginia Antiquities (APVA) advanced $4,500 for purchase of the property. A branch of the APVA was then formed in Fredericksburg and the money repaid. Since then the property has been owned and administered by the Mary Washington Branch, which restored the house to the architectural period of Mary's occupancy. An appeal made to The Garden Club of Virginia to rehabilitate the garden was approved May 23, 1968. Before approval the Restoration Committee spent over two years in research. Of particular value were George Washington's diary and old Fredericksburg court records, which list the garden's measurements. Responsibility for the design of an appropriate garden was given to Ralph E. Griswold, landscape architect.

No documentary or archaeological trace was found of the original garden. There were, however, legends on which the design of a garden could be predicated. The most important one was that an extant double row of dwarf boxwood had been planted by Mary; it borders a well-worn brick walk that she herself had ordered laid for her daily visits to Kenmore, her daughter Betty Lewis's home. Less important, but equally attractive as a garden ornament was an old sundial legend says had been Mary's.

The apparent age of the boxwood and brick walk made the first legend sufficiently plausible to accept it as the main axis of the garden. Without disturbing it, the boxwood

Boxwood walk said to be Mary Washington's own creation

was cautiously trimmed back to make the walk passable and the fragile old brick leveled on a new base. Some overgrown tree boxwood was severely cut back and retained as a screen against a neighboring garage. Beyond this boxwood the walk is abruptly cut off by other properties. Here a gate was placed to suggest continuance to Kenmore.

Mary's legendary sundial was made the focal center of a rectangular grass panel edged with boxwood-bordered flower beds and newly created brick walks. These walks lead to an inevitable structure in all eighteenth-century gardens, a "necessary." Tucked away, as it should be, in the rear corner, it has the appearance of a garden house.

Fortunately, there were still standing two of the original outbuildings—a quaint swaybacked kitchen with a big brick chimney at one end of the house and another small structure at the other end. These were used as the anchor points for the simple rectangular shape of the new design. Between the kitchen and the house a brick-paved work area was partially screened from the pleasure garden by a strategically placed well house.

Back of the kitchen, separated by Mary's walk from the rest of the garden, a small herb and vegetable garden was laid out, and where the stable might have been a storage yard was fenced off.

In order to create a sense of separation from the abutting properties, yet without revealing the restricted size of the present holding, an open, unpainted cedar trellis was erected to support espaliered fruit trees along one property line and sweetbay magnolias along another. Bittersweet was planted at the posts.

Huge pecan trees cast shade over most of the central area of this garden, making the growing of flowers difficult but providing comfortable spots for benches. Existing perennials and roses were salvaged for the beds wherever possible. These were augmented by new plantings of tulips, narcissus, lenten roses, violets, sweet william, Madonna lilies, shasta daisies, mint, and many old-fashioned annuals that were started in the cutting garden. Eighteenth-century roses were added, and white crape myrtles and dogwood were used to accentuate important corners in the design. The bloom is doubly effective against the deep green of dwarf boxwood that surrounds the beds.

The sundial, when lifted to be reset in the center of the new design, proved to be one monolithic piece of Aquia stone five feet long. The pedestal that was exposed above ground was a three-foot octagonal column expertly carved with a very subtle silhouette and molded architectural base. The base had been hidden beneath the ground. Obviously this was the work of a very knowledgeable stone carver. The Aquia quarry from which this stone came and which supplied stone for many of the early government buildings in Washington was open during Mary's lifetime but closed in 1830; thus the pedestal could well have been hers. The brass plate that supported the gnomon is stamped with the manufacturer's name "F. W. and R. King, Baltimore." This firm started in business long after Mary's death, operating from 1851 to 1875. When the plate was lifted to reorient it with the new position of the sundial, another set of anchor holes was found in the top of the shaft, indicating that at some time this plate had been changed. It is known that this sundial was sold and taken away from the garden and later returned, which may account for the change in the plate. Presumably the original plate, which would have been thin copper, was lost, stolen, or worn out and replaced by a later model. Though the mystery of the gnomon remains, this sundial is still a most extraordinary piece of garden ornament. The expert design of the shaft makes it a fitting embellishment for the garden of Mary Ball Washington, mother of this nation's first president.

The recreated garden

Simulated necessary, a privy

Aquia stone sundial pedestal, original eighteenth century

TREES

Aesculus hippocastanum, Horse-Chestnut
Amelanchier canadensis, Service-Berry,
    Shad-Bush
Chionanthus virginicus, Fringe-Tree
Cornus florida, Flowering Dogwood

Ilex opaca, American Holly
Magnolia virginiana, Swamp Bay, Sweet
    Bay Magnolia
Malus var., Apple (Espalier)
Pyrus var., Pear (Espalier)

SHRUBS

Buxus sempervirens suffruticosa, Dwarf
    Boxwood (true dwarf)
Chaenomeles lagenaria, Japanese Flowering
    Quince
Clethra alnifolia, Summer Sweet
Gaylussacia dumosa, Bush Huckleberry
Gelsemium sempervirens, Carolina Yellow
    Jessamine

Hydrangea arborescens grandiflora, Hills-of-
    Snow
Hypericum densiflorum, Shrubby St. Johns-
    Wort
Ilex vomitoria, Yaupon
Lagerstroemia indica, Crape-Myrtle
Myrica cerifera, Bayberry, Wax Myrtle
Ribes rubrum, Red Currant

Syringa vulgaris, Common Lilac
Virburnum Opulus, European Cranberry-
    Bush
Viburnum prunifolium, Black-Haw Vibur-
    num

VINES

Campsis radicans, Trumpet-Vine
Celastrus scandens, Bittersweet

Hedera helix, English Ivy
Lonicera semperflora, Coral Honeysuckle

HERBACEOUS PLANTS—ANNUALS AND PERENNIALS

Achillea millefolium, Common Yarrow
Allium schoenprasum, Chives
Althea rosea, Hollyhock
Alyssum saxatile, Golden-Tuft
Amaranthus caudatus, Love-Lies-Bleeding
Anemone coronaria, Poppy-Flowered
    Anemone
Anethum graveolens, Dill
Anthemis tinctoria, Golden Camomile
Aquilegia canadensis, American Columbine
Artemisia Dracunculus, Tarragon
Asparagus officinalis, Asparagus
Aster sp., Michaelmas Daisy
Callistephus chinensis, China Aster
Camassia scilloides, Wild Hyacinth
Campanula persicifolia, Peach-Leaved
    Bell-Flower
Carum Carvi, Caraway
Celosia argentea cristata, Cockscomb
Celosia plumosa, Feather Cockscomb
Centaurea cyanus, Cornflower

Centaurea moschata, Sweet Sultan
Chrysanthemum maximum, Shasta Daisy
Chrysanthemum parthenium, Feverfew
Cleome spinosa, Spider-Flower
Colchicum autumnale, Fall Crocus
Convallaria majalis, Lily-of-the-Valley
Coreopsis lanceolata, Coreopsis
Crocus var., Crocus
Daucus carota, Carrot
Dianthus barbatus, Sweet William
Dianthus sp., Dwarf Pink
Dictamnus albus, Fraxinella, Gas-Plant
Digitalis purpurea, Foxglove
Eupatorium coelestinum, Mist-Flower
Foeniculum vulgare, Fennel
Fritillaria imperialis, Crown Imperial
Gaillardia pulchella, Gaillardia
Galanthus nivalis, Snowdrop
Galax aphylla, Galax
Helianthus annuus, Common Sunflower
Helleborus orientalis, Lentenrose

Hemerocallis flava, Lemon Day-Lily
Hemerocallis fulva, Tawny Day-Lily
Hibiscus palustris, Rose Mallow
Hypericum calycinum, St. Johns-Wort
Hyssopus officinalis, Hyssop
Iris sibirica, Siberian Iris
Lactuca sativa, Lettuce
Lavandula spica, Lavender
Lilium candidum, Madonna Lily
Limonium latifolium, Sea Lavender
Lunaria annua, Honesty
Majorana hortensis, Marjoram
Mentha spicata, Spearmint
Monarda didyma, Oswego-Tea, Bee-Balm
Narcissus var., Daffodil
Nicotiana alata grandiflora, Flowering Tobacco
Ocimum Basilicum, Sweet Basil
Penstemon hirsutus, Hairy Penstemon
Petroselinum hortense, Parsely
Phaseolus vulgaris, Pole Bean

Phlox paniculata, Summer Phlox
Pimpinella Anisum, Anise
Platycodon grandiflora, Balloon-Flower
Polianthes tuberosa, Tuberose
Primula veris, Cowslip
Rheum rhaponticum, Rhubarb
Rudbeckia hirta, Blackeyed Susan
Salvia officinalis, Sage
Scilla hispanica, Spanish Bluebell
Scilla sibirica, Siberian Squill
Solanum lycopersicum, Tomato
Sternbergia lutea, Autumn-Flowering Sternbergia
Teucrium Chamaedrys, Germander
Thymus vulgaris, Thyme
Tulipa Clusiana, Tulip
Veronica longifolia subsessilis, Clump Speedwell
Veronica maritima, Maritime Veronica
Vinca minor, Periwinkle
Viola odorata, Sweet Violet

Viola tricolor hortensis, Pansy

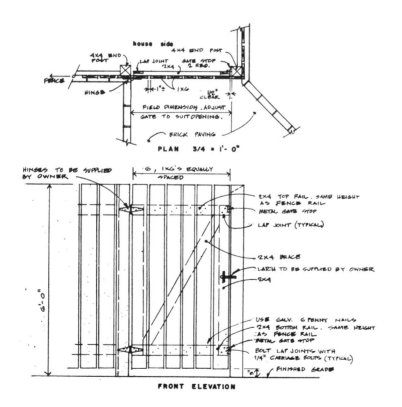

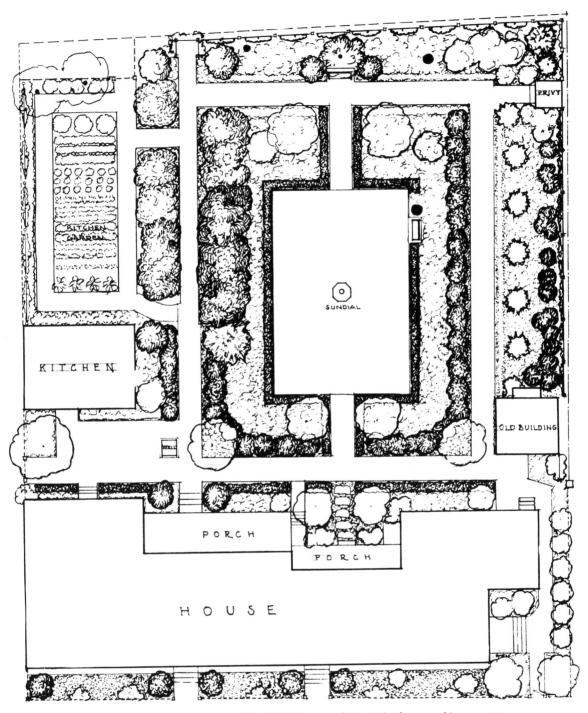

Presentation plan, Mary Washington House, Griswold, Winters, and Swain, landscape architects, 1968

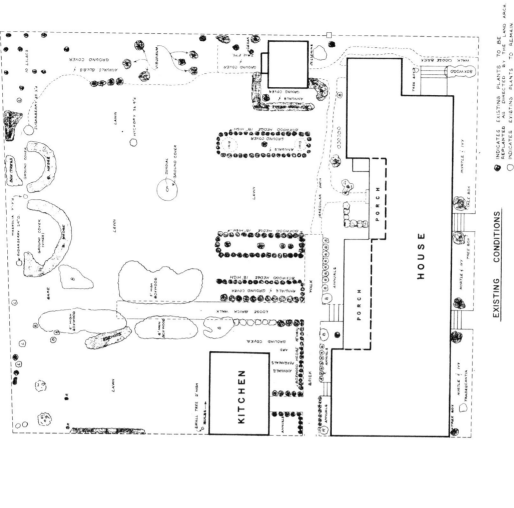

EXISTING CONDITIONS

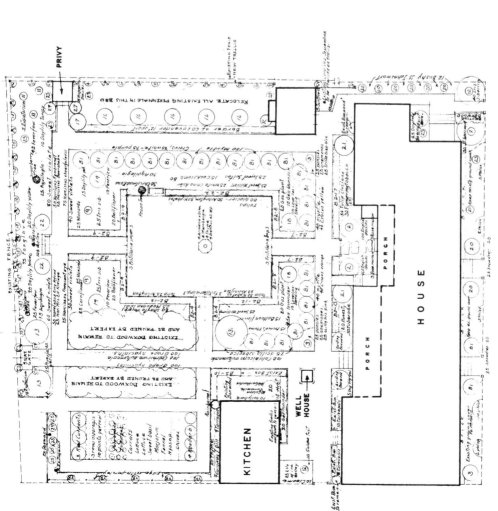

PLANTING PLAN

Planting plan, Mary Washington House, Griswold, Winters, and Swain, landscape architects, 1968

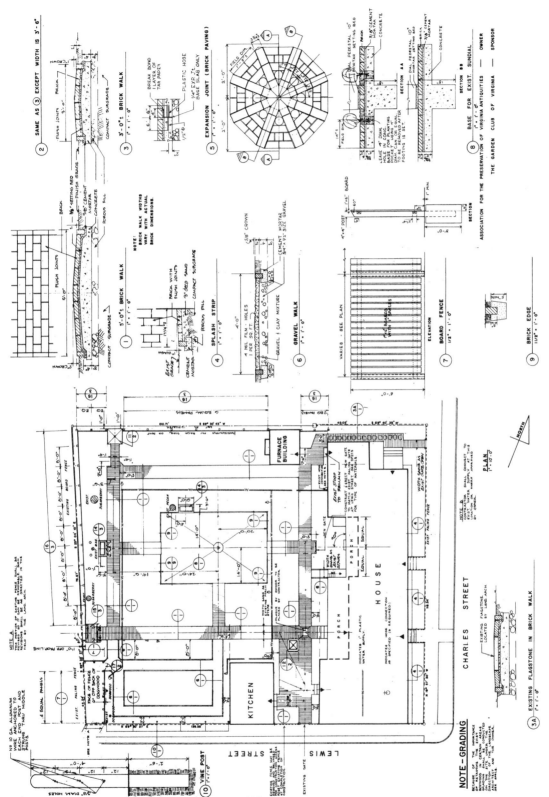

Construction plan for the garden and details for the Mary Washington House, Griswold, Winters, and Swain, landscape architects, 1968

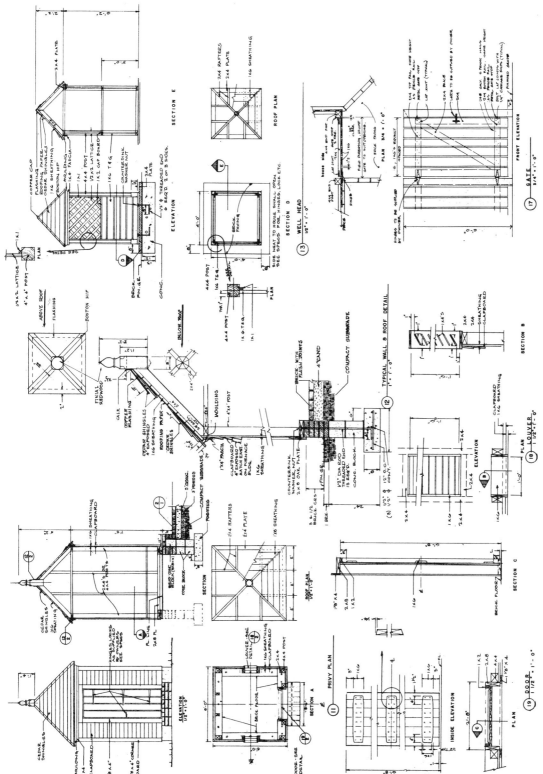

Construction details for the privy, well house, and gate, Mary Washington House, Griswold, Winters, and Swain, landscape architects, 1968

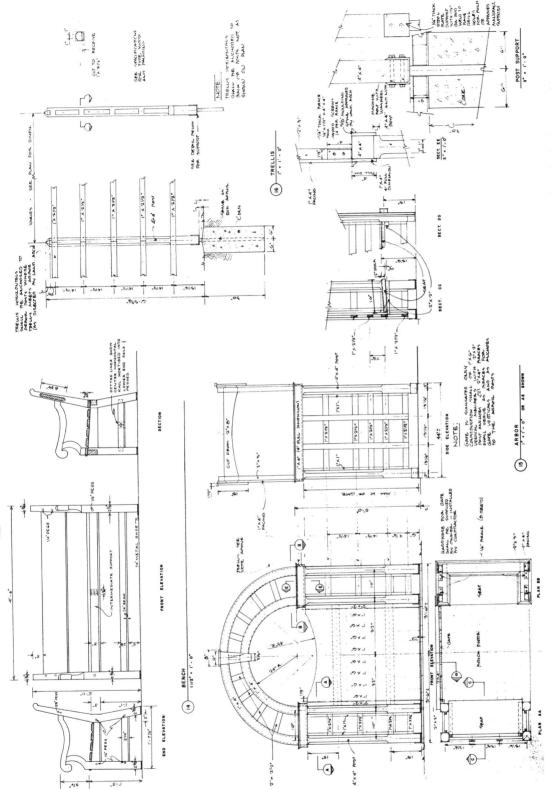

Construction plans and details for the arbor gate, bench, and trellis at the Mary Washington House, Griswold, Winters, and Swain, landscape architects, 1968

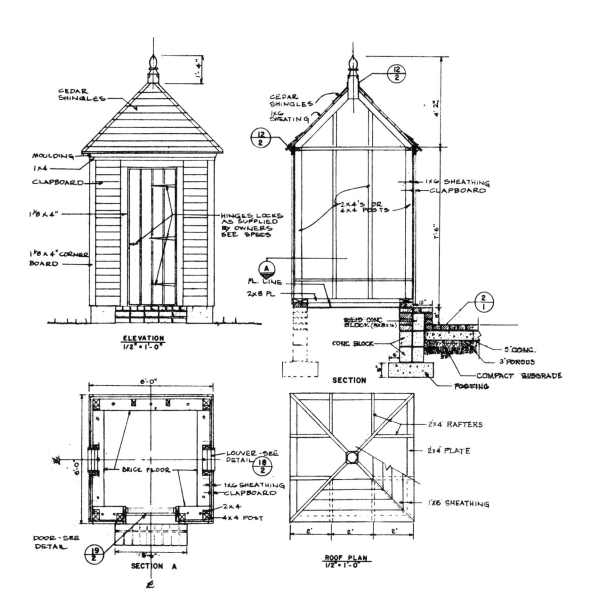

CEDAR SHINGLES

MOULDING 1x4

CLAPBOARD

1⅛ x 4"

1⅛ x 4" CORNER BOARD

HINGES LOCKS AS SUPPLIED BY OWNERS SEE SPECS

ELEVATION
1/2" = 1'-0"

CEDAR SHINGLES

1x6 SHEATING

2x4'S OR 4x4 POSTS

1x6 SHEATHING
CLAPBOARD

FL. LINE
2x8 PL

SOLID CONC. BLOCK (8x8x16)

CONC. BLOCK

5" CONC.
3" POROUS
COMPACT SUBGRADE
FOOTING

SECTION

6'-0"

6'-0"

LOUVER - SEE DETAIL

BRICK FLOOR

1x6 SHEATHING
CLAPBOARD

2x4
4x4 POST

DOOR - SEE DETAIL

SECTION A

2x4 RAFTERS

2x4 PLATE

1x6 SHEATHING

ROOF PLAN
1/2" = 1'-0"

A very old English boxwood was probably there in Henry's time.

Scotchtown

IN 1717 Charles Chiswell patented a holding of 9,976 acres on which he built a house, a tannery, and a mill. He called this holding Scotchtown. Only the house remains today; the exact date of its building is unknown, but it was probably about 1719. For that era and location it was an exceptionally spacious, elegant house with a unique architectural plan, obviously designed for entertaining as well as comfort.

Twenty years later ownership was transferred by Colonel Chiswell to his son, Col. John Chiswell, a member of the House of Burgesses. He sold it to his son-in-law, John Robinson, treasurer of the colony and speaker of the House of Burgesses, after whose death the original large acreage was divided into smaller segments. The house was bought by John Payne, father of Dolley Payne Madison. From him, in 1771, Patrick Henry bought the house and 960 acres.

Patrick Henry owned Scotchtown from 1771 until 1778 during the most important political period of his life. From Scotchtown he went to Saint John's Church to make his famous freedom statement and to Williamsburg to become the first governor of Virginia. Preoccupied as he was with political interests and also with the consequences of his wife's tragic illness, he could have had little opportunity or inclination to leave any impact on the buildings or grounds he occupied. It is not surprising, therefore, that documentary research and archaeological excavations failed to reveal any evidence of Henry's influence on the original plantation grounds; still, it was his occupancy that gave historic significance to this remarkable old mansion, prompting its designation as a National Historic Landmark.

Not until the tenure of the next owner, Col. Wilson Miles Cary, was there any record of there having been a garden at Scotchtown. A visitor to the Cary home in the late eighteenth century, Baron Ludwig Von Closen, wrote in his journal, February 19, 1782, "This Plantation which is called Scotchtown, is charmingly situated in the midst of a plain six leagues from Porter. The house is spacious and handsome, extremely well furnished and delightfully well ordered. In a word, it is one of the most pleasant establishments in America. An English garden below adds a great deal to the charm of the estate." Returning in July 1782, he wrote, "The grounds at Scotchtown are very pretty and there are little woods in the shade of which we took some country walks. The garden is an attractive sight. There are several pretty flower-beds although these are still rather neglected in this country." These descriptions, written four years after Henry's departure, might have referred to a previously existing garden, but in the absence of any corroborating evidence there was no basis for restoration.

Following Colonel Cary's ownership Scotchtown passed through many hands, some careful, some neglectful. When the photograph of a goat standing at the foot of the entrance steps, a stray from the herd living in the basement, was shown by J. Ambler Johnson in 1955 to the Association for the Preservation of Virginia Antiquities (APVA), the old mansion was at its lowest ebb. "The plaster is falling . . . windows on the first floor are nearly all gone . . . a sad picture," reported Johnson. Three more years passed before the Hanover County Branch of the APVA came to the rescue by purchasing Scotchtown and 26.6 acres. More land was purchased later, making the total 41.6 acres, and during the 1950s extensive restoration of the mansion was directed by Walter M. Macomber.

Such was the status when in 1968 The Garden Club of Virginia agreed to "undertake archaeological research to determine any and all possible facts about the existence of a garden at Scotchtown." For this research Barbara Liggett of Philadelphia, a trained archaeologist, was employed by the Restoration Committee to conduct a feasibility study of the area. After a summer of field excavation under the direction of Harvard Ayers in 1969, no evidence of a garden of any period was produced. Discouraging as this report was, it freed facts from traditional fiction that had long confused thinking about this proposed restoration. As a result a project to create the appearance of an eighteenth-century plantation without any pretense to fanciful gardening or recreation of theoretical outbuildings was authorized at the 1970 annual meeting of The Garden Club of Virginia. The landscape architectural firm of Griswold, Winters and Swain was retained to produce such a design.

The mansion stands on a slight rise of land, closely surrounded by open fields on three sides, with a fringe of woods to the rear. When the planting began there was no defined enclosure, no well-marked entrance road. Only a few unkempt trees, a modern colonial-styled office building, and caretaker's house existed. The approach was through a small parking lot connected with the adjacent county road. The ornamental planting consisted of large tree boxwood flanking both main entrance stairs and a cluster of very old dwarf boxwood that might have been the center of some sort of garden in front of the east entrance. Nothing suggested the period of Patrick Henry's life here. The project had to be entirely reconstructed from contemporary plantation precedent.

An entrance drive as bold and simple as the architecture of the house was directed straight from the highway toward the east entrance. A country gravel road, it was fenced with post-and-rail on both sides and shaded with rows of southern red oaks. Dogwood, sourwood, serviceberry, and clusters of Scotch broom, common to the area, were planted along the fences. What seemed to be a logical space for a yard was enclosed with a post-and-rail with gates at four points of entrance.

Approaching the dwelling, visitors bypass the lawn enclosure by a road that detours them into a parking space, where their cars are out of sight of the mansion. Down the center of the large gravel parking area a strip of pines alternated with goldenrain trees is underplanted with periwinkle and Saint-John's-wort.

In contrast to the impressive first head-on view from the entrance drive, a diagonal path through the foot gate from the parking area gives an informal view of the house.

The main entrance is a straight, oak-shaded gravel road centered on the mansion. It is paralleled by post-and-rail fence and clumps of Scotch broom, shadbush, and sourwood.

The approach is through a grass-covered courtyard in which visitors once arrived by carriage or on horseback. This usage is now indicated by a hitching rail and mounting block beside the circular gravel drive. Somewhere around this drive the outbuildings essential to a plantation were once clustered. Now, a gate leading in the direction of the old barn and another presumably leading to the mill add the impression of extension into the larger area of the plantation. The existing trees were pruned and supplemented with new sweet gum, ash, pecan, redbud, sweet bay magnolia, and, beyond the fence, by crab apples and deciduous holly. An apple orchard and a kitchen garden with some blueberries, rhubarb, and asparagus give a utilitarian domestic appearance. Wild strawberries were planted as ground cover beneath the apple trees. A row of pear trees borders the road to the mill gate. There is no superimposed pretense to gardening in the grand manner.

False hopes were aroused twice that clues to the existence of a garden had been found. The book *Paths of Glory* by Nelly Preston described Scotchtown gardens of

The view down the entrance road from the mansion is framed by existing boxwood. The gate to the plantation yard defines this enclosure.

A casual approach from the parking space to the mansion shows it to advantage.

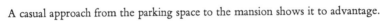

Henry's time, but it was proved to be unauthentic storytelling. Three insurance declarations were discovered, but their dates (1802, 1805, and 1806) made them irrelevant.

Hollies, beech, black gum, and magnolias were used to relieve the barrenness of the entrance side and to enhance views of the house. As was the contemporary English custom, no plants except a broad band of English ivy were used close to the house. The structure appears to rest solidly on the ground. In front of the house a cluster of existing boxwood, some of which seemed old enough to have been planted by Henry, was cleaned up, fed, and retained as a shelter for a wooden bench. The bench simulates the fanciful description by Nelly Preston that "inside [this old boxwood] is a wooden seat and a comfortable rest for the back, very closely concealed. Here Patrick loved to sit and smoke, or sometimes to play a little on his flute."

On the fence around the lawn native white clematis, coral honeysuckle, trumpet vine, and Virginia creeper, with a few scuppernong grapes, are distributed casually. An undulating bed of wild flowers borders the lawn inside the fence—butterfly weed, bouncing bet, wild phlox, native coreopsis, rough-leaved sunflower, and tickseed. All flowers seen in the surrounding countryside are gathered here for seasonal display.

On October 10, 1970, the completed project was presented to the APVA at a modest ceremony in the house to which the guests retreated from the mist of a day that "dawned rainy, and remained most Scottish in aspect as bagpipers piped in the many guests who had come despite the weather." As time matures this landscape, it will bring ever-increasing honor to Patrick Henry, whose most immortal words were conceived here.

A mounting block and a token orchard were characteristic plantation items.

TREES

Amelanchier canadensis, Shad-Bush,
  Service-Berry
Carya pecan, Pecan
Cercis canadensis, Eastern Redbud
Cornus florida, Flowering Dogwood
Crataegus oxyacantha, English Hawthorn
Fagus sylvatica, European Beech
Fraxinus americana, American Ash
Ilex opaca, American Holly
Juniperus virginiana, Eastern Red Cedar
Koelreuteria paniculata, Goldenrain-Tree
Liquidambar Styraciflua, Sweet Gum
Liriodendron Tulipifera, Tulip-Tree

Magnolia grandiflora, Southern Magnolia
Magnolia virginiana glauca, Sweet Bay
  Magnolia
Malus coronaria, Wild Sweet Crab
Malus var., Apple
Nyssa sylvatica, Black Gum
Oxydendron arboreum, Sourwood
Pinus Strobus, White Pine
Pinus Taeda, Loblolly Pine
Prunus avium var., Black Sweet Cherry
Prunus cerasus var., Sour Cherry
Pyrus var., Pear
Quercus falcata, Southern Red Oak

SHRUBS

Buxus sempervirens suffruticosa, Dwarf
  Boxwood (true dwarf)
Chionanthus virginicus, Fringe-Tree
Clethra alnifolia, Summer Sweet
Cytissus scoparius, Scotch Broom
Hydrangea paniculata grandiflora, Hydrangea
  Peegee
Hypericum calycinum, St. Johns-Wort

Hypericum densiflorum, St. Johns-Wort
Ilex verticillata, Winterberry
Ilex vomitoria, Yaupon
Kalmia latifolia, Mountain Laurel
Myrica cerifera, Southern Wax Myrtle
Vaccinium corymbosum, Highbush Blueberry
Viburnum prunifolium, Black-Haw
  Viburnum

VINES

Campsis radicans, Trumpet-Vine
Celastrus scandens, American Bittersweet

Clematis virginiana, Virgins-Bower
Hedera helix, English Ivy

Parthenocissus quinquefolia, Virginia Creeper
Vitis rotundifolia var. *scuppernong*,
  Scuppernong Grape

HERBACEOUS PLANTS—ANNUALS AND PERENNIALS

Asclepias tuberosa, Butterfly-Weed
Asparagus officinalis, Asparagus
Bidens coronaia, Tickseed
Convallaria majalis, Lily-of-the-Valley
Dianthus Barbatus, Sweet William
Fragaria virginiana, Wild Sweet Strawberry

Helianthus strumosus, Rough-Leaved
  Sunflower
Rheum rhaponticum, Rhubarb
Saponaria officinalis, Bouncing Bet
Solidago altissima, Tall Goldenrod
Viola papilonacea, Common Violet

Yucca filamentosa, Adams-Needle

ROSES

Rosa virginiana, Virginia Rose

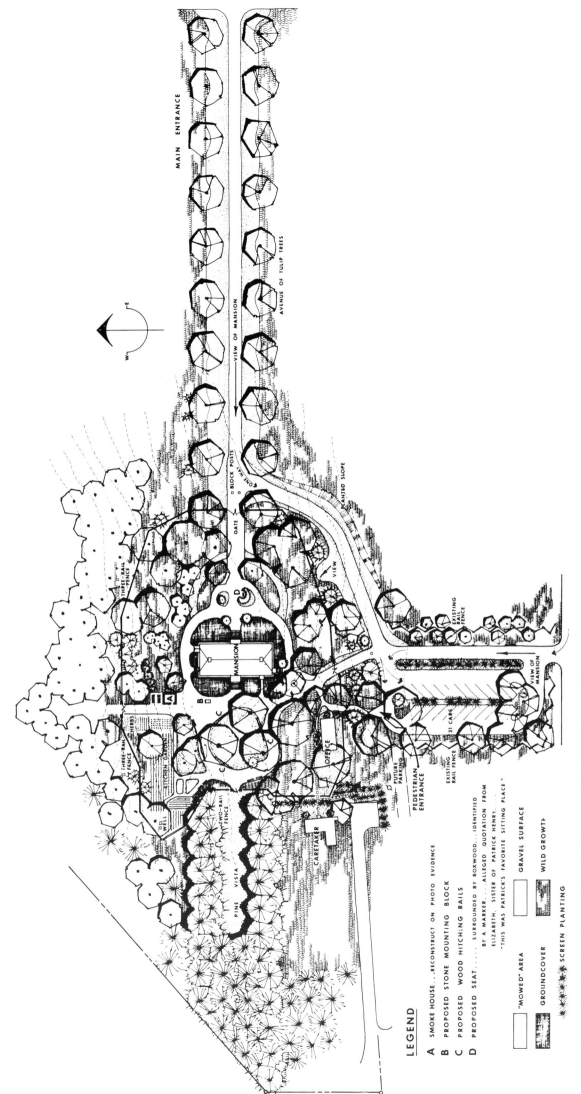

LEGEND

A SMOKE HOUSE...RECONSTRUCT ON PHOTO EVIDENCE

B PROPOSED STONE MOUNTING BLOCK

C PROPOSED WOOD HITCHING RAILS

D PROPOSED SEAT.....SURROUNDED BY BOXWOOD....IDENTIFIED
BY A MARKER....ALLEGED QUOTATION FROM
ELIZABETH, SISTER OF PATRICK HENRY.
"THIS WAS PATRICK'S FAVORITE SITTING PLACE."

"MOWED" AREA   GRAVEL SURFACE

GROUNDCOVER   WILD GROWTH

SCREEN PLANTING

MAIN ENTRANCE

VIEW OF MANSION

AVENUE OF TULIP TREES

GATE

ONE WAY

BLOCK POSTS

THREE-RAIL FENCE

THREE-RAIL FENCE

KITCHEN GARDEN

HERBS

OLD WELL

TWO-RAIL FENCE

PINE VISTA

CARETAKER

OFFICE

PEDESTRIAN ENTRANCE

FUTURE PARKING

EXISTING RAIL FENCE

21 CARS

VIEW OF MANSION

EXISTING RAIL FENCE

PLANTED SLOPE

VIEW

MANSION

Presentation plan, Scotchtown, Griswold, Winters, and Swain, landscape architects, 1970

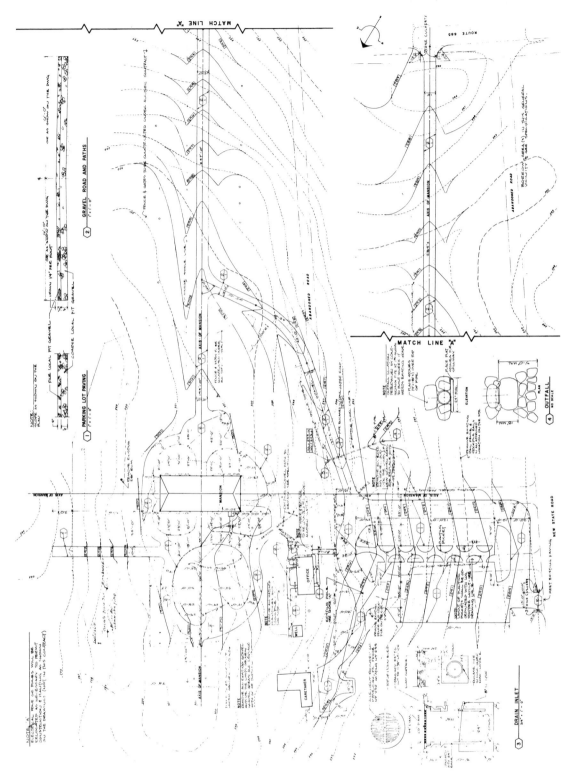

Construction plan, Part I, Scotchtown, Griswold, Winters, and Swain, landscape architects

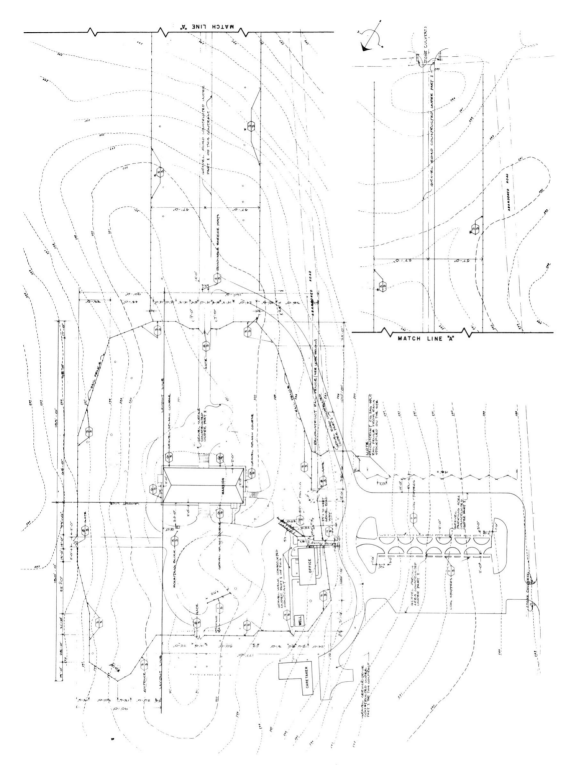

Construction plan, Part II, Scotchtown, Griswold, Winters, and Swain, landscape architects

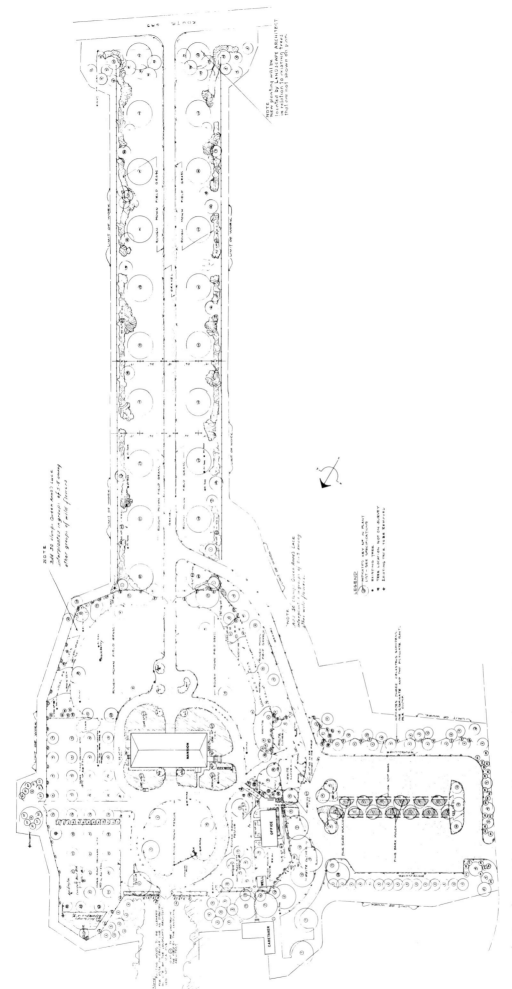

Planting plan, Scotchtown, Griswold, Winters, and Swain, landscape architects

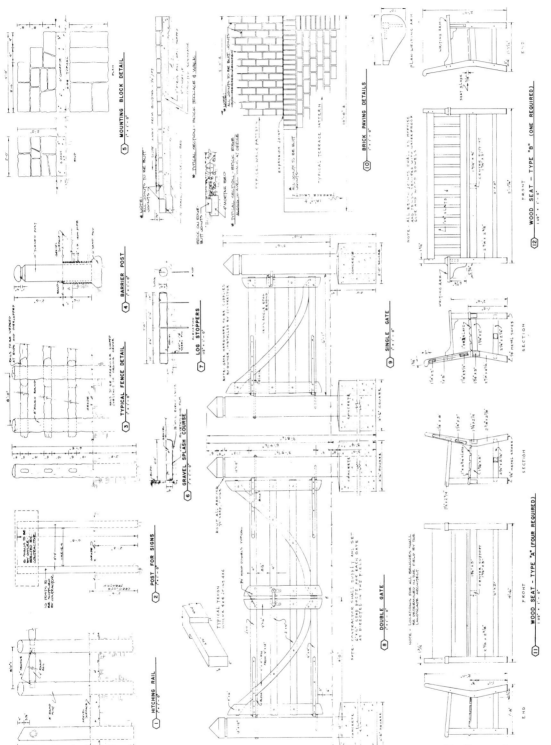

Construction details, gates, seats, and fences, Scotchtown, Griswold, Winters, and Swain, landscape architects

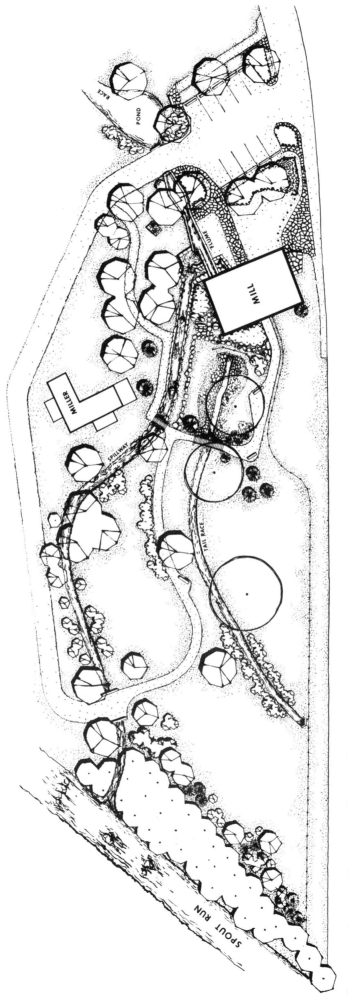

Presentation plan, Burwell-Morgan Mill, Griswold, Winters, and Swain, landscape architects, 1972–73

Burwell-Morgan Mill

IN THE GREAT VALLEY, west of the Shenandoah River, is the village of Millwood. Once a busy crossroads of commerce and warfare, this Clark County town is now a quiet oasis. Here stands the Burwell-Morgan Mill, a monument to two great patriots.

In 1964 the Clarke County Historical Association acquired the mill and six surrounding acres. The mill was in ruinous condition, but the Society felt that the significance of its historic past justified restoration. The restored structure retains an upper story that was a later addition to the original one-story building of 1782. That the mill machinery once more operates is a feat made possible by the gift of original wooden gears from another mill near Middleburg. Restoration of the control dam and the headrace brought back the water needed to operate the waterwheel. This waterwheel is unusual as it is located inside the mill. Protected by the building, the original shaft of the twenty-foot wheel has been preserved for almost two hundred years.

The Burwell-Morgan Mill is a memorial to the two men who built and operated it for mutual benefit. Nathaniel Burwell, of Carter's Grove on the James, was an aristocratic landowner. Daniel Morgan was a frontiersman and a superb military tactician. Both were outstanding business men. In 1771 the young Burwell realized that the uncertainty of the tobacco market and the depletion of the soil along the James made the future of the planter problematical. He turned his attention to the development of property he owned in the Shenandoah Valley. Here he became acquainted with General Morgan and formed a business association with him. Morgan's life, unlike Burwell's, began in poverty, but he was a man of great resourcefulness. His early career as a wagoner gave him a familiarity with all the roads in and out of the valley. He fought Indians and understood their guerrilla tactics that he, in turn, drilled into his unit of Virginia riflemen. These tactics enabled his unit to turn the tide of battle at Saratoga and Cowpens.

After the battle of Saratoga Morgan was placed in command of Hessian prisoners held in a camp near Winchester. With Hessian labor he built this great mill in 1782. His observations made during early days of hauling flour from valley mills to eastern shipping points had made him familiar with the milling business; so the great mill soon prospered. Creation of this successful business and the subsequent development of the village of Millwood by the combined talents of Burwell and Morgan form an interesting chapter of post-Revolutionary War history.

Lower exit to the meadow

Resting place to view the overflow cascade

In 1970 the Clark County Historical Association requested The Garden Club of Virginia to rehabilitate the grounds around the mill. This request was granted in May 1971 and plans were drawn by Ralph Griswold, of the firm of landscape architects Griswold, Winters and Swain.

Before work could be started rank overgrowth had to be removed to open up views of the mill. A post-and-rail fence was built along the highway, and a new parking area was created. A flagstone path was built from the parking court along the millrace to the upper floor of the mill, where an impressive view of the grinding operation may be seen. Other paths invite wandering along the overflow stream through fields of wild flowers.

No embellishment was needed to make this a beautiful landscape. Controlling the natural growth and restoration of the watercourse were the essential requirements. The ample flow of water is the dominant feature of the landscape as it progresses from mill-pond to mill race to cascading overflow. Massive stones guide the water along its course, their rugged forms softened by native growth. Great care has been taken to merge paths and bridges unobtrusively with the natural landscape. Native trees were planted to provide shade for picnic spots; wild flowers, shrubs, and vines mingle natural-ly; and everywhere the sound of water creates a feeling of power and dynamic beauty.

Bridges over spillway and overflow

TREES

Acer rubrum, Red Maple
Acer saccharum, Sugar Maple
Amelanchier canadensis, Service-Berry, Shad-Bush
Betula lutea, Yellow Birch
Cercis canadensis, Eastern Redbud
Cornus florida, Flowering Dogwood
Liquidambar Styraciflua, Sweet Gum
Liriodendron Tulipifera, Tulip-Tree
Magnolia acuminata, Cucumber-Tree
Magnolia macrophylla, Big-Leaf Magnolia

Magnolia virginiana, Swamp Bay, Sweet Bay Magnolia
Malus coronaria, Wild Sweet Crab
Oxydendron arboreum, Sourwood
Paulownia tomentosa, Empress-Tree
Pinus Strobus, White Pine
Pinus Taeda, Loblolly Pine
Plantanus occidentalis, Sycamore
Quercus falcata, Southern Red Oak
Salix babylonica var. *Salamonii*, Weeping Willow

Tsuga canadensis, Canadian Hemlock

SHRUBS

Chionanthus virginicus, Fringe-Tree
Cornus Amomum, Silky Dogwood
Hibiscus Moscheutos var., Rose-Mallow
Hypericum prolificum, Shrubby St. Johns-Wort
Ilex verticillata, Winterberry
Kalmia latifolia, Mountain Laurel

Leucothoë Catesbaei, Drooping Leucothoë
Rhododendron nudiflorum, Pinxter Bloom
Rhododendron viscosa, White Swamp Azalea
Rhus aromatica [*R. canadensis*], Fragrant Sumac
Syringa vulgaris, Common Lilac

VINES

Bignonia radicans, Trumpet Creeper
Celastris scandens, American Bittersweet

Clematis virginiana, Virgins-Bower
Hedera helix baltica, Baltic English Ivy

Parthenocissus quinquefolia, Virginia Creeper

HERBACEOUS PLANTS—ANNUALS AND PERENNIALS

Aquilegia canadensis, American Columbine
Asclepias incarnata, Swamp Milkweed
Aster puniceus, Swamp Aster
Caltha palustris, Marsh Marigold
Coreopsis lanceolata, Lance Coreopsis
Eupatorium purpureum, Joe-Pye-Weed
Eupatorium urticaefolium, American Ageratum
Helianthus stumosus, Sunflower
Hemerocallis flava, Lemon Lily

Iris pseudacorus, Yellow Flag
Iris versicolor, Blue Flag
Liatris spicata, Spike Gayfeather
Mertensia virginica, Virginia Bluebell
Monarda didyma, Oswego-Tea, Bee-Balm
Phlox divaricata, Blue Phlox
Thalictrum polygonum, Tall Meadow Rue
Trillium grandiflorum, Snow Trillium
Vinca minor, Periwinkle
Viola cuculata, Blue Marsh Violet

FERNS

Dennstaedtia punctilobula [*Disconia punctilobula*], Hayscented Fern

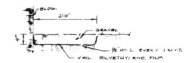

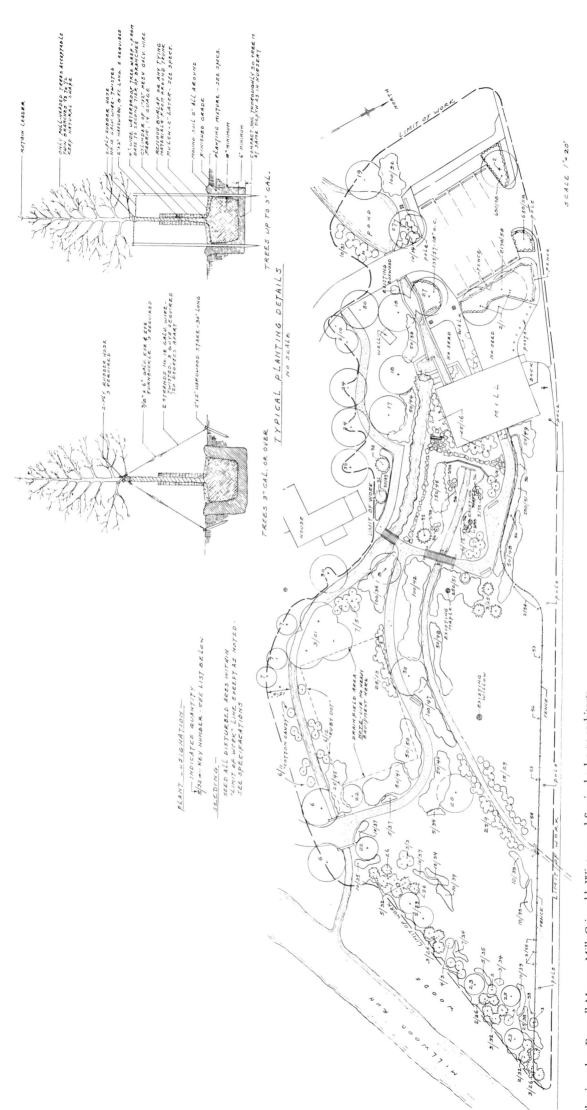

Planting plan, Burwell-Morgan Mill, Griswold, Winters, and Swain, landscape architects

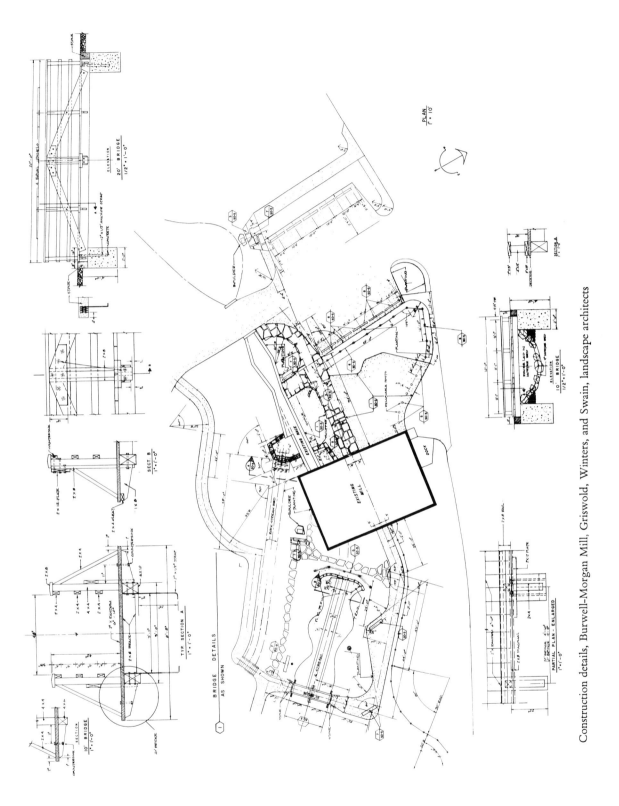

Construction details, Burwell-Morgan Mill, Griswold, Winters, and Swain, landscape architects

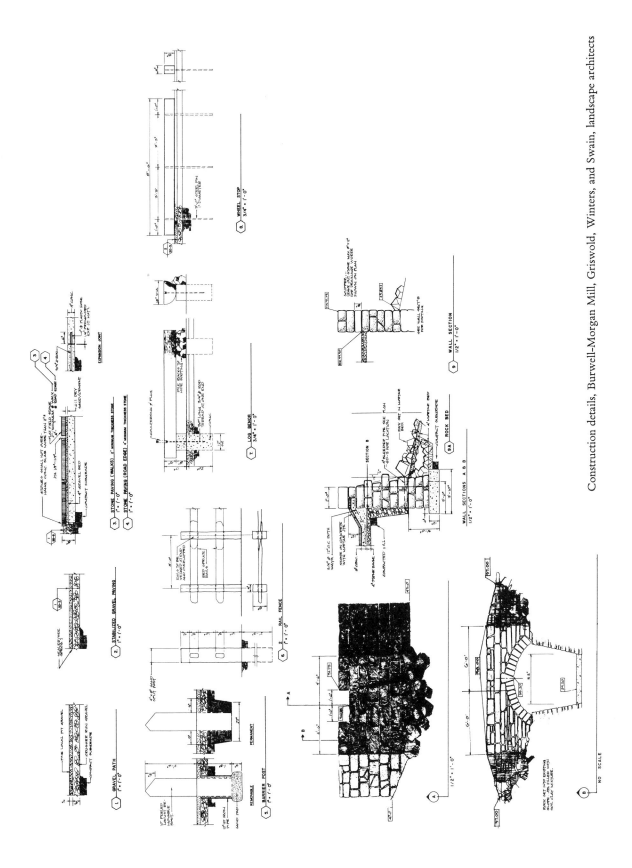

Construction details, Burwell-Morgan Mill, Griswold, Winters, and Swain, landscape architects

Franklin Street entrance gate

Kent-Valentine House

THE KENT-VALENTINE HOUSE, an eighteen-room antebellum residence situated at 12 East Franklin Street, Richmond, was acquired by The Garden Club of Virginia in the spring of 1971. Across First Street and to the east of the Kent-Valentine House is Linden Row, a range of eight outstanding Greek Revival townhouses. This range, together with the house at 12 East Franklin, now preserves an important area of historic character in downtown Richmond.

This is an architecturally handsome house. It is carried in the Virginia Landmarks Register; it is listed on the National Register of Historic Places, and the Landmarks Commission holds an open space easement on the property. The original portion of the mansion was built in 1845 for Horace Kent, the most important wholesale importer and jobber of dry goods in Virginia. The plans were drawn by Isaiah Rogers of Boston, a noted designer of the Greek Revival period. It is the only identified residence standing attributed to Rogers.

In 1875 title to this property passed by purchase to Charles Talbott, a Richmond merchant whose widow sold it in 1904 to Granville G. Valentine. Valentine made the alterations and additions responsible for the present architectural appearance of the house.

Originally a one-story iron porch extended the full length of the front and around the west corner. Valentine removed this porch and added Ionic columns, using the beautiful cast-iron railings from the former porch between the new columns. At the same time he added a two-story wing to the west and to the rear of the mansion. With the exception of the details of the double parlor, Valentine altered the interior details of the house in accordance with the Colonial Revival tastes of the time. The handrail of the triple flight of stairs that leads from the central hall rises from a curved volute at the newel. To the right of the hall a drawing room opens through a wide door framed by Corinthian columns and pilasters, supporting a classical lintel. The mantel is elegantly ornamented with classical motifs. The double parlor on the opposite side of the hall retains its original Gothic features. The marble mantel is ornamented with clustered colonnettes, having modified Tudor arches.

The mansion, flanked by magnificent southern magnolia trees, stands in the midst of a big handsome lawn. With the single exception of the Governor's Mansion in

Gravel parking lot

The former Carriage House

Capitol Square, this is the last mansion in downtown Richmond surrounded by trees.

Purchase of the property was made possible by the generosity of a loan from a member of The Garden Club of Virginia. The cost of preservation and restoration was met from Historic Garden Week proceeds. In this project a twofold gain was realized. The restoration of the house and grounds assures that future generations will be able to enjoy the classic grandeur of a disappearing age of architectural importance and beauty. At the same time The Garden Club of Virginia gained a place in which to draw together its records and memorabilia, ample office space for the Historic Garden Week office, space for a horticultural library, and a central meetingplace for the convenience and pleasure of the membership.

Restoration of the grounds was more preservation of what was there at the time of purchase than actual restoration, but it required careful handling by the landscape architects Griswold, Winters and Swain. The carriage house at the northwest corner of the property was renovated for use as an office by an architect. A garage attached to this carriage house was removed. Limited parking area was carefully worked in among existing holly trees at the rear of the mansion. The surrounding brick walls and iron fence were repaired. A wood fence was built along the west property line and faced with a row of Burford hollies running the length of the house. Original iron gates at the First Street entrances were found to be basically sound and were repaired. New gates were made for the back entrances to match the existing ones. New brick walks were laid for convenience. Under the trees English ivy was used in profusion to replace thin grass. Mansion and grounds now stand as resplendent as they were in their original era of elegance.

West Lawn

East Lawn

TREES

Cornus kousa chinensis, Chinese Dogwood
Koelreuteria paniculata, Goldenrain-Tree
Lagerstroemia indica, Crape-Myrtle

Magnolia grandiflora, Southern Magnolia
Magnolia virginiana glauca, Sweet Bay
  Magnolia

SHRUBS

Buxus sempervirens, Common Boxwood
  (true tree)
Buxus sempervirens suffruticosa, Dwarf
  Boxwood (true dwarf)

Ilex cornuta burfordi, Burford Holly
Ilex cornuta burfordi nana, Dwarf Burford
  Holly
Ilex vomitoria, Yaupon

Rhododendron sp., Rhododendron

VINES

Euonymus radicans, Winter Creeper
Hedera helix baltica, Baltic English Ivy

Hydrangea petiolaris, Climbing Hydrangea
Pyracantha sp., Firethorn

HERBACEOUS PLANTS—ANNUALS AND PERENNIALS

Hemerocallis flava, Lemon Day-Lily

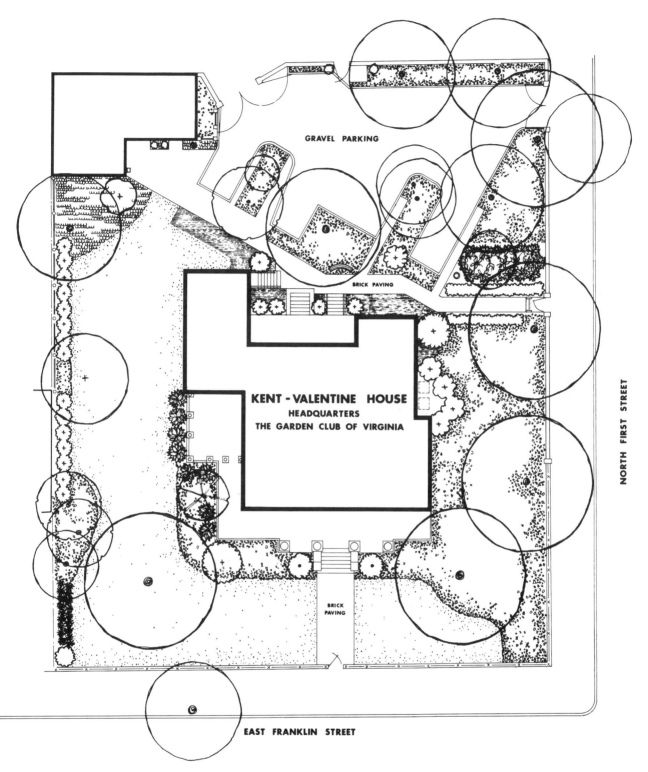

GRAVEL PARKING

BRICK PAVING

KENT - VALENTINE HOUSE
HEADQUARTERS
THE GARDEN CLUB OF VIRGINIA

BRICK
PAVING

NORTH FIRST STREET

EAST FRANKLIN STREET

Presentation plan, Kent-Valentine House, Griswold, Winters, and Swain, landscape architects

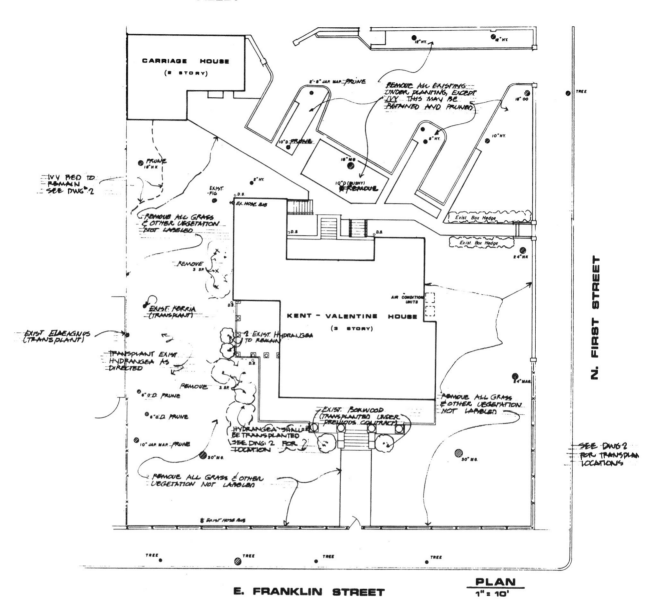

Planting plan showing existing and proposed planting, Kent-Valentine House,
Griswold, Winters, and Swain, landscape architects

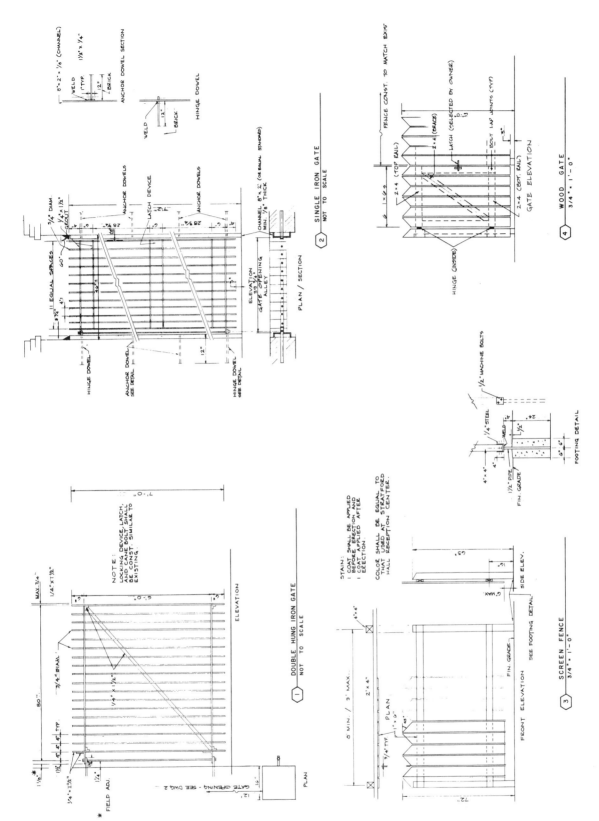

Construction details, gate, and fence, Kent-Valentine House, Griswold, Winters, and Swain, landscape architects

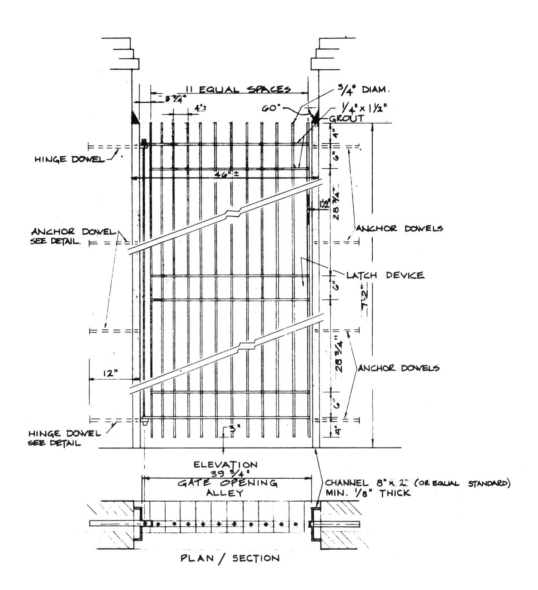

ELEVATION

GATE OPENING
ALLEY

PLAN / SECTION

Historic

Virginia Gardens

in

Color

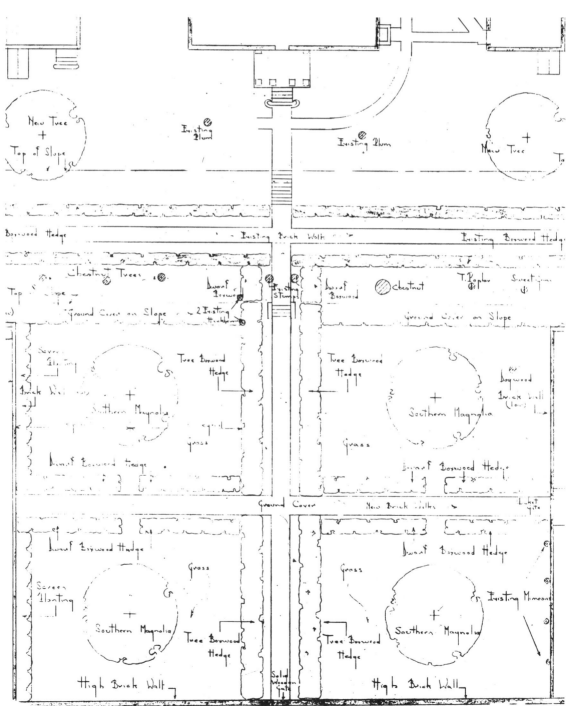

Kenmore

Stratford

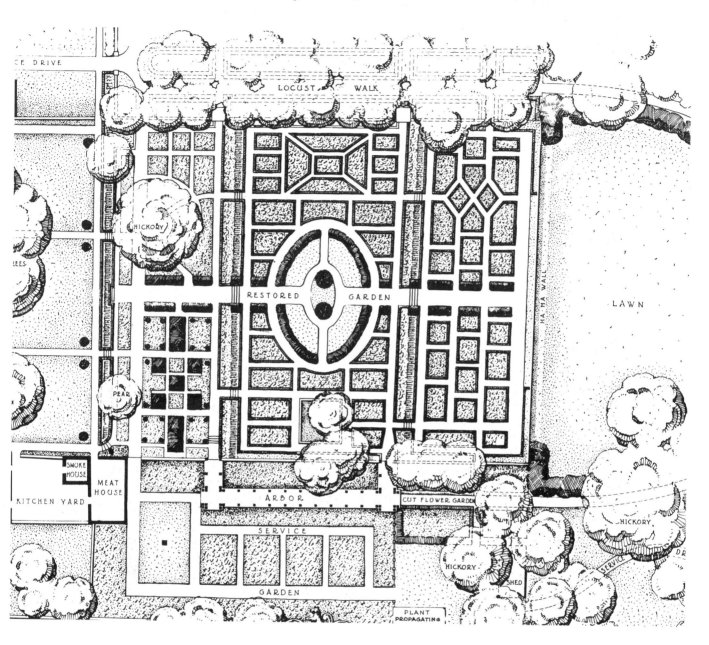

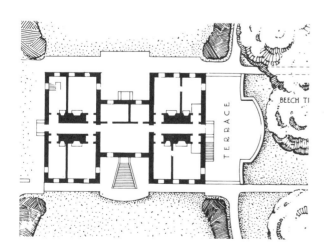

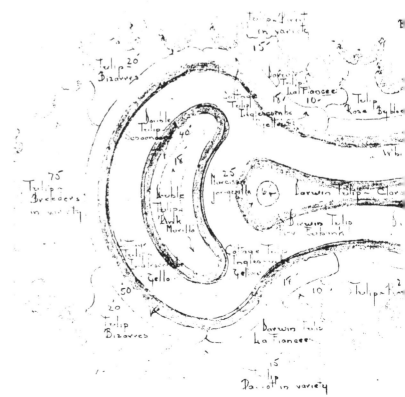

Woodrow Wilson Birthplace: The Manse

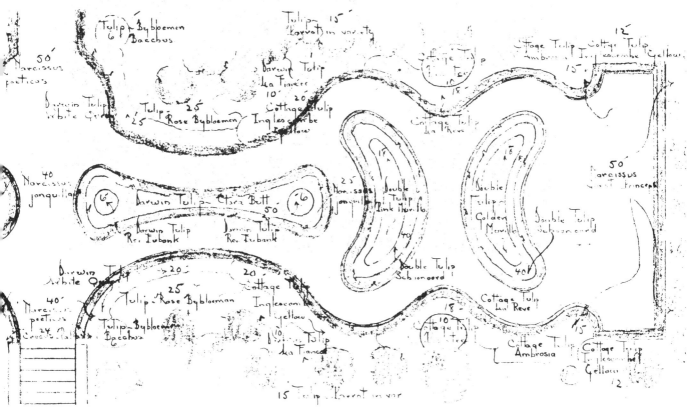

Lee Memorial Chapel

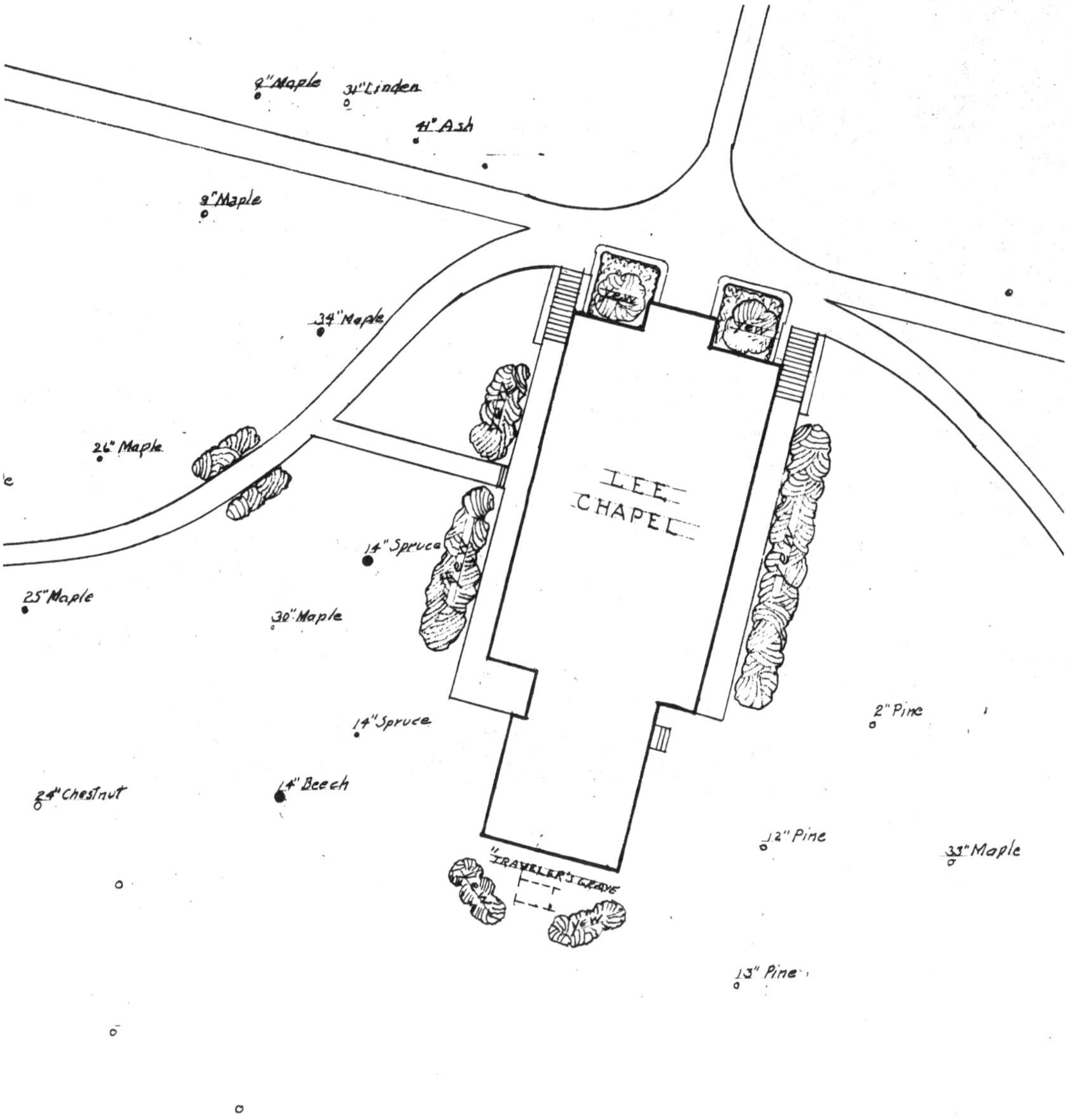
9" Maple
31" Linden
41" Ash
8" Maple
34" Maple
26" Maple
14" Spruce
25" Maple
30" Maple
14" Spruce
24" Chestnut
14" Beech
LEE
CHAPEL
YEW
YEW
"TRAVELER'S GRAVE"
YEW
2" Pine
12" Pine
33" Maple
13" Pine

NOTE
• Trees listed by Gillette marked thus •

Rolfe-Warren House: Smith's Fort Plantation

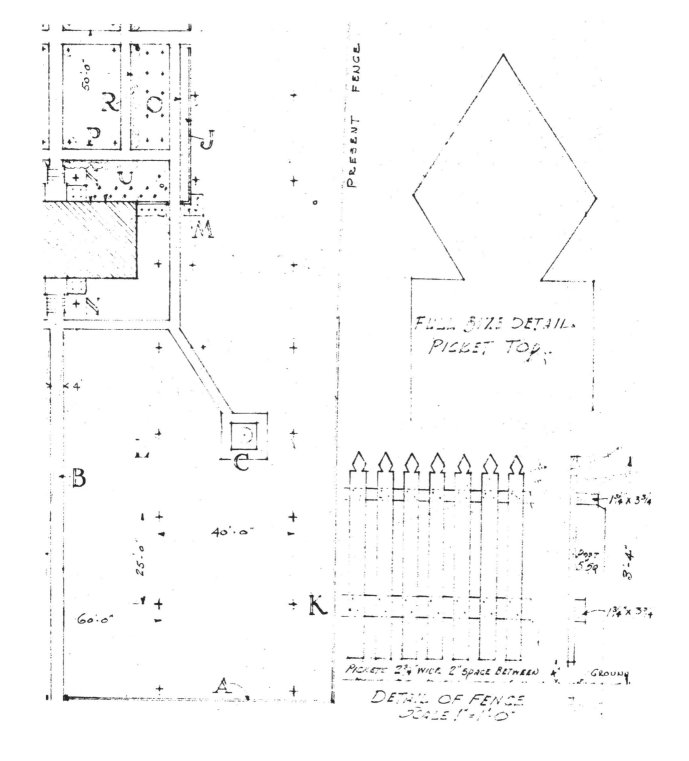

PRESENT FENCE

FULL SIZE DETAIL
PICKET TOP.

PICKETS 2¾" WIDE 2" SPACE BETWEEN   GROUND

DETAIL OF FENCE
SCALE 1"=1'0"

1¾" X 3¾"

1¾" X 3¾"

3'-4"

50'-0"

60'-0"

25'-0"

40'-0"

B

A

C

K

J

M

N

U

R

O

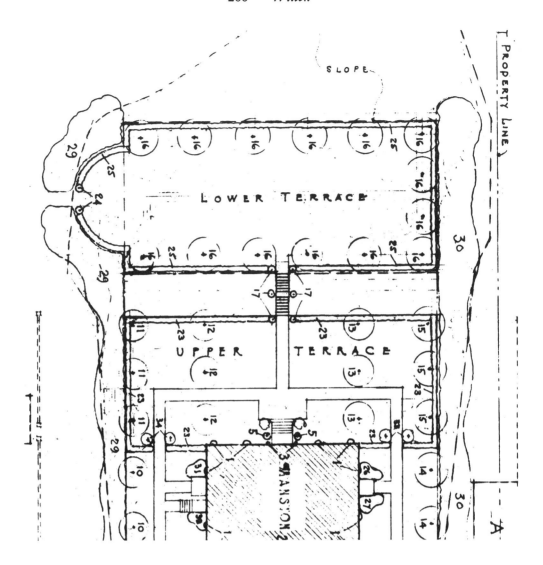

Wilton

Bruton Parish Church

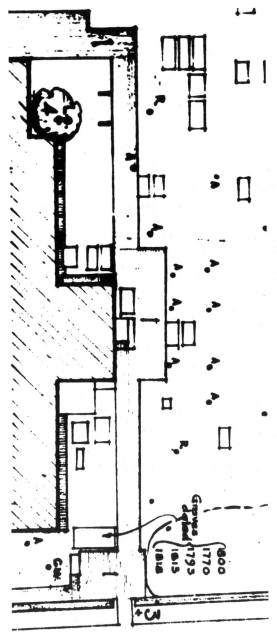

Mary Washington Monument

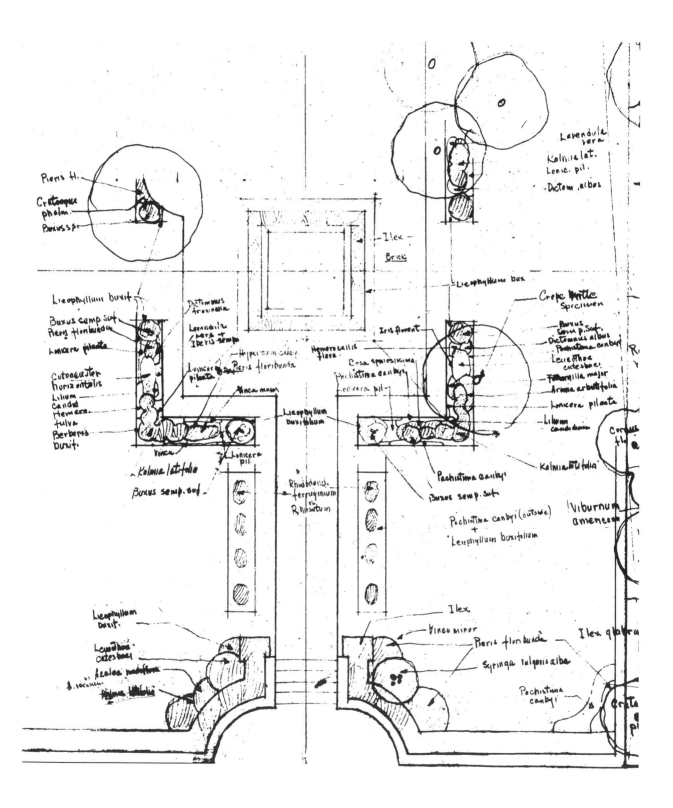

Monticello

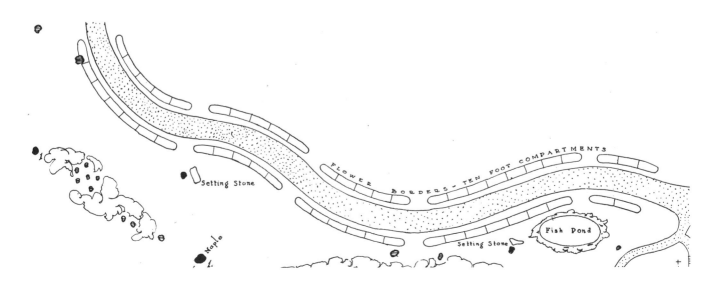

Christ Church: Middlesex

Christ Church: Fincastle

Barter Theatre: Abingdon

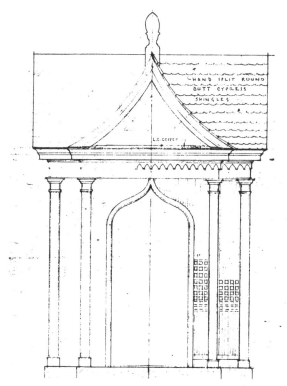

Gunston Hall

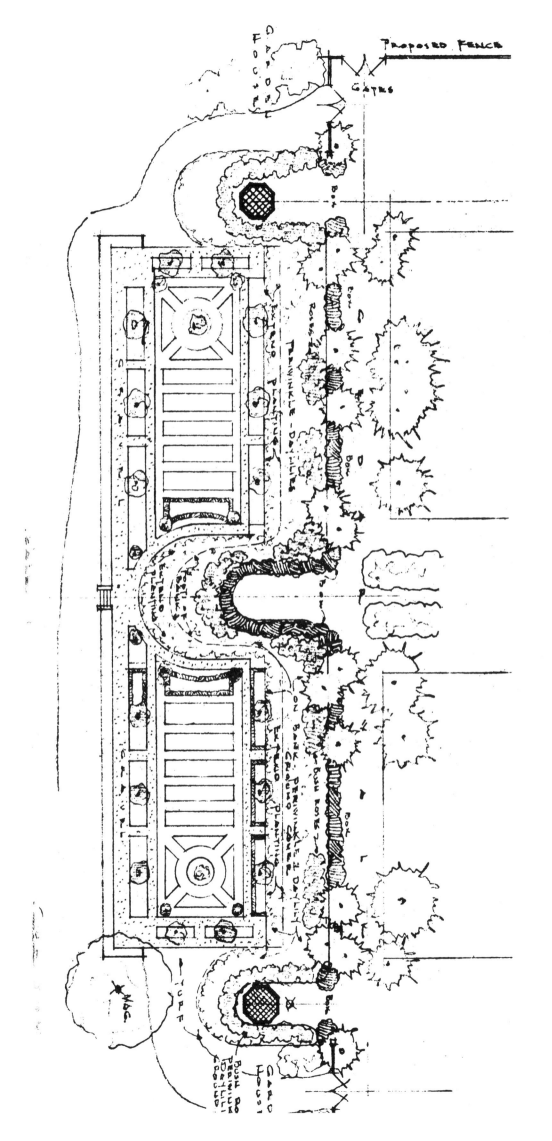

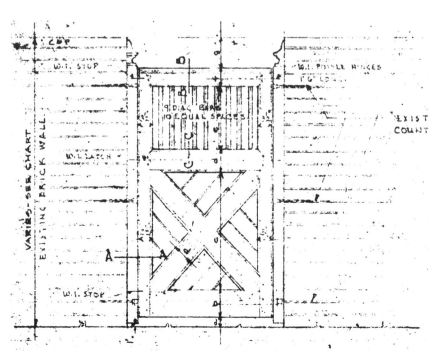

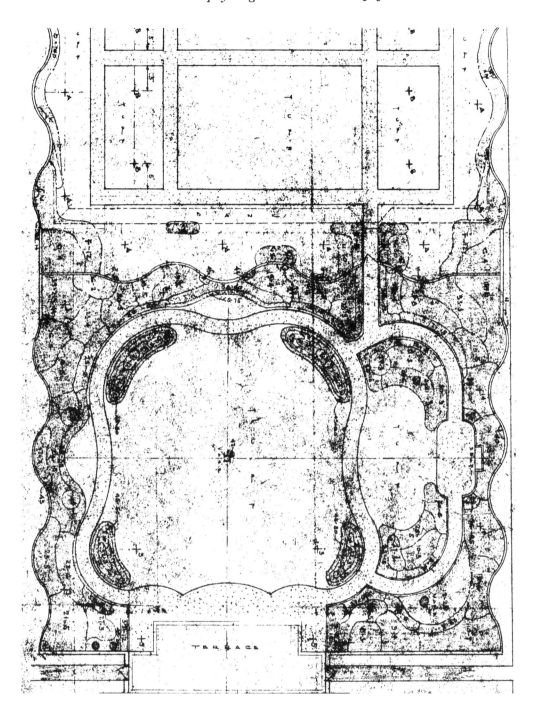

University of Virginia: Pavilion I

ELEVATION OF WEST WALL

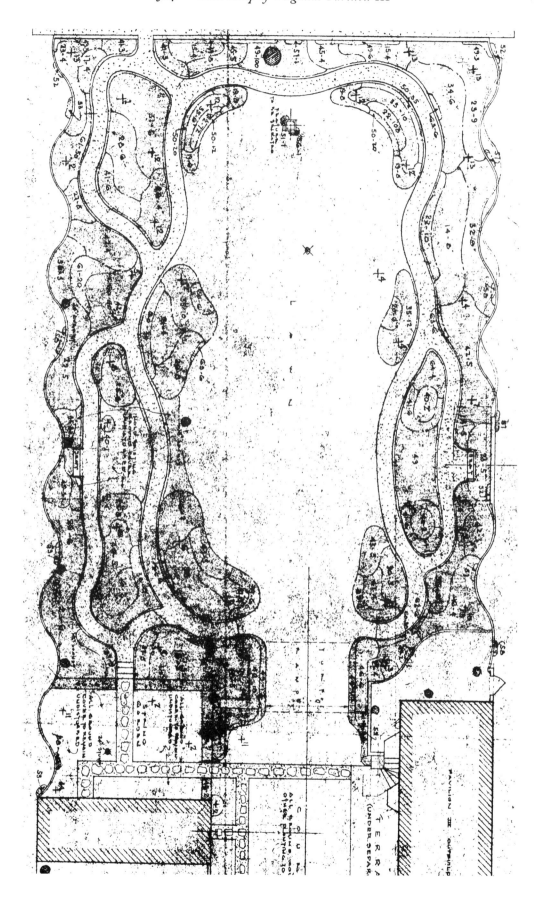

University of Virginia: Pavilion III

University of Virginia: Pavilion V

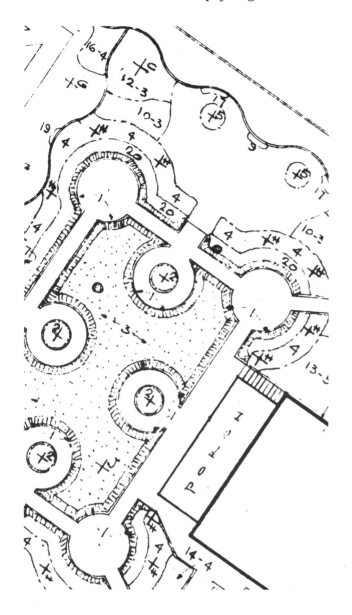

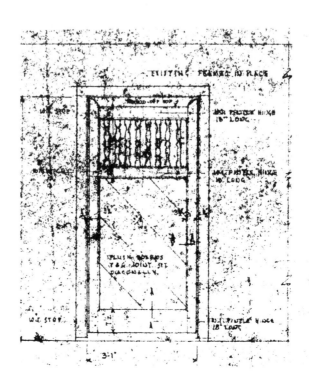

University of Virginia: Pavilion VII

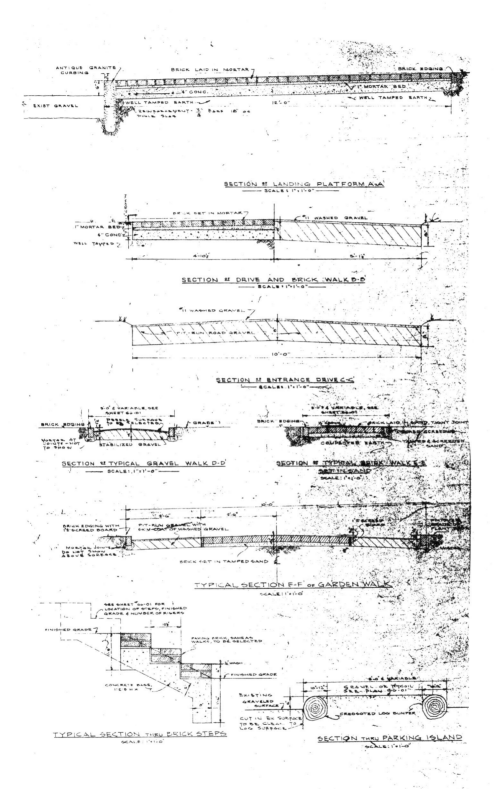

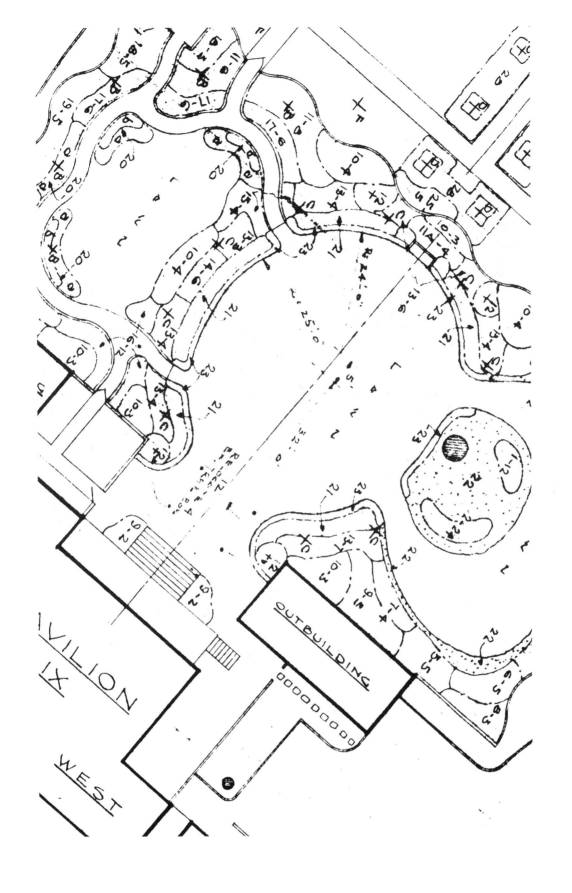

University of Virginia: Pavilion IX

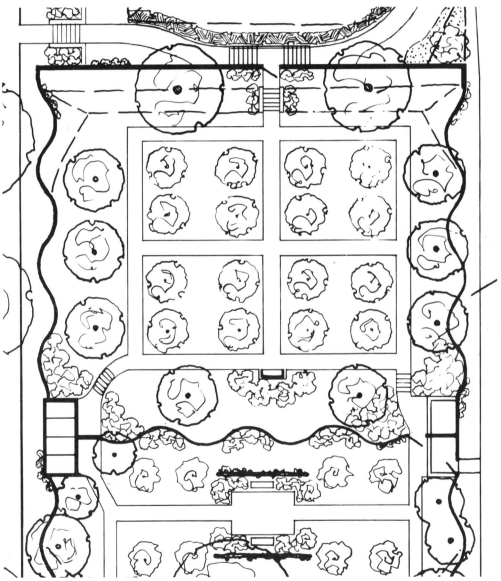

University of Virginia: Pavilion II

University of Virginia: Pavilion IV

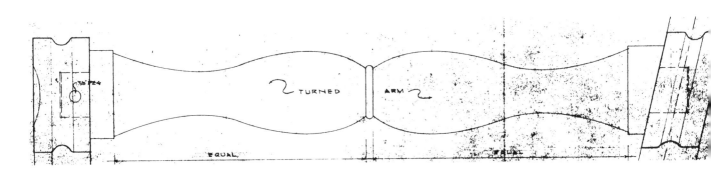

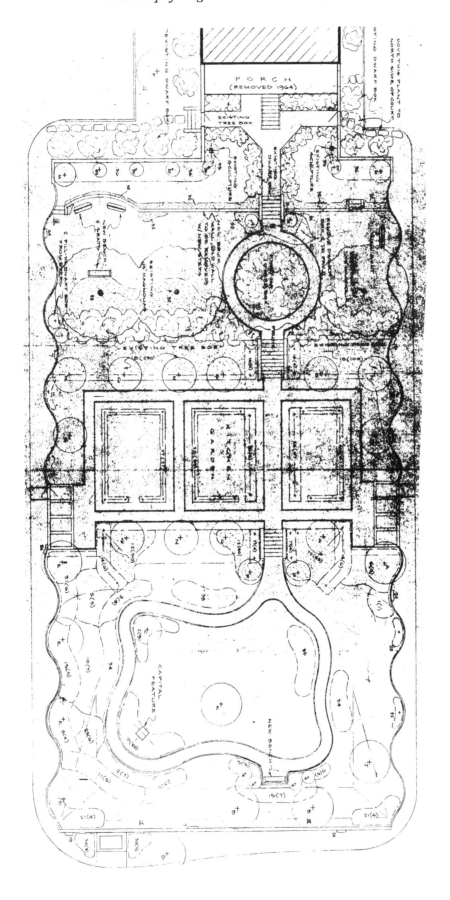

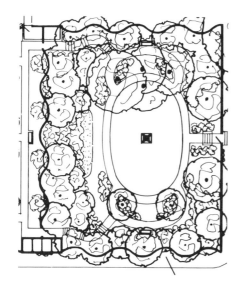

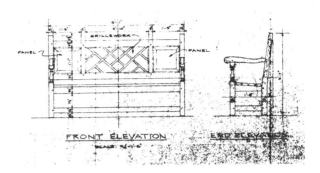

University of Virginia: Pavilion VI

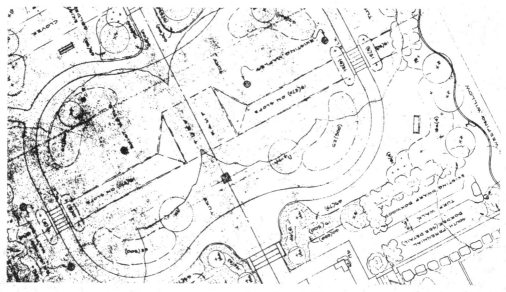

University of Virginia: Pavilion VIII

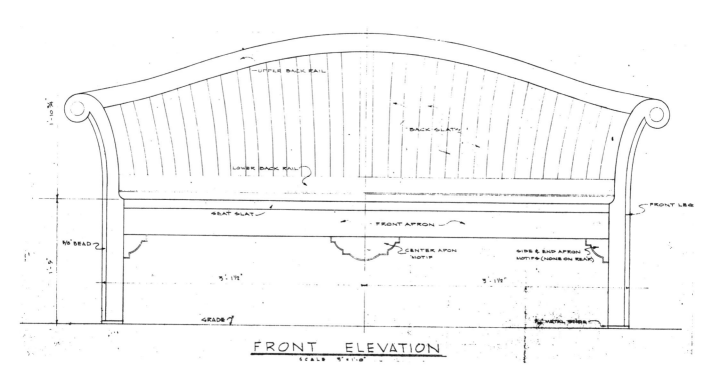

FRONT   ELEVATION
SCALE 3"=1'-0"

University of Virginia: Pavilion X

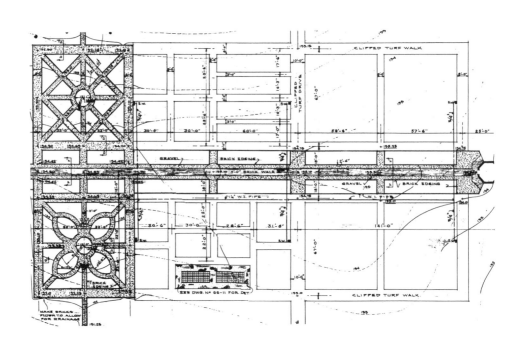

Woodlawn

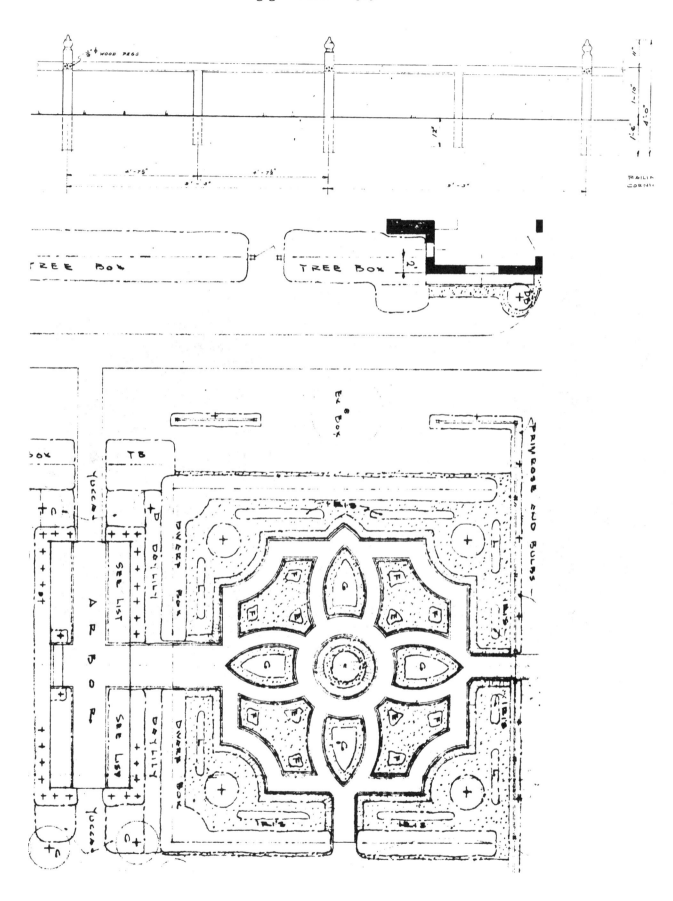

Adam Thoroughgood House

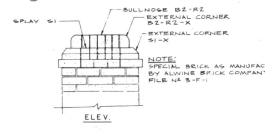

The Mews: Richmond

Christ Church: Lancaster

Mary Washington House

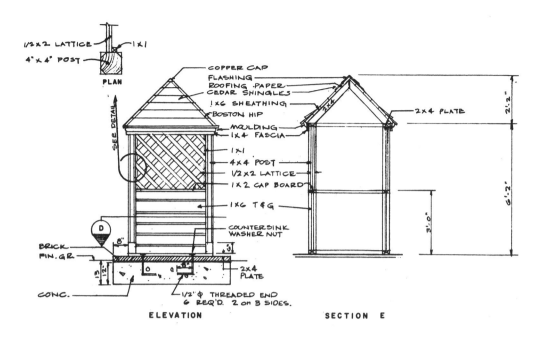

1/2x2 LATTICE — — 1x1
4" x 4" POST
PLAN

SEE DETAIL

COPPER CAP
FLASHING
ROOFING PAPER
CEDAR SHINGLES
1x6 SHEATHING
BOSTON HIP
MOULDING
1x4 FASCIA
1x1
4x4 POST
1/2x2 LATTICE
1x2 CAP BOARD
1x6 T&G
COUNTERSINK
WASHER NUT

2x4 PLATE

2x4 PLATE

2'-2"
3'-0"
6'-2"

BRICK
FIN. GR.
CONC.

13
12

8"

3"

2x4 PLATE

1/2" Ø THREADED END
6 REQ'D. 2 on 3 SIDES.

ELEVATION   SECTION E

Scotchtown

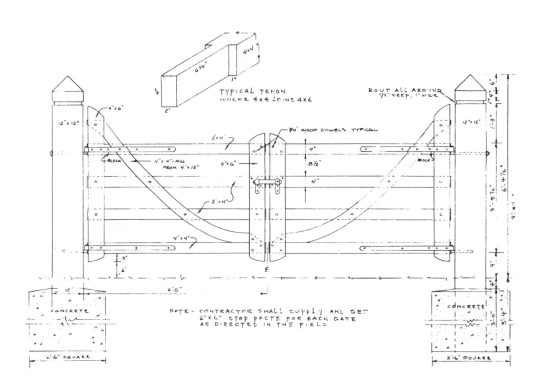

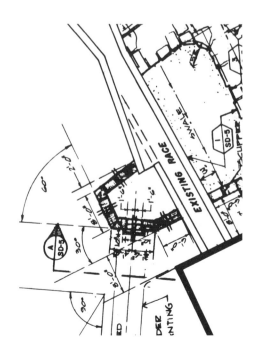

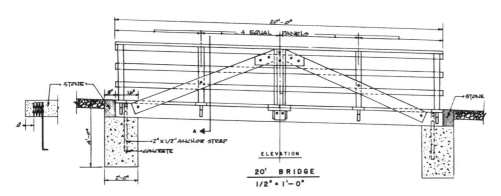

STONE

2" X 1/2" ANCHOR STRAP

CONCRETE

STONE

A

ELEVATION

20' BRIDGE

1/2" = 1'-0"

20'-0"

4 EQUAL PANELS

Burwell-Morgan Mill

Kent-Valentine House

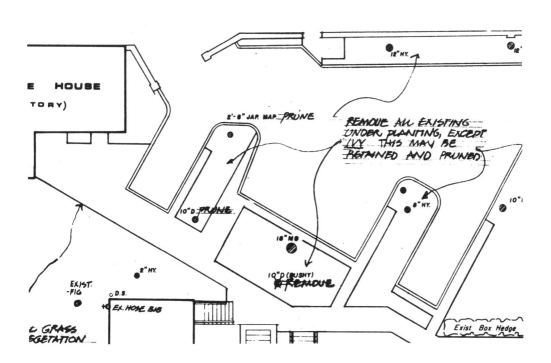

Bibliography

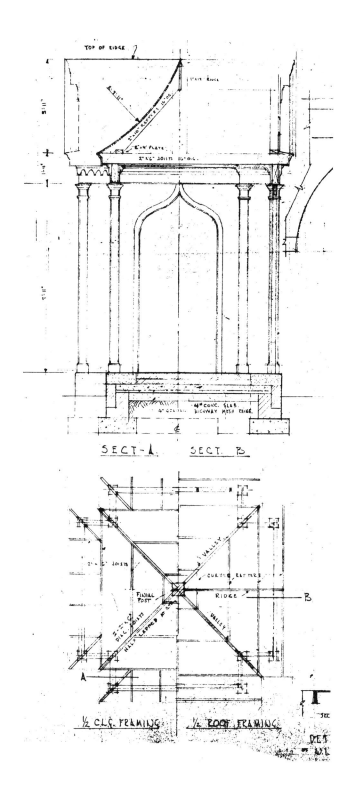

TOP OF RIDGE

STAIR RIDGE

R.1'-1"

2"X10" RAFTERS @ 16" O.C.

6"X6" PLATE

2"X6" JOISTS 16" O.C.

4" CONC. SLAB.
HIGHWAY MESH REINF.
4" GRAVEL

5'-11"

1'-4"

7'-11"

SECT-A.   SECT. B

VALLEY

CURVED RAFTERS

FINIAL POST

RIDGE   B

2"X6" JOISTS

2"X12" CLG.
DIAG. JOISTS
HALF LAPPED AT C.

VALLEY

A

½ CLG. FRAMING   ½ ROOF FRAMING

SEE

DET
N.1

Bibliography

Abercrombie, John. *Every Man His Own Gardener*. London: S. Crowder, 1779.

Allan, Mea. *The Tradescants, their Plants, Gardens and Museum*. London: Michael Joseph, n.d.

American Association of Architectural Bibliographers. *Papers*. Edited by William B. O'Neal. 10 vols. Charlottesville: University Press of Virginia, 1965–73.

Ayrton, Maxwell. *Wrought Iron and its Decorative Use*. New York: Scribner's, 1929.

Bailey, Liberty Hyde. *Standard Cyclopedia of Horticulture*. 3 vols. New York: Macmillan Co., 1928.

—— and Ethel Zoe. *Hortus: A Concise Dictionary of Gardening, General Horticulture and Cultivated Plants in North America*. New York: Macmillan Co., 1930.

Bartram, William. *Travels of William Bartram*. Philadelphia: Dover Publications, 1928.

Benjamin, Asher. *The American Builder's Companion or a New System of Architecture*. Boston: Etheridge and Bliss, 1806.

Betts, Edwin Morris, ed. *Thomas Jefferson's Farm Book*. Princeton: Princeton University Press, 1953.

——. *Thomas Jefferson's Garden Book*. Philadelphia: American Philosophical Society, 1944.

——, and Hazelhurst Bolton Perkins. *Thomas Jefferson's Flower Garden at Monticello*. Charlottesville: University Press of Virginia, 1971.

Boggs, Kate Doggett. *Prints and Plants of Old Gardens*. Richmond: Garrett & Massie, 1932.

Bréhout, Thomas Collings. *Cordon Training of Fruit Trees*. Boston: Hovey & Co., 1864.

Brooklyn Botanic Garden. *Handbook on Herbs* (a special printing of *Plants and Gardens*, vol. 14, no. 2). Committee from the New York Unit of the American Herb Society, 1958.

Bullock, Orin M., Jr. *The Restoration Manual*. Norwalk, Conn.: Silvermine Publishers, 1966.

Byrd, William. *Another Secret Diary of William Byrd*. Edited by Maude H. Woodfin and Marion Tinling. Richmond: Dietz Press, 1942.

Cabell, Nathaniel Francis. *Early History of the University of Virginia as Contained in the Letters of Thomas Jefferson and Joseph C. Cabell*. Edited by J. W. Randolph. Richmond: n.p., 1856.

Carson, Jane. *Travelers in Tidewater Virginia 1700–1800*. Charlottesville: University Press of Virginia, 1965.

Chastellux, Jean-Francois, Marquis de. *Travels in North America in the Years 1780, 1781, 1782*. Translated and edited by Howard C. Rice, Jr. 2 vols. Chapel Hill: University of North Carolina Press, 1963.

Claiborne, Herbert A. *Comments on Virginia Brickwork before 1800*. N.p.: The Walpole Society, 1957.

Downing, Andrew Jackson. *The Fruit and Fruit Trees of America*. New York: J. Wiley, 1851.

——. *Theory and Practice of Landscape Gardening*. The 1859 6th ed. supplemented by Henry Winthrop Sargent. New York: Funk & Wagnalls, 1967.

Dutton, Joan Parry. *The Flower World of Williamsburg*. New York: Holt, Rinehart & Winston, 1962.

——. *The Flower World of Williamsburg*. Rev. ed. with color photography by Frank J. Davis. New York: Holt, Rinehart & Winston, 1973.

Earle, Swepson. *The Chesapeake Bay Country*. Baltimore: Thomsen-Ellis Co., 1929.

Foster, F. Gordon. *The Gardener's Fern Book*. Princeton: Van Nostrand, 1964.

Frick, George Frederick, and Raymond Phineas Stearns. *Mark Catesby, the Colonial Audubon*. Urbana: University of Illinois Press, 1961.

Garden Club of America. *Gardens of Colony and State*. Edited by Alice G. B. Lockwood. 2 vols. New York: Scribner's, 1934.

Garden Club of Virginia. *Historic Garden Week in Virginia*. Richmond: 1929—A guide book published annually.

——. *Homes and Gardens in Old Virginia*. Edited by Frances Archer Christian and Sussanne Williams Massie. Richmond: Garrett & Massie, 1950.

Gardiner, John, and David Hepburn. *The American Gardener*. Washington, D.C.: Samuel H. Smith, 1804.

Gothein, Marie Luise. *A History of Garden Art*. Edited by Walter P. Wright. Translated by Mrs. Archer-Hind. New York: E. P. Dutton & Co., 1928.

Halfpenny, William. *The Modern Builder's Assistant*. London: Robert Sayer, 1747.

Hay, Roy, and Patrick M. Synge. *The Color Dictionary of Flowers and Plants for Home and Garden*. New York: Crown Publishers, 1969.

Hosmer, Charles Bridgham. *Presence of the Past*. New York: Putnam, 1965. A history of the preservation movement in the United States before Williamsburg.

Hume, Ivor Nöel. *Historical Archaeology*. New York: Alfred A. Knopf, 1969.

International Registration Authority for Roses, The American Rose Society, and The McFarland Company, comps. *Modern Roses 7: The International Check-list of Roses*. Harrisburg, Pa.: McFarland Co., 1969.

James, John [Dezallier d'Argentville, Antoine Joseph]. *James on Gardening*. London: Bernard Lintot, 1728.

James River Garden Club. *Historic Gardens of Virginia*. Richmond: William Byrd Press, 1923.

Kimball, Sidney Fiske. *Thomas Jefferson, Architect*. New York: Da Capo Press, 1968.

Kocher, Lawrence A., and Howard Dearstyne. *Colonial Williamsburg, Its Buildings and Grounds*. New York: Holt, Rinehart & Winston, 1949.

Lambeth, William Alexander, and Warren R. Manning. *Thomas Jefferson as an Architect and a Designer of Landscape*. Boston: Houghton Mifflin Co., 1913.

Langley, Batty. *New Principles of Gardening*. London: A. Bettesworth and J. Batley, 1728.

La Quintinie, Jean de. *The Complete Gard'ner*. Abridged by George London and Henry Wise. 6th ed. London: A. and W. Bell, 1717.

Lee, Frederick P. *The Azalea Book*. New York: Van Nostrand, 1958.

Le Rouge, George Louis. *Jardins Anglo-Chinois*. Paris: Le Rouge, 1776–85; 1777.

Little, Bryan. "Cambridge and the Campus: An English Antecedent for the Lawn of the University of Virginia." *Virginia Magazine of History and Biography* 79 (1971), 190–201.

Loudon, John Claudius. *Encyclopedia of Gardening*. London: Longman, Brown, Green, and Longmans, 1835.

——. *Hints on the Formation of Gardens and Pleasure Grounds*. London: Gale Curtis and Fenner, 1813.

——. *The Landscape Gardening and Landscape Architecture of the Late Humphrey Repton, esq*. London: Longman & Co., 1840.

——. *A Treatise on Farming, Improving and Managing Country Residences*. 1806. Westmeade, England: Gregs International, 1971.

Martin, Mrs. James Bland. *Follow the Green Arrow*. Richmond: Dietz Press, 1970.

Miller [Millar], Philip. *Dictionaire des Jardiniers*. London: N.p., 1731.

M'Mahon, Bernard. *The American Gardener's Calendar*. 11th ed. Philadelphia: J. B. Lippincott & Co., 1857.

National Register of Historic Places. Washington, D.C.: National Park Service, 1969. For sale by the Superintendent of Documents, U.S. Government Printing Office.

National Trust for Historic Preservation and Colonial Williamsburg. *Historic Preservation Today: Essays Presented to the Seminar on Preservation and Restoration, Williamsburg, Virginia*. Charlottesville: University Press of Virginia, 1966.

Nichols, Frederick Doveton. *Thomas Jefferson's Architectural Drawings*. Charlottesville: Thomas Jefferson Memorial Foundation and University Press of Virginia, 1961.

——, and James A. Bear, Jr. *Monticello*. Monticello, Va.: Thomas Jefferson Memorial Foundation, 1967.

Niederer, Frances J. *The Town of Fincastle, Virginia*. Charlottesville: University Press of Virginia, 1965.

Palladio, Andrea. *The Architecture of A. Palladio in Four Books*. Revised. N.p.: Giacoma Leoni, 1715.

Patton, John Shelton. *Jefferson's University*. Charlottesville: Michie Co., 1915.

Peden, William, ed. *Thomas Jefferson: Notes on the State of Virginia*. Chapel Hill: University of North Carolina Press, 1955.

Preston, Nelly. *Paths of Glory*. Richmond: Whittet & Shepperson, 1961.

Primatt, Stephen. *The City and Country Builder*. London: John Wright and Assignes of Sam Speed, 1680.

Randolph, John, Jr. *A Treatise on Gardening by a Citizen of Virginia*. Reprinted from *The American Gardener*, by John Gardiner and David Hepburn. 3d ed., 1826. Edited by M. F. Warner. Richmond: Appeals Press for William Parks Club, 1924.

Rath. Frederick L. *NYSHA Selective Reference Guide to Historic Preservation*. Cooperstown, N.Y.: New York State Historical Association, 1966.

Rehder, Alfred. *Manuel of Cultivated Trees and Shrubs Hardy in North America.* New York: Macmillan Co., 1934.

Reid, John. *The Scots Gard'ner.* Edinburgh: D. Lindsay and his partners, 1683.

Roberts, Edith Adelaide. *American Plants for American Gardens—1881.* New York: Macmillan Co., 1929.

Roop, Guy. *Villas and Palaces of Andrea Palladio.* Milan: Ghezzi, 1968.

Salmon, William. *Palladio Londinensis.* London: S. Birt et al., 1748. Typical handbook of the kind borrowed by Jefferson from a cabinetmaker near the College of William and Mary while he was a student there.

Schmidt, Carl F. *Fences, Gates and Garden Houses.* Rochester, N.Y.: Published by the author, 1963.

Stemler, Dorothy. *The Book of Old Roses.* Boston: Bruce Humphries Publishers, 1966.

Stotz, Charles Morse. *The Early Architecture of Western Pennsylvania.* New York: William Helbrun for the Buhl Foundation, Pittsburgh, 1936.

Swem, E. G., ed. *Brothers of the Spade.* Barre, Mass.: Barre Gazette, 1957. Correspondence of Peter Collinson of London and John Custis of Williamsburg.

Taylor, Raymond Leech. *Plants of Colonial Days.* Richmond: Dietz Press, 1952.

Thomas, Graham Stuart, F.L.S. *The Old Shrub Roses,* rev. ed. London: Phoenix House, 1965.

Three Centuries of Botany in North America. New York: Rockefeller University Press, 1967. Catalogue of an Exhibit.

U.S. National Park Service. *Historic American Building Survey.* Washington, D.C.: Library of Congress, 1938. Catalogue of the measured drawings and photographs.

Waterman, Thomas Tileston. *The Mansions of Virginia.* Chapel Hill: University of North Carolina Press, 1945.

Wayland, John W. *Historic Homes of Northern Virginia.* Staunton, Va.: McClure Co., 1937.

Whateley, Thomas. *Observations on Modern Gardening.* London: N.p., 1770.

Wigginton, Brooks E. *Trees and Shrubs for the Southeast.* Athens: University of Georgia Press, 1963.

Wright, Richardson. *The Story of Gardening.* New York: Dover Publications, 1934.

Wyman, Donald. *Shrubs and Vines for American Gardens.* Rev. ed. New York: Macmillan Co., 1969.

Zucker, Isabel. *Flowering Shrubs.* Princeton: Van Nostrand Co., 1966.

For sources of authentic period plant material, information may be supplied by writing The Chairman of the Horticultural Committee, The Garden Club of Virginia, Kent-Valentine House, 12 East Franklin Street, Richmond, Virginia 23226.

On-Site Brochures. Practically all the projects included in this book have their own printed brochures with brief histories that can be found in Virginia travel agencies as well as on the sites.

Index

Page numbers in *italics* refer to illustrations.

Abingdon, Barter Theatre, 95–96

"Academical Village," 115, *123*

Adam Thoroughgood House, 205–15, *324–25*; arbor, 206, *207*, *213*; architectural style, 205; "beasties," 206; "beasties" support, *215*; bench, 206, *208*; boxwood, *204*; brickwork, 205; espalier, *208*, *214*; fence, 206, *213*; The Garden Club of Virginia and, 205; gate, *213*; Alden Hopkins and, 205; landholdings, 205; parterres, 205, *211*, *212*; plant species, 209; planting plan, 205–6; presentation plan, *210*; site, 205; topiary, 206; well house, *207*

Adam Thoroughgood House Foundation, 205

Albemarle Garden Club, 157

American Gardener, The (Gardiner and Hepburn), 118

American Revolution: Fielding Lewis and, 3; Daniel Morgan and, 261

Aquia stone, 237

Arbor: Adam Thoroughgood House, 206, *207*, *213*; Mary Washington House, *246*; Woodrow Wilson Birthplace, 30

Archaeological survey: Bruton Parish Church, 61; Gunston Hall, 101; Rolfe-Warren House, 43, 45, *49*, *50*; Scotchtown, 249, 250; Stratford Hall, *14*, 18–19, *25*; University of Virginia gardens, 117, 149; Wilton, 54; Woodlawn, 191–92, *196*

Architects: William Buckland, 99; Samuel Darst, 39; John Jordan, 39; William Thornton, 189

Architecture: Classic Revival style, 39; Corinthian order, 15–16, 125, 157, 269; Doric order, 91, 118; Georgian style, 53, 76, 189, 229; Gothic style, 61, 269; of great houses, 15; Greek Revival style, 29, 269; H-plan, 15; Ionic order, 269; Jacobean style, 15; Palladian style, 76, 99, 118; Revival styles, 269; Roman Revival style, 76; Tudor style, 269; University of Virginia pavilions, 118; *see also specific buildings*

Arms, for American Revolution, 3

Association for the Preservation of Virginia Antiquities (APVA), 45, 46, 235, 250

Augusta Academy, 39

Augusta Female Seminary, 29

Ayres, Harvard, 250

Baldwin, Mary Julia, 29

Barrier post, Wilton, *58*

Barter Theatre (Abingdon), *94*, 95–96, *298–99*; The Garden Club of Virginia and, 95; plant species, 96; planting plan, 95; site, 95; terrace, 95

Baths of Diocletian, 118

Battle of Fredericksburg, 3

"Beasties," Adam Thoroughgood House, 206, *215*

Benches and benchwork: Adam Thoroughgood House, 206, *208*; Mary Washington House, *246*; The Mews (Richmond), *219*, 220, *224*; Scotchtown, 253, *259*; University of Virginia gardens, 125, 131, 139, 142, 151, 157, 161, 167, 173, *179–87*; Wilton, *56*

Betts, Edwin Morris, 77, 78; *Thomas Jefferson's Flower Garden at Monticello*, 84; *Thomas Jefferson's Garden Book*, 75n

Betts, Mary Hall, *123*

Blenheim, 131, 161

Blue Ridge Garden Club, 39

Boone, Daniel, 95

Boxwood and boxwood borders: Adam Thoroughgood House, *204*; Gunston Hall, 99, 101, 103–4; Mary Washington House, 235, *236*, 237; Mary Washington Monument, *72*; Scotchtown, *248*, *252*; Stratford Hall, *18*

Brick construction, 15

Brickwork: Adam Thoroughgood House, 205; Bruton Parish Church, 61, 62; Christ Church (Lancaster), 231; Christ Church (Middlesex), *86*; Mary Washington Monument, 70; The Mews (Richmond), *226*; Stratford, 15, 16, 19, 20; Wilton, 53, 57; Woodrow Wilson Birthplace, 29

Bridges, Burwell-Morgan Mill, *263*

Bruton Parish Church, 61–67, *290–91*; architectural styles, 61; brickwork, 61, 62; churchyard, *60*, *66*, *67*; churchyard restoration funding, 62; Civil War and, 53; excavation, 61; The Garden Club of Virginia and, 61–62; pavement, *62*; plant species, 63; planting plan, 62; planting plan for maintenance, 64–65; Arthur Shurcliff and, 62; site, 61; Alexander Spotswood and, 61; walks, 62; walls, 61, 62

Buckland, William, 99

Burwell, Nathaniel, 261

Burwell-Morgan Mill, 261–67, *262*, *263*, *332–33*; bridges, *263*; construction details, *266*, *267*; fence, *263*; The Garden Club of Virginia and,

Burwell-Morgan Mill (*cont.*)
263; Ralph Griswold and, 263; grounds rehabilitation, 263; parking area, 263; paths, 263; plant species, 264; planting plan, *265*; presentation plan, *260*; restoration, 261; site, 261

Capitals: Corinthian order, 125, 157; at Stratford Hall, 16; University of Virginia garden ornaments, 125, *126*, 131, 139, 157, *158*
Caroline, queen of England, 15
Carriage house, Kent-Valentine House, *270*, 271
Carter, John, 229
Carter, Robert ("King"), 229, 231
Carter's Grove, 261
Cary, Wilson Miles, 249
Cedars, Christ Church (Lancaster), 231, *232*
Charlottesville: Monticello, 75; University of Virginia, 115
Cheatham, B. F., III, *27*
Chicheley, Sir Henry, 87
Chippendale bench, 157
Chiswell, Charles, 249
Chiswell, John, 249
Christ Church (Fincastle), 91–93, *297*; fence, 91, *92*; front elevation, *90*; The Garden Club of Virginia and, 91, 92; gate, 91; pavement, 91; plant species, 93; planting plan, 92; site, 91; street lamp, 91, *92*; structural alterations, 91; terrace, 91; walks, 91; walls, 91, *92*
Christ Church (Lancaster), 229–33, *231*, *232*, *327*; architectural style, 229, 231; brickwork, 231; cedars, 231; dogwood planting, *228*; The Garden Club of Virginia and, 229; gates, 229; Ralph E. Griswold and, 229; parking area, *230*, 231; plant species, 232, planting plan, 229, 231, *233*; site, 229; splash course, 231; walks, 229
Christ Church (Middlesex), 87–89, *296*; cemetery, 87; churchyard sketch, 87, *89*; The Garden Club of Virginia and, 87; parish vestry book, 87; plan, 89; site, 87; walls, *86*, 87, *88*
Christchurch (Middlesex), 87
Church architecture: Christ Church (Fincastle), 91–93, *297*; Christ Church (Lancaster), 229–33, *231*, *232*, *327*; Christ Church (Middlesex), 87–89, *296*; Lee Memorial Chapel, *41*, *284–85*; Saint John's Church, Richmond, *227*
City and County Builder, The (Primatt), 15
Civil War: Bruton Parish Church and, 53; Kenmore and, 3, 5; Mary Washington Monument and, 69
Claiborne, Herbert, 19, 53
Claiborne & Taylor, 53
Clarke County Historical Association, 261, 263
Cleveland, Grover, 70
Closen, Ludwig Von, 249
Collected Works (Shenstone), 75
Colonial Dames, *see* National Society of the Colonial Dames of America

Conn, William Young, 95
Corinthian order, 15–16, 125, 157, 269

Darst, Samuel, 39
Daughters of the American Revolution, Washington-Lewis Chapter, 5
DeVere, Schele, 157
Dezallier d'Argentville, Antoine Joseph, *The Theory and Practice of Gardening*, 118, 135, 157, 167
Dick, Charles, 3
Doric order, 91, 118

Encyclopedia of Gardening (Loudon), 135
English landscape style, 75, 99, 101, 161, 206, 253
Episcopalians, 229
Espalier: Adam Thoroughgood House, 206, *208*, *214*; Stratford Hall, *19*
Excavations: Bruton Parish Church, 61; Gunston Hall, 101; Rolfe-Warren House, 43, 45, 49, *50*; Scotchtown, 249, *250*; Stratford Hall, *14*, 18–19, *25*; University of Virginia gardens, 117, 149; Wilton, 54; Woodlawn, 191–92, *196*

F. W. and R. King (Baltimore), 237
Fairfax, Lord, 229
Federal Hill, garden pavilion, *6*, 8
Fences: Adam Thoroughgood House, 206, *213*; Burwell-Morgan Mill, 263; Christ Church (Fincastle), 91, *92*; Kent-Valentine House, 271, *275*; Mary Washington Monument, 71; The Mews (Richmond), *224*; Rolfe-Warren House, 45, 47; Scotchtown, 250, *259*; Woodlawn, 191, *202*, *203*
Fern species: Burwell-Morgan Mill, 264; The Mews (Richmond), 221; University of Virginia gardens, 153, 159, 162
Ferry Farm, 235
Fifer, John, 29
Fincastle, Christ Church, 91
Fincastle Declaration, 91
Fish pond, Monticello, 78–79
Foundation for Historic Christ Church, 229
Fredericksburg, 3; gun factory, 3; Kenmore, 69; Mary Washington House, 235; Mary Washington Monument, 69
Fry-Jefferson map, 53

Garden Club of Virginia: Adam Thoroughgood House and, 205; Barter Theatre and, 95; Bruton Parish Church and, 61–62; Burwell-Morgan Mill and, 263; Christ Church (Fincastle) and, 91, 92; Christ Church (Lancaster) and, 229; Christ Church (Middlesex) and, 87; Gunston Hall and, 101; Kenmore and, 5, 7–8; Kent-Valentine House and, 269, 271; Lee Memorial Chapel and, 39, 40; Mary Washington House and, 235; Mary Washington Monument and,

Garden Club of Virginia (*cont.*)
  70, 71; The Mews (Richmond) and, 217; Monticello and, 77–78, 80; Rolfe-Warren House and, 45, 46; Scotchtown and, 250; Stratford and, 18, 20; University of Virginia gardens and, 117, 118, 123, 149; Wilton and, 53, 57; Woodlawn and, 189; Woodrow Wilson Birthplace and, 30, 32
Garden design: formal style, 75, 77, 99, 101, 118, 206; naturalistic style, 75, 77, 118, 157, 161; *see also* Planting plan
Garden furniture: The Mews (Richmond), *219*, 220; Woodrow Wilson Birthplace, 32
Garden ornament: Mary Washington House, 237; The Mews (Richmond), 220; University of Virginia, 125, 131, 139, 157, *158*, *161*
Garden planting plan, *see* Planting plan
Garden presentation plan, *see* Presentation plan
Garden structures, *see specific structures*
Gardening (Langley), 192
Gardiner, John, *The American Gardener*, 118
Gas lamp, The Mews (Richmond), *219*
Gate: Adam Thoroughgood House, *213*; Christ Church (Fincastle), 91; Christ Church (Lancaster), 229; Kenmore, *13*; Kent-Valentine House, *268*, 271, *275*; Mary Washington House, 237, *245*, *246*; The Mews (Richmond), 220; Scotchtown, 250, 251, *252*, *259*; Stratford Hall, *17*, 20; University of Virginia gardens, *119*, 125, *129*, 135, *137*, *138*, *147*, 151, 161, *172*; Wilton, *54*, 57; Woodlawn, 192, *202*, *203*
Gazebo, Gunston Hall, *102*
Geddy, Vernon M., 62
Gibboney, Stuart, 77, 78
Gillette, Charles F., 7, *9*, *10*, *12*, *13*, 30, 32, *33*, *36*, 39–40, *41*
Goldenrain tree, 167
Goodwin, William Archer Rutherfoord, 61
Gordon, Samuel, 3
Great houses on U.S. 1, 189
Greenleaf, James, 5, 7
Griswold, Ralph E., 32, *41*, 118, *154–56*, *160*, *171*, *178*, *179*, *181–87*, 217, 229, 235, 263
Griswold, Winters, & Swain, 37, *222–26*, 233, *242–46*, 250, *260*, 263, *265–67*, 271, *273–75*
Grymes family, 87
Gunston Hall, 99–113, 189, *300–301*; boxwood, 99, 101, 103–4; William Buckland and, 99; central allée, *103*; entrance, *100*, *107*; excavations, 101; The Garden Club of Virginia and, 101; garden design, 99, 101; garden restoration, 101; garden view, *104*; gazebo, *102*; Louis Hertle and, 99, 101; Alden Hopkins and, 101; landholdings, 99; landscape plan, *109*; National Society of the Colonial Dames of America and, 101; owners, 99, 101; Palladian drawing room, 99; parking plan, *107*; parterres, 101, *105*, *110*, *111*; pavilions, 101, 103, *112*, *113*; plant list, *110*, *111*; plant species, 106; planting plan, 101, 103, *109*, *110*,

111; Potomac River vista, 99, 103; presentation plan, *108*; site, 99; terrace, 103; topiary, 101; willow oaks, *100*; woodcarvings, 99

Hampton, 118, 125
Harvard University, Clark Fund for Research in Landscape Design, 19
Henry, Patrick, 217, 249
Hepburn, David, *The American Gardener*, 118
Herbaceous plant species: Adam Thoroughgood House, 209; Bruton Parish Church, 63; Burwell-Morgan Mill, 264; Christ Church (Fincastle), 93; Christ Church (Lancaster), 232; Gunston Hall, 106; Kenmore, 9; Kent-Valentine House, 272; Lee Memorial Chapel, 40; Mary Washington House, 240–41; Mary Washington Monument, 71; The Mews (Richmond), 221; Monticello, 83–84; Scotchtown, 254; Stratford Hall, 22; University of Virginia gardens, 145, 153, 159, 162, 168, 175–76; Woodlawn, 194–95; Woodrow Wilson Birthplace, 34
Hertle, Louis, 99, 101
Historic Garden Week, 8, 18, 78, 123, 149, 271
Historic Richmond Foundation, 217
Hopkins, Alden, 20, *26*, 46, 57, 70, 73, 101, *107–13*, 117, 118, *120*, 125, *127–29*, *133*, *136–38*, *141*, *146*, *147*, 149, *154*, *164*, 189, 192, *196*, *201*, *202*, *205*, *210–15*
Hotel de Salm (Paris), 76
Howard, William Key, 5

Innocenti, Umberto, 20
Ionic order, 269
Ironwork: Kent-Valentine House, 269; The Mews (Richmond), *216*, *218–20*, *225*; Wilton, 54
Irvington, Christ Church, 229

Jackson, Andrew, 69
James, John, *James on Gardening*, 118
James River vista, Wilton, *55*
Jardins Anglo-Chinois (Le Rouge), 139, 173
Jefferson, Thomas, 139; "Academical Village," 115, *123*; as architect, 75–76; Blenheim garden visits, 131, 161; English naturalistic garden design and, 75, 77, 118, 157, 161; family cemetery, 80; garden sketches, 75, 78; goldenrain tree and, 167; grave, 80; horticultural diary, 75; as horticulturist, 80; landholdings, 75, 77; library on gardening, 118; as minister to France, 76; Monticello and, 75–80; notes on English gardens, 118; plant importation, 151; University of Virginia and, 115, 117–18, 125
Johnson, J. Ambler, 250
Jordan, John, 39

Kenmore, 3–13, 235, *278–79*; bowers, 8; Civil War and, 3, 5; entrance lawn, 5; The Garden Club of Virginia and, 5, 7–8; garden pavilion,

Kenmore (*cont.*)

6, 8; garden plan, *9, 12*; gate, *13*; Charles Gillette and, 7; James Greenleaf and, 5, 7; kitchen restoration, 8; landholdings, 3, 5, 8; landscape restoration funding, 7–8; owners, 3, 5; plant species, 9; planting plan, 8; restoration land purchases, 8; restoration plan, 8; site, 3; terraces, 8; walks, *4, 7, 11*; walls, *6*, 8, *10*, 13, 70

Kenmore Association, 5, 7, 8

Kent, Horace, 269

Kent-Valentine House, 269–76, *334–36*; architectural style, 269; carriage house, *270,* 271; construction details, *275*; East Lawn, *271*; fence, 271, *275*; The Garden Club of Virginia and, 269, 271; Griswold, Winters, & Swain and, 271; ironwork, 269; owners, 269; parking area, *270,* 271; plant species, 272; planting plan, *274*; presentation plan, 273; restoration funding, 271; site, 269; walks, 271; walls, 271; West Lawn, *271*

Kimball, Sidney Fiske, 15, 20, 77

Kitchen garden: Mary Washington House, 237; Scotchtown, 251; University of Virginia, 157

Knight, James, 117, 118

Knight, William C., 53

Lamp: Christ Church (Fincastle), *92*; The Mews (Richmond), *219*

Lancaster, Christ Church, 229

Landscape architects: B. F. Cheatham III, 27; Charles F. Gillette, 7, *9, 10, 12, 13*, 30, 32, *33, 36*, 39–40, *41*; James Greenleaf, 5, 7; Ralph E. Griswold, 32, *41*, 118, *154–56, 160, 171, 178, 179, 181–87*, 217, 229, 235, 263; Griswold, Winters, & Swain, 37, *222–26, 233, 242–46,* 250, *260*, 263, *265–67*, 271, *273–75*; Alden Hopkins, 20, *26*, 46, 57, 70, *73*, 101, *107–13*, 117, 118, *120*, 125, *127–29, 133, 136–38, 141, 146, 147, 149, 154, 164*, 189, 192, *196, 201, 202*, 205, *210–15*; Umberto Innocenti, 20; W. W. LaPrade & Bros., *23*; Donald H. Parker, 118, *154–56, 160, 171, 178–87*; Arthur A. Shurcliff, 18, 19, 45, *49–51, 59*, 62, *67*; Morley J. Williams, 19, 20, *24, 25*; Garland A. Wood, 85

Langley, Batty, *Gardening*, 192

Le Rouge, George Louis, *Jardins Anglo-Chinois,* 139, 173

Lee, Henry, 16

Lee, Mrs. Henry (Anne Hill Carter), 16

Lee, Henry (son of Henry), 16

Lee, Mrs. Henry (Anne McCarty), 16

Lee, Philip Ludwell, 16; inventory, 18

Lee, Robert E., 16; tomb sculpture, 39; Washington and Lee University and, 39; *see also* Lee Memorial Chapel

Lee, Thomas, 15, 16; inventory, 18

Lee Memorial Chapel, *38*, 39–41, *284–85*; construction of, 39; entrance, 40, *41*; The Garden

Club of Virginia and, 39, 40; Charles Gillette and, 39–40; memorial planting for, 39–40; parking area, 40; pavement, 39, 40; plant species, 40; site, 39; walks, 39

Levy, Uriah Phillips, 77

Lewis, Fielding, 3, 69, 189

Lewis, Mrs. Fielding (Betty Washington), 3, 69, 189, 235

Lewis, John, III, 3

Lewis, Lawrence, 189

Lewis, Mrs. Lawrence (Eleanor Parke [Nelly] Custis), 189, 191, 192

Lexington: Lee Memorial Chapel, 39; Washington and Lee University, 39

Liberty Hall, 39

Liggett, Barbara, 250

Loudon, John Claudius, *Encyclopedia of Gardening,* 135

Lynnhaven River, 205, 206

McGuffey, William A., 142

"McGuffey Ash," 142, *143*

Macomber, Walter M., 250

Madison, Mrs. James (Dolley Payne), 249

Manse, The (Staunton), *see* Woodrow Wilson Birthplace

Mary Baldwin College, 29–30

Mary Washington House, 235–47, *328–29*; arbor, *246*; Association for the Preservation of Virginia Antiquities and, 235; bench, *246*; boxwood, 235, *236*, 237; documentary research, 235; garden, *238*; The Garden Club of Virginia and, 235; garden construction plan, *244*; garden ornament, 237; garden restoration, 235; gate, 237, *245, 246*, Ralph E. Griswold and, 235; kitchen garden, 237; necessary (privy), 237, *239, 245*; outbuildings, 237; owners, 235; plant species, 240–41; planting plan, 237, *243*; presentation plan, *242*; site, 235; sundial, 235, 237, *239*; trellis, 237, *246*; walks, 235, 237; well house, 237, *245*

Mary Washington Monument, 69–73, *292–93*; boxwood-bordered entrance walk, *72*; brickwork, 70; Civil War and, 69; cornerstone, 69; entrance, *70*; fence, 71; The Garden Club of Virginia and, 70, 71; Alden Hopkins and, 70; paving, 70; plant species, 71; planting plan, 71, *73*; site, 69; walk, 70; walls, 70

Mary Washington Monument Association of Fredericksburg, 69

Mason, George, 99, 104, 189

Mason, Mrs. George (Ann Eilbeck), 99

Maverick, Peter, *114*, 115, 117, 149

Merton College, Oxford, stone spire, *161*

Mews, The (Richmond), 217–27, *326*; benches, *219*, 220, *224*; brickwork, *226*; entrance gate, 220; fence, *224*; The Garden Club of Virginia and, 217; garden furniture, *219*, 220; garden

Mews, The (Richmond) (*cont.*)
ornament, 220; gas lamp, *219*; Ralph E. Griswold and, 217; ironwork, *216, 218, 219*, 220, *225*; pavilion, *216*, 220, *224*; paving, 217, *219*, 220, *226*; plant species, 221; planting plan, 220, *222, 223*; railings, *218*; restoration area, 217; steps, *225*; terrace, 220; toolhouse, *226*; view of Saint John's Church, *227*; walks, 220; walls, *218*, 220, *225*
Middlesex County, Christ Church, 87
Mill, Burwell-Morgan, 261–67, *262, 263, 332–33*
Millwood, Burwell-Morgan Mill, 261
Monticello, 75–85, 118, 131, 167, *294–95*; architectural style, 76; East Front, 79; Ellipse, 79; fairs at, 78; family cemetery, 80; fish pond, 78–79; flower beds, *77*; garden, *74*; The Garden Club of Virginia and, 77–78, 80; garden loggia, 76; garden restoration, 78; Jefferson's garden sketches for, 75, 78; John Jordan and, 39; landholdings, 75; naturalistic garden design at, 76–77; original gardens, 75, 76–77; owners, 77; plant species, 80, 81–84; planting plan, 78–80, *85*; roundabout, *80*; silkworm mulberry culture, 77; site, 75; tulip beds, *79*; walks, 78, 79; West Lawn, 78, 80
Monticello Restoration Committee, 77
Morgan, Daniel, 261
Mount Airy, 75
Mount Pleasant, 15
Mount Rogers, 95
Mount Vernon, 20, 131, 189, 192
Mounting block, Scotchtown, 251, *253*

National Historic Landmarks, 39, 249
National Mary Washington Memorial Association, 69, 70, 71
National Society of the Colonial Dames of America, 53, 101
National Trust for Historic Preservation, The, 189, 205
Necessary (privy): Mary Washington House, 237, *239, 245*; Rolfe-Warren House, 45; University of Virginia, *117, 122, 149, 152, 169, 173*

Observations on Modern Gardening (Whateley), 75, 77
Osborne, Sir Thomas, 205

Palladio, Andrea, 118
Parish vestry book, Christ Church (Middlesex), 87
Parker, Donald H., 118, *154–56, 160, 171, 178–87*
Parking area: Burwell-Morgan Mill, 263; Christ Church (Lancaster), *230*, 231; Gunston Hall, *107*; Kent-Valentine House, *270*, 271; Lee Memorial Chapel, 40; Scotchtown, 250; Wilton, 58; Woodlawn, 192, *197, 202*; Woodrow Wilson Birthplace, 32

Parterre(s): Adam Thoroughgood House, 205, *211, 212*; Gunston Hall, 101, *105, 110, 111*; Stratford Hall, *18*, 20, 21; University of Virginia gardens, 135; Woodlawn, 192, *193*; Woodrow Wilson Birthplace, *35*
Paths, *see* Walks
Paths of Glory (Preston), 251
Pavement: Bruton Parish Church, 62; Christ Church (Fincastle), 91; Lee Memorial Chapel, 39, 40; Mary Washington Monument, 70; The Mews (Richmond), 217, *219*, 220, *226*; Stratford Hall, *18, 19*; Woodrow Wilson Birthplace, 30
Pavilion (garden): Federal Hill, *6, 8*; Gunston Hall, 101, 103, *112, 113*; Kenmore, *6, 8*; The Mews (Richmond), *216*, 220, *224*; Woodlawn, *190*; Woodrow Wilson Birthplace, *32*
Pavilion (residential), University of Virginia, 115, 118
Payne, John, 249
Perkins, Hazlehurst Bolton, *Thomas Jefferson's Flower Garden at Monticello*, 84
Pinkney, Charles Coatsworth, 14
Plant list: Gunston Hall, *110, 111*; University of Virginia gardens, *128, 133, 136, 141, 146, 155, 160, 171*, 178
Planting plan: Adam Thoroughgood House, 205–6; Barter Theatre, 95; Bruton Parish Church, 62, *64–65*; Burwell-Morgan Mill, *265*; Christ Church (Fincastle), 92; Christ Church (Lancaster), 229, 231, *233*; Gunston Hall, 101, 103, *109, 110, 111*; Kenmore, *8, 9*; Kent-Valentine House, *274*; Lee Memorial Chapel, 39–40; Mary Washington House, 237, *243*; Mary Washington Monument, 71, *73*; The Mews (Richmond), 220, *222, 223*; Monticello, 78–80, *85*; Rolfe-Warren House, 45–46; Scotchtown, 250–51; *253, 258*; Stratford Hall, 20–21, *26*; University of Virginia gardens, 125, *128*, 131, *133*, 135, *136*, 139, *141*, 142, *146*, 151, *155*, 157, *160*, 161, *164*, 167, *171*, 173, *178*; Wilton, 57, *59*; Woodlawn, 192, *197, 200*; Woodrow Wilson Birthplace, 30, 32
Pocahontas, 43
Porterfield, Robert, 95
Potomac River, Gunston Hall vista, 99, 103
Powhatan, 43
Presbyterians, 29, 91, 95
Presentation plan: Adam Thoroughgood House, *210*; Burwell-Morgan Mill, *260*; Gunston Hall, *108*; Kent-Valentine House, *273*; Mary Washington House, *242*; Scotchtown, *255*; University of Virginia gardens, 118, *154, 157, 163, 170, 177*
Preston, Nelly, *Paths of Glory*, 251
Primatt, Stephen, *The City and Country Builder*, 15
Privy, *see* Necessary

Railings, The Mews (Richmond), *218*
Randolph, Anne Cary, 78, 79

Randolph, William, III, 53

Randolph, Mrs. William, III (Ann Carter Harrison), 53

Reggi, Giacomo, 125

Reggi, Micheli, 125

Richmond: Carrington Square, 217; Church Hill Historic Zone, 217; Kent-Valentine House, 269; Linden Row, 269; The Mews, 217; Saint John's Church, 217; Wilton, 53

Roanoke Valley Garden Club, 91

Robert E. Lee Memorial Foundation, 18, 20

Robinson, John, 249

Rockefeller, John D., Jr., 45, 61

Rogers, Isaiah, 269

Rolfe, Henry, 43

Rolfe, John, 43

Rolfe, Mrs. John (Pocahontas), 43

Rolfe, Thomas, 43

Rolfe-Warren House, 43–51, *286–97*; archaeological survey, 43, 45, 49, *50*; dating of, 43; entrance road, *44, 46*; fences, 45, *47*; garden area, *46*; The Garden Club of Virginia and, 45, 46; garden entrance, *45*; grounds, *51*; Alden Hopkins and, 46; plant species, 47; planting plan, 45–46; privy, 45; restoration, 45; Arthur Shurcliff and, 45; site, 43; tulip trees, *44*; well, *48*

Roman Pantheon, 118

Rose species: Christ Church (Lancaster), 232; Gunston Hall, 106; The Mews (Richmond), 221; Monticello, 84; Rolfe-Warren House, 47; Scotchtown, 254; Stratford Hall, 22; University of Virginia gardens, 127, 135, 139, 145, 153, 159, 168, 176; Woodlawn, 195; Woodrow Wilson Birthplace, 34

Rosewell, 15

Roundabout, Monticello, *80*

Saint John's Church, Richmond, 217, *227*

Scotchtown, 249–59, *330–31*; archaeological survey, 249, 250; bench, 253, *259*; boxwood, *248*, *252*; construction plan, *256, 257*; documentary research, 249, 253; entrance, 250–51, *252*; fences, 250, *259*; The Garden Club of Virginia and, 250; gates, 250, 251, 252, *259*; Griswold, Winters, & Swain and, 250; kitchen garden, 251; landholdings, 249, 250; mounting block, 251, *253*; orchard, *253*; owners, 249–50; parking area, 250; plant species, 254; planting plan, 250–51, 253, *258*; presentation plan, *255*; site, 249, 250; views, *252*

Serpentine walls, University of Virginia, 115, *121*, 135, 149, 151, 161, *163*, 173

"Setting stones," 167

Shenstone, William, *Collected Works*, 75

Shippen, Thomas Lee, 20

Shirley, 75

Shrub species: Adam Thoroughgood House, 209; Barter Theatre, 96; Bruton Parish Church, 63; Burwell-Morgan Mill, 264; Christ Church (Fincastle), 93; Christ Church (Lancaster), 232; Gunston Hall, 106; Kenmore, 9; Kent-Valentine House, 272; Lee Memorial Chapel, 40; Mary Washington House, 240; Mary Washington Monument, 71; The Mews (Richmond), 221; Monticello, 82; Rolfe-Warren House, 47; Scotchtown, 254; Stratford Hall, 22; University of Virginia gardens, 127, 131, 135, 139, 145, 153, 159, 162, 168, 175; Wilton, 58; Woodlawn, 194; Woodrow Wilson Birthplace, 34

Shurcliff (Shurtleff), Arthur, 18, 19, 45, *49–51*, 53, 57, *59*, 62, *67*

Silkworm mulberries, 77

Smith, John, 43

Smith's Fort Plantation, *see* Rolfe-Warren House

Somerville, William C., 16

Spotswood, Alexander, 61

Spurr, Samuel, 61

Staunton, Woodrow Wilson Birthplace, 29

Steps: The Mews (Richmond), *225*; University of Virginia gardens, *121*, 151, 157, 161, 167, *173*; Woodlawn, *202*; Woodrow Wilson Birthplace, *30*

Stone spire, Merton College, Oxford, *161*

Stonewall Jackson College, 95

Stratford Hall, 15–27, *280–81*; archaeological survey, *14*, 18, *25*; architectural plan, *15*; boxwood parterre, *18*; brickwork, 15, 16, 19, 20; building chronology, 15–16; capitals, 16; Herbert Claiborne and, 19; crape myrtle, *16*; documentary research, 18–19; espalier, *19*; The Garden Club of Virginia and, 18, 20; garden maintenance fund, 20; garden plan, *23, 24, 26*; garden restoration period, 20; garden topographic survey, 19; gate, *17*, 20; hickory tree, *21*; Alden Hopkins and, 20; Umberto Innocenti and, 20; octagon house, 20; orchard plan, *27*; outbuildings, *17*; owners, 15, 16; parterres, 20, 21; pavements, 18, 19; plant species, 21–22; planting plan, 20–21, *26*; Arthur Shurcliff and, 18, 19; site, *15*; staircase, 16; toolhouse, 20; walk, *16*; 20; walls, 16, 17, 19, 20; Morley Williams and, 19, 20

Street lamp, Christ Church (Fincastle), 91, *92*

Stratford Foundation, 15

Summerhouse: Woodlawn, 192, *201*; Woodrow Wilson Birthplace, 30, *36*

Sundial, Mary Washington House, 235, 237, *239*

Talbott, Charles, 269

Temple of Fortuna Virilis, 118

Terrace: Barter Theatre, 95; Christ Church (Fincastle), 91; Gunston Hall, 103; Kenmore, 8; The Mews (Richmond), 220; University of Virginia gardens, *121*, 125, *150–52*, 157, 161; Wilton, 54, *56*, 57; Woodrow Wilson Birthplace, 30, *31*, 32, *37*

Theater of Marcellus, 118

Theory and Practice of Gardening, The (Dezallier d'Argentville), 118, 135, 157, 167

Thomas Jefferson Memorial Foundation, 77, 80

Thomas Jefferson's Flower Garden at Monticello (Betts and Perkins), 84

Thomas Jefferson's Garden Book (Betts), 75n

Thornton, William, 189

Thoroughgood, Adam, 205, 206; *see also* Adam Thoroughgood House

Thoroughgood, Mrs Adam (Sarah Offly), 205

Thoroughgood, William, 205

Tobacco economy, 43

Toolhouse: Stratford Hall, 20; The Mews (Richmond), *218, 226*

Topiary: Adam Thoroughgood House, *206*; Gunston Hall, 101

Tree species: Adam Thoroughgood House, 209; Barter Theatre, 96; Bruton Parish Church, 63; Burwell-Morgan Mill, 264; Christ Church (Fincastle), 93; Christ Church (Lancaster), 232; Gunston Hall, 106; Kenmore, 9; Kent-Valentine House, 272; Lee Memorial Chapel, 40; Mary Washington House, 240; Mary Washington Monument, 71; The Mews (Richmond), 221; Monticello, 81–82; Rolfe-Warren House, 47; Scotchtown, 254; Stratford Hall, 21; University of Virginia gardens, 127, 131, 135, 139, 145, 153, 159, 162, 168, 175; Wilton, 58; Woodlawn, 194; Woodrow Wilson Birthplace, 34

Trellis, Mary Washington House, 237, *246*

Tucker, George, 142

United Daughters of the Confederacy, William Alexander, Jr., Chapter, 17

U.S. route 1, great houses on, 189

University of Virginia, 115–87; allée, 142; alleys, *116, 134*; architectural design, 115, 118; Colonnade Club, 139; cornerstone, 139; East Lawn gardens, 118–19, 149–87; East Range, 115; engraved ground plan, *114*; The Garden Club of Virginia and, 117, 118, 123, 149; Ralph E. Griswold and, 118; Alden Hopkins and, 117, 118, 125, 149; Thomas Jefferson and, 115, 117–18, 125; John Jordan and, 39; James Knight and, 117, 118; the Lawn, 115; "McGuffey Ash," 142, *143*; Peter Maverick engraving, *114*, 115, 117, 149; necessary (privy), *117, 122*, 149, *152*, 169, 173; Donald Parker and, 118; pavilions, 115; pavilions facade design, 118; perspective in architectural design, 118; serpentine walls, 115, *121*, 135, 149, 151, 161, *163*, 173; site, 115; West Lawn gardens, 118, 123–48; West Range, 115

University of Virginia gardens, 115–19; allée, *142*; alleys, *116, 134*; archaeological survey, 117, 149; arrangement, 115, 117; benches and seats, 125, 131, 139, 151, 157, 161, 167, 173, *179–87*; gates, *119*, 125, *129*, 135, *137*, *138*, *147*, 151, 161, *172*; ornaments, 125, *126*, 131, 139, 157, *158*, 161;

parterre, 135; plans, 118, *123*; plant species, 131; prototypes, 118; restoration design, *120*; restoration funding, 123, 149; steps, *121*, 151, 157, 161, 167, *173*; terraces, *121*, 125, *150*, 151, *152*, 157, 161; walks, *121*, 125, 131, *134*, 135, 140, 151, 157, *158*, 173; walls, *117*, 118, 157, *163*

University of Virginia gardens: Pavilion I, *124*, 125–29, *302–3*; construction plan, *127*; hotel area, *126*; plant species, 127; planting plan and plant list, 125, *128*; prototype, 125; residential area, *126*; restoration, 125–29

University of Virginia gardens: Pavilion II, 151–56, *312–13*; grading and layout plan, *156*; plant species, 153; planting plan and plant list, *155*; presentation plan, *154*; restoration, 151–56

University of Virginia gardens: Pavilion III, *130*, 131–33, *132*, *304–5*; planting plan and plant list, 131, *133*; prototype, 131; restoration, 131–33

University of Virginia gardens: Pavilion IV, 157–60, *314–15*; plant species, 159; planting plan and plant list, 157, *160*; presentation plan, *157*; prototype, 157

University of Virginia gardens: Pavilion V, 135–38, *306–7*; plant species, 135; planting plan and plant list, 135, *136*; prototype, 135

University of Virginia gardens: Pavilion VI, 161–64, *316–17*; plant species, 162; planting plan, 161, *164*; presentation plan, *163*

University of Virginia gardens: Pavilion VII, 139–41, *140*, *308–9*; planting plan and plant list, 139, *141*; prototype, 139

University of Virginia gardens: Pavilion VIII, 167–72, *318–19*; garden connection, *166*; plant species, 168; planting plan and plant list, 167, *171*; presentation plan, *170*; prototpye, 167

University of Virginia gardens: Pavilion IX, 142–47, *144*, *310–11*; plant species, 145; planting plan and plant list, 142, *146*; residential area, *144*

University of Virginia gardens: Pavilion X, 173–78, *320–21*; approach, *176*; holly trees, *174*; plant species, 175–76; planting plan and plant list, 173, *178*; presentation plan, *177*; prototype, 173; upper level design, *174*

University of Virginia Rotunda, 115, 118; annex, 157; annex capital, *158*; architectural style, 118; capitals for, 125

Valentine, Edward, 39

Valentine, Granville, G., 269

Vine species: Adam Thoroughgood House, 209; Bruton Parish Church, 63; Burwell-Morgan Mill, 264; Christ Church (Fincastle), 93; Christ Church (Lancaster), 232; Kenmore, 9; Kent-Valentine House, 272; Lee Memorial Chapel, 40; Mary Washington House, 240; The Mews (Richmond), 221; Monticello, 82; Rolfe-Warren House, 47; Scotchtown, 254; Stratford Hall, 22; University of Virginia gardens, 127, 131, 135,

Vine Species (*cont.*)
139, 153, 159, 162, 168, 175; Wilton, 58; Woodrow Wilson Birthplace, 34

Virginia Beach Garden Club, 205

Virginia State Theatre, 95

W. W. LaPrade & Bros., *23*

Walks, Bruton Parish Church, 62; Burwell-Morgan Mill, 263; Christ Church (Fincastle), 91; Christ Church (Lancaster), 229; Kenmore, *1, 4, 11*; Kent-Valentine House, 271; Lee Memorial Chapel, 39; Mary Washington House, 235, 237; Mary Washington Monument, 70, *72*; The Mews (Richmond), 220; Monticello, 78, 79; Stratford Hall, *16*, 20; University of Virginia gardens, *121*, 125, 131, *134*, 135, *140*, 142, 151, 157, *158*, 173; Wilton, 54, 57; Woodlawn, 192, *194*; Woodrow Wilson Birthplace, 30, 32

Walls: Bruton Parish Church, 61, 62; Christ Church (Fincastle), 91, *92*; Christ Church (Middlesex), *86*, 87, *88*; Kenmore, 6, 8, *10, 13*, 70; Kent-Valentine House, 271; Mary Washington Monument, 70; The Mews (Richmond), *218*, 220, *225*; Stratford, 16, 17, 19, 20; University of Virginia gardens, 115, *117*, 118, *121*, 135, 149, 151, 157, 161, *163*, 173; Ware Church, 70; Wilton, 54, 57–58; Woodlawn, *202*; Woodrow Wilson Birthplace, 30, 32

Ware Church (Gloucester), 8, 70

Warren, Thomas, 43

Washington, George, 3, 39, 69, 189, 235

Washington, Mrs. George (Martha Custis), 189

Washington, Mary Ball (Mrs. Augustine), 3; domestic arrangements, 235, 237; grave site, 69; *see also* Mary Washington House; Mary Washington Monument

Washington and Lee University, 39; architectural design, 39; construction, 39; Robert E. Lee and, 39; Washington Hall at, 39

Washington College, 39

Well: Adam Thoroughgood House, *207*; Mary Washington House, 237, *245*; Rolfe-Warren House, *48*; Woodrow Wilson Birthplace, 30, *36*

Whateley, Thomas, *Observations on Modern Gardening*, 75, 77

White Top Mountain, 95

Williams, Morley J., *14*, 19, 20, *24*, 25

Williamsburg (colonial): Bruton Parish Church, 61; Governor's Palace, 15; restoration, 61, 62

Williamsburg Garden Club, 61

Wilson, Woodrow, 29; *see also* Woodrow Wilson Birthplace

Wilson, Mrs. Woodrow (Edith Bolling), 30, 32

Wilton, 53–59, *288–89*; archaeological survey, 54; architectural style, 53; barrier post, *58*; brickwork, 53, 57; Claiborne & Taylor and, 53; The Garden Club of Virginia and, 53, 57; gate, *54*, 57; Alden Hopkins and, 57; interior design, 53; ironwork, 54; James River vista, *55*; landholdings, 53; memorial bench, *56*; owner, 53; parking area, 58; plant species, 58; planting plan, 57, *59*; river view terraces, *56*; Arthur Shurcliff and, 53, 57; sites, 53, 54, 58; terraces, 54, *56*, 57; transplantation of, 53; walks, 54, 57; walls, 54, 57–58

Wood, Garland A., *85*

Woodcarving, Gunston Hall, 99

Woodlawn, 189–203, *322–23*; archaeological survey, 191–92, *196*; architectural style, 189; construction details of fences, gates, walls, drives, parking islands, and steps, *202–3*; documentary sources, 189, 191; entrance, *188*, 197, *198–99*; fence, 191; The Garden Club of Virginia and, 189; garden construction plan, *198–99*; garden pavilion, *190*; garden prototypes, 192; garden vista, *190*; gate, 192; Alden Hopkins and, 189, 192; landholdings, 189; orchard plan, *200*; owners, 189; parking area, 192, *197*; parterres, 192, *193*; paths, *194*; plant species, 194–95; planting plan, 192, *200*; serpentine drives, 191–92, *202*; serpentine walks, 192; site, 189; summerhouse, 192, *201*

Woodrow Wilson Birthplace, 29–37, *30, 282–83*; arbor, 30; architectural plan, 29; brickwork, 29; builder, 29; bulb planting, *33*; front porch, 32; The Garden Club of Virginia and, 30, 32; garden entrance, *37*; garden furniture, 32; Charles Gillette and, 30, 32; Ralph Griswold and, 32; Mary Baldwin College and, 29–30; parking area, 32; parterre, *35*; pavilion, 32; plan 13 detail, *31*; plant species, 34; planting plan, 30, 32; purchase for historic site, 30; site, 29; steps, *30*; summerhouse, 30, *36*; terraces, 30, *31*, 32, *37*; walks, 30, 32; walls, 30, 32; well, 30, *36*

Woodrow Wilson Foundation, 30, 32

Wren, Christopher, 15

Yates family, 87

Historic Virginia Gardens

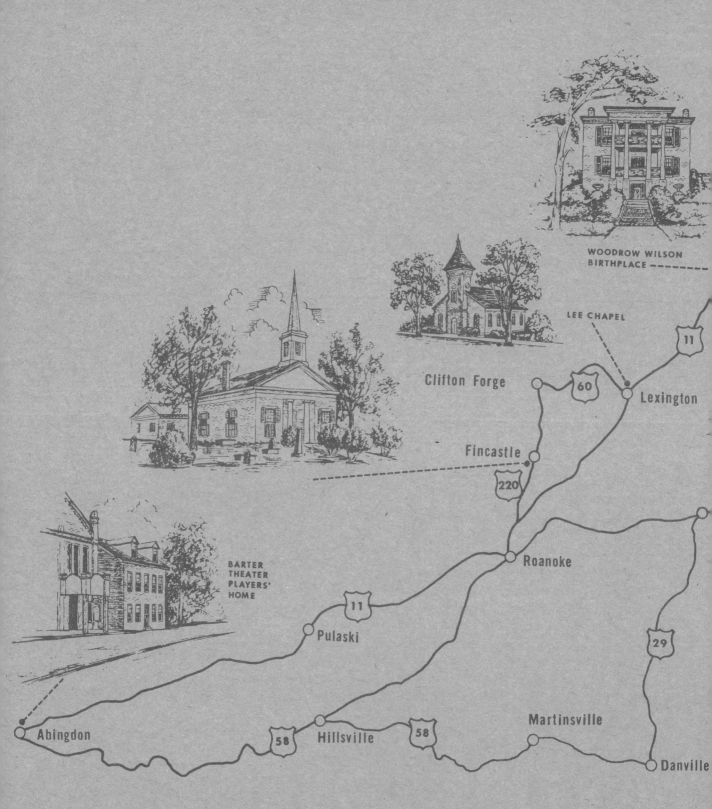

Winche

WOODROW WILSON
BIRTHPLACE ---------

LEE CHAPEL

11

Clifton Forge

60

Lexington

Fincastle

220

BARTER
THEATER
PLAYERS'
HOME

Roanoke

29

11

Pulaski

Martinsville

Abingdon

58

Hillsville

58

Danville

D.C.Hensley